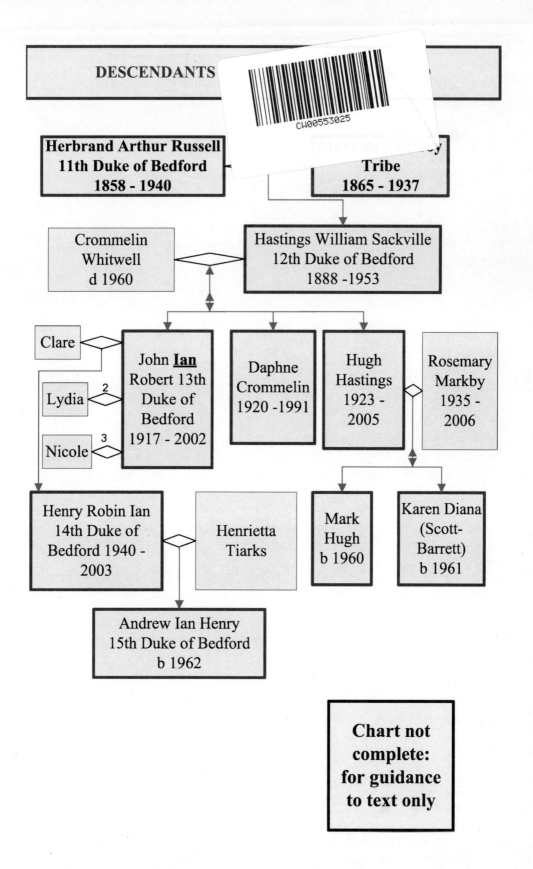

DESCENDANTS

Herbrand Arthur Russell
11th Duke of Bedford
1858 - 1940

Tribe
1865 - 1937

Crommelin
Whitwell
d 1960

Hastings William Sackville
12th Duke of Bedford
1888 -1953

Clare

John **Ian**
Robert 13th
Duke of
Bedford
1917 - 2002

Daphne
Crommelin
1920 -1991

Hugh
Hastings
1923 -
2005

Rosemary
Markby
1935 -
2006

Lydia 2

Nicole 3

Henry Robin Ian
14th Duke of
Bedford 1940 -
2003

Henrietta
Tiarks

Mark
Hugh
b 1960

Karen Diana
(Scott-
Barrett)
b 1961

Andrew Ian Henry
15th Duke of Bedford
b 1962

**Chart not
complete:
for guidance
to text only**

THE HIGH-FLYING DUCHESS

BY THE SAME AUTHOR

Ladies of the Chase

The World of Hunting

The Pony Club: Dream and Reality

David Livingstone

THE HIGH-FLYING DUCHESS

MARY DU CAURROY BEDFORD
1865-1937

MERIEL BUXTON

Meriel J Buxton

FOREWORD BY
THE DUKE OF BEDFORD

WOODPERRY BOOKS

First published in Great Britain in 2008
by
Woodperry Books

A CIP Catalogue of this book is available from the British Library

ISBN 978-0-9558925-0-9

Printed and bound in
Great Britain by
Biddles Ltd.
King's Lynn, Norfolk

In memory of

H.H.R.

CONTENTS

Front Cover - Mary in 1934

FOREWORD
BY THE 15TH DUKE OF BEDFORD

Mary du Caurroy Tribe, who married my great-great grandfather Herbrand, 11th Duke of Bedford, had probably one of the most outstanding lives of any great Victorian lady. She is best known for her exploits in the field of aviation, having taken up flying in the 1920's at a little over the age of 60 and earning herself the title of the "Flying Duchess" in the popular press.

However this was only one facet of a remarkable life. She was also a highly trained surgical nurse and a qualified radiologist using these skills to great advantage in her Cottage Hospital in Woburn village until her death in 1937 and also at Woburn Abbey Military Hospital during the First World War. Her other main interests included ornithology and zoology and she spent a considerable amount of time in keeping detailed accounts of the many exotic animals introduced by the Duke to Woburn in the early twentieth century. Added to this she was a competent watercolourist and photographer who enjoyed skating, fishing, sailing and shooting, at all of which she excelled.

Since her death in a flying accident over the Fens in 1937, she has inspired succeeding generations of my family with a desire to know more about her. My grandfather wrote his own biography of her and my father declared her to be the relative he would most have liked to meet. Lord Hugh Russell, my great uncle, who knew and greatly admired his grandmother, was a frequent visitor to Woburn and was 14 years old at the time of her death. Almost 70 years later he appreciated that the achievements which had impressed him as a child were more not less remarkable than they had then appeared and he wanted them to be appreciated by a wider audience. That is why Meriel Buxton wrote this book and why I, too, am full of admiration for this remarkable lady.

INTRODUCTION

Lord Hugh Russell

I first heard about Mary from her grandson, Hugh Russell. Hearing him talk about his early life and the different members of his family always held me spellbound, though for many years I took most interest in those whom I had met. In the last years of his life, his mind went back with increasing frequency to the grandmother whom he had adored. At the time, I was helping him to put an account of his own life on paper and he told me of his wish for an accurate record of Mary's life to be written.

None of the three previous accounts of her life reveals the full picture of this extraordinary woman. Born into an ordinary middle class family, she married one of the richest aristocrats of her age, broke world flying records and established two hospitals where she worked for many years as theatre sister and radiologist. Dubbed the Flying Duchess in the 1930s, she became the darling of the press, who covered their front pages with full details of her 'every new and daring exploit.' Mary herself was amazed and somewhat appalled by the popular enthusiasm, pointing out quietly to anyone willing to listen that, although she held a pilot's licence for some years, her record breaking flights were always undertaken with a professional pilot at the controls and that her motives were private and personal: she enjoyed being in the air, loved the challenge of the adventures she met with and obtained relief in the air from the tinnitus which plagued most of her adult life. She marvelled that this hobby attracted so much attention, while her life's work in the medical field went largely unnoticed. Even today, most of what has been written about her relates to flying. Despite efforts at her old home at Woburn Abbey to portray all the different aspects of her life, this soubriquet remains the dominant image. The booklet about her by Tim Jennings bears this name.

Lettice Curtis gave an excellent account of her flying career in her 1993 book *Winged Odyssey*. Two full biographies of Mary have been written. The first, by John Gore, was commissioned after her death by her husband. It was made available only to her family and close friends. The writer was allowed no word of criticism. Gore later wrote a short piece on the centenary of her birth, long after her husband too was dead, giving an interesting and more balanced reflection on her strengths and weaknesses.

The third account which has helped to shape her memory was that given by Hugh's older brother John, known to the family as Ian, 13th Duke of Bedford. Ian's autobiography, *A Silver-Plated Spoon*, formed part of his spectacularly successful publicity campaign which eventually did so much to save Woburn Abbey. Unfortunately he occasionally found it necessary to sacrifice accuracy to the telling of a good story. More than forty years later, his brother was surprised to find the Duke's obituary writers still taking at face value his account of how, when he was sixteen, a garrulous housemaid inadvertently informed the astonished young man that this Flying Duchess, featured so prominently in the newspapers, was in fact his grandmother.

By the time of the 13th Duke's death, few people except his brother recalled how, as boys, both brothers had been invited, I believe on separate occasions, to their ancestral home to stay with their grandparents. The older brother did not find his grandparents' way of life, and in particular his grandfather's rigid insistence on absolute punctuality, to his taste and so became a less frequent visitor. Ian's own biography of his grandmother, *The Flying Duchess*, was professionally researched and does paint a different picture which is rather more sympathetic than *A Silver-Plated Spoon*. Sadly, it has not been as widely read and still includes much material from the earlier work, although Gore's reflections are included as an appendix.

Hugh was only 14, and his grandmother 72, when she met her death, at the controls of her own aeroplane, two years before the outbreak of the Second World War. During the Thirties, Hugh frequently stayed at Woburn with his grandparents. The world was in the grip of the Depression, yet four motor cars and eight men were deemed necessary, on every occasion, to transport one small boy some 45 miles from London. Every family member and guest was still attended at meals by an individual footman, even if those footmen were now more frequently attired in practical dark brown, rather than the rose coloured coats, white breeches and powdered hair prevalent when Mary and her husband Herbrand, the 11th Duke of Bedford, first took over the Abbey in 1893.

Woburn Abbey in Bedfordshire is one of the great country houses of Britain. It has belonged to the Russell family, Earls and later Dukes of Bedford, since 1547, following the Dissolution of the Monasteries, and became the family home some 70 years later. Woburn was one of the last houses still to be run in 19th or even 18th century style, up to the death of Herbrand in 1940. Fifteen years later, after Herbrand and Mary's grandson Ian became the 13th Duke, he transformed it with all the flare of the natural showman into perhaps the most popular tourist attraction of the time. I first visited Woburn two years later as a ten year old bridesmaid at Hugh's wedding.

If Woburn Abbey in Mary's lifetime was reminiscent of a fairytale world of princes and princesses living a life of unimaginable luxury, Hugh soon learnt that discipline too was important. Breakfast was at 7 a.m. every morning: any guest, old or young, arriving even a minute late incurred the displeasure of the Duke, who was a stickler for punctuality. The reason for the early hour was that the Duchess, even in her seventies, started her working day, in the hospital she had founded, at 8.30. Her shift lasted into the afternoon. During that time, she would not only attend to all the more major issues of administration and personnel, but she was also Theatre Sister whenever an operation was scheduled, as well as an expert of national standing in radiology and radiography. She still managed to find time to take a personal interest in the welfare of every patient, yet she had no formal training or qualifications in medicine.

Mary, like the house she lived in, seems to bridge the centuries in a remarkable fashion. Her lifestyle at home was decreed by her husband. She acquiesced, without enthusiasm or interest, although in her many interests she certainly both appreciated and made full use of the almost unlimited money lavished on her by her devoted husband. Yet psychologically she was more akin to the 21st century career woman than to the pampered wife of an 18th century aristocrat. Her hospital work was an obsession. Despite, or perhaps in consequence of, her lack of qualifications, she set herself, and all those with whom she worked, almost impossibly high standards. John Gore later wrote: 'If she had never married, she would have risen to the top in the profession of nursing.' Her most conspicuous failure, in her relationship with her son, probably owed as much to her commitment to her profession as to the idiosyncrasies of her family life. If few modern career women enjoy her opportunities, few have the breadth of interest and ability to excel in such diverse fields. Her intellectual curiosity, determination and sense of humour were as important to her success as her husband's fortune.

After she came off duty in the afternoon, she would go for long walks with the Duke in the park, both of them teaching their grandson about the remarkable collection of deer which Herbrand had built up. The Duke originally hoped to have examples of every species of deer in the world at Woburn. He did not achieve this, but his breeding programme was so successful with certain varieties that descendants of the Père David deer, which he imported from China, have recently been taken back to that country to re-establish the breed, which had become extinct in the wild.

Mary, though interested, was less knowledgeable about mammals than her husband. She specialised instead in ornithology. She delighted in sharing her knowledge and enthusiasm with the young, including not only her grandson, but boys from the village who joined her Bird Watching Club. She and her chauffeur between them (the chauffeur was a former member of the Boys' Bird Watching Club) not only taught Hugh about birds. They also introduced him to mechanics and the workings of the internal combustion engine, enabling him to earn his living as a mechanic during the Second World War.

He learned from others how she won a gold medal for ice skating, and saw for himself her skill with a shotgun. She showed him her superb photographs, drawings and needlework; she told him thrilling tales of her life in India before her marriage, plunging down ravines on a pony or watching the procession of elephants in a great Durbar held for a Maharajah. More exciting still were the tales of her recent adventures, accompanying her pilot as they established world record times for flights across the world. He heard of the time when they were forced to land in the desert, where local tribesmen shot at them, or had an even closer brush with death, when the cabin filled with carbon monoxide fumes. To the end of his life, Hugh remembered with pleasure how, when he was at home with his mother near Hastings, his grandmother flew low over the house, wiggling the plane's wings in greeting to her grandson, at the start of one of her epic flights.

Yet Hugh knew too that between his father and his grandparents there was an almost insuperable chasm. Long years of bitterness, misunderstanding, inability to see one another's point of view and, perhaps most depressing of all, a total lack of interest, separated them. Hugh, alone, struggled to build bridges, with some success, perhaps because his presence made his grandmother at last appreciate a little of what she had, almost carelessly, sacrificed a generation earlier. Relations between Mary and Herbrand and their son were never to become close, but at least there was some communication, unlike the icy, impenetrable gulf which separated Hugh's father from his mother. Hugh, a very gentle, kindly boy, moved quietly between the three households, mother, father and grandparents, loved in each, appreciative of what was good in every member of his family, preferring not to dwell on aspects others deplored. Almost seventy years later, looking back with a more mature judgement, his eyes still lit up at the memory of the grandmother he adored. Conscious of the terrible damage caused to his family by her failure to develop a close relationship with her only child, Hugh yet appreciated that the achievements which had impressed him as a child were more, not less, remarkable than they had then appeared to him. He wanted them to be appreciated by a wider audience. Above all, he still loved her as deeply as he had done as a boy. That is why I started to write this book.

LIST OF ILLUSTRATIONS

THE DUKES OF BEDFORD

Five successive Dukes of Bedford featured in Mary's life. To minimise confusion, they are listed below.

The 9th Duke of Bedford   1819 – 1891
Father of Herbrand.
He is not referred to in this book by his Christian name, Hastings, to avoid confusion with his grandson, the 12th Duke, who was also Hastings.

The 10th Duke of Bedford: *George*   1852-1893
Brother of Herbrand.

The 11th Duke of Bedford: *Herbrand*   1858-1940
(Married Mary du Caurroy Tribe)
Commissioned John Gore to write his biography of Mary after her death, allowing no criticism of Mary to be included.

The 12th Duke of Bedford: *Hastings*   1888-1953
Son of Herbrand and Mary
Wrote his autobiography, *The Years of Transition.*

The 13th Duke of Bedford: *Ian*   1917-2002
Registered as John but Christened and always known as *Ian.*
Eldest grandson of Herbrand and Mary.
Wrote *A Silver-Plated Spoon* (a sensationalised account of his own life and family) and *The Flying Duchess* (a biography of his grandmother Mary).

NOTE
In the spelling of place names, I have followed the spellings used by Mary herself in her diaries and letters.

ACKNOWLEDGEMENTS

I am most grateful to the Duke of Bedford for his support and encouragement throughout this project, and in particular for writing the Foreword.

Everyone at Woburn Abbey with whom I have had any contact has gone out of their way to be helpful. Ann Mitchell especially has been a tower of strength with her detailed knowledge of the archives and her willingness to discuss every aspect of Mary's life with me in detail, frequently casting new light on issues which had previously puzzled me. She and the assistant archivist June Day have consistently made me feel welcome in the Archives Department. Christopher Gravett as Curator and his predecessor Lavinia Wellicome, assisted by Marilyn Buckley, have used their encyclopaedic knowledge to help me to find the best illustrations.

Other members of Mary's family who have been particularly helpful to me include my God-daughter Karen Scott-Barrett, Mary's great granddaughter, and Martin Beaver, a grandson of Mary's sister Zoë. Both made many constructive comments on the text, Karen provided some fascinating photographs and Martin's research and personal recollections have been invaluable. Zoë's granddaughter Kate Rae and great granddaughter Alice Bird have also helped to give me a rounded picture of Mary.

I am especially grateful to those who have read and commented upon the text, including Ashley Stokes, Jack Spence, Nicholas Watkins, Susie Brankin Frisby and my daughter Rose Smail. My thanks are also due to Rosemary Manning for proof reading; Kath Boothman and Rachel Roberts of Cheltenham Ladies' College; Deborah Quare, Librarian and Archivist at St. Hugh's College, Oxford; Christopher Gosnell and Helen and Ian Longworth for helping me to trace the Carpendale family tree; and to Jeanette Hurworth and Nicky Prentis and their team at Biddles Ltd., the printers, also graphic designer John Chandler.

My son Hugh has enabled me to resolve the inevitable technical problems with which I have been faced and my husband James has supported and encouraged me at every turn, always with sound advice. My only sadness is that Mary's grandson Hugh Russell and his wife Rosemary, two of my dearest friends, did not live long enough to read this book.

ILLUSTRATIONS

All the illustrations are reproduced by kind permission of the Duke of Bedford and the Trustees of the Bedford Estates, with the following exceptions.

Pages 64 (group including Jemima Green), 152 (Hastings with parakeets), 157 (Three generations) and 222 (Herbrand at home) are reproduced by kind permission of Karen Scott-Barrett.

Page xi, the portrait of Lord Hugh Russell by Lenare, is © reserved: despite strenuous enquiries, including the National Portrait Gallery, I have been unable to trace the current copyright holders and must apologise for any inadvertent infringement.

Page 108 (Maryland) is by kind permission of Ian Church.

Page 182 ('Spider') is by kind permission of Martin Beaver.

Pages 123, 144, 198 and 225 were taken, by the author, of books included in Mary's collection bequeathed to St. Hugh's College, Oxford.

Inside cover (the author) is by kind permission of James Buxton

A FAMILY TRADITION

Woburn Abbey has long had a tradition of strong and independent women. A remarkable exception was Anne Carr, wife of William, the 1st Duke and first of the Russell family to live all his life at Woburn. Anne's quiet, sweet nature was remarkable, for her mother, the 1st Duke's mother-in-law, was not only strong and independent, she was also probably the most terrifying woman of her time. Anne Carr, wife of the 1st Duke of Bedford, was the daughter of two convicted murderers. Her parents, Robert Carr, Viscount Rochester and Earl of Somerset and former adored favourite of James I, and his wife Frances, spent the early years of Anne's life imprisoned in the Tower of London under sentence of death for the murder of Sir Thomas Overbury by poisoning. Despite a murky saga of financial and sexual corruption, blackmail, witchcraft and murder, in which the wife was the dominant partner, neither was eventually executed. Surprisingly, their daughter Anne became a charming, kind and gentle wife and mother.

Anne and William's second son, also named William after his father, was one of those people whom everyone, family, friends and, as he became more widely known, the citizens of London and elsewhere, loved and admired. He was courageous, kind, thoughtful and intelligent. His friends spoke of his loyalty, great virtue and integrity, describing him as honourable and modest.

His wife Rachel was the first of the succession of strong, independent women who married members of the Russell family. An heiress who brought Bloomsbury into the family, her marriage to William was as much a true love match as that of William's parents, the older William and Anne Carr. Both were devout Protestants who were deeply concerned over the way in which the country was being governed. William in particular found the behaviour of the King's brother, the Duke of York, later King James II, unacceptable, and thus provoked York's bitter enmity.

In 1683 the Rye House Plot, an alleged conspiracy to kill the King, was uncovered. William had some connections with a few of those involved in the plot but had taken no part in it. Despite this, he was charged with high treason and stood trial for his life. The trial was a travesty of justice. William was allowed no proper legal advice. He had only one support.

'The Attorney-General, in order to prevent him from getting the aid of counsel, told him he might use the hand of one of his servants in writing.

'"I asked none," answered the prisoner, "but that of the lady who sits by me."

'When the spectators, at these words, turned their eyes and beheld the daughter of the virtuous Southampton, rising up to assist her Lord in this his utmost distress, a thrill of anguish ran through the assembly.'[1]

The trial lasted only a single day. William was executed eight days later. He had every reason to complain that 'he was hardly used.'

During that week Rachel moved heaven and earth to save her husband's life. She did not, however, move the King, despite throwing herself at his feet and reminding him of his close friendship with her late father and of the consequences for her small children and herself as well as for her husband. When this failed, she resolved to show no more weakness. Even at their final farewell, after the children had paid him their last visit, Rachel did not break down, so determined was she to avoid upsetting her 'dear lord' in any possible way.

Her efforts did achieve two concessions. William had been sentenced to be hanged, drawn and quartered, with the sentence read out by the judge in all its macabre detail, but he was in fact more mercifully beheaded. Secondly, the Duke of York, in his vindictive fury, had wanted the sentence to be carried out in front of Bedford House in the Strand. Again the King refused.

Rachel's courage impressed even her enemies. In her widowhood she became a remarkably astute businesswoman, determined that her three children should lack for nothing. All were married before their 16th birthdays, the girls to the future Dukes of Devonshire and Rutland, her son Wriothesley, the 2nd Duke, to a rich heiress. But life again was cruel to Rachel: two of her children predeceased her and she lived on to a lonely old age.

After her death, the family was for a time dominated by an even more formidable matriarch, Sarah, Duchess of Marlborough. Two of Sarah's granddaughters, cousins to each other, married the brothers who became successively the 3rd and 4th Dukes of Bedford. The first, Anne, had the double misfortune of marrying the feckless and dissolute elder brother, a spendthrift who, had he survived beyond his 25th birthday, would have destroyed his inheritance with his extravagant way of life, and thus incurring her grandmother's displeasure. Sarah eventually made her dislike of the young Duchess manifest in a particularly vicious, almost childlike, fashion. The face in a portrait of Anne, which belonged to Sarah, was painted over in black paint, and Sarah had written underneath 'But she is much blacker inside.'[2]

Sarah's other granddaughter, Lady Diana Spencer, remained in favour with Sarah until Diana's own untimely death. A beautiful, gentle girl, her husband, Lord John, who became the 4th Duke, also remained popular with Sarah until he had the temerity to remarry. From that moment, Sarah's influence at Woburn was finished. John became a successful politician and statesman: he was described by Horace Walpole as 'the merry little Duke.' His second wife, Gertrude Leveson-Gower, became the most dictatorial Duchess ever to hold sway at Woburn.

All was well during her husband's lifetime. But then history repeated itself and Gertrude found herself grandmother of two little brothers who eventually became 5th and 6th Dukes. She miscalculated and overstepped the mark. The older boy, Francis, returned from the Grand Tour, accompanied by his mistress, who was closer in age to his grandmother than to Francis himself, and the Dowager Duchess was forced to leave Woburn. She lived a further nine years, no doubt coming to regret at least the consequences of her behaviour.

Despite his lifestyle, Francis found himself pursued by the mothers of eligible daughters and had almost decided on Georgiana, daughter of the Duchess of Gordon, when, tragically and unexpectedly, he suddenly died. Undeterred, the Duchess of Gordon transferred her attentions to Francis' younger brother John, the new Duke, a widower with three small boys, the youngest of whom was the future Prime Minister, Lord John Russell. John married Georgiana little more than a year after his brother's death.

Georgiana, on her marriage, burst into Woburn like a bunch of balloons released during a solemn Board meeting. She was full of life, energy and enthusiasm, attractive, flirtatious, sometimes bawdy, extravagant and determined to make her mark. She entertained in style, on a grand scale. Life was a constant round of sporting activities during the day, with shooting and racing predominating. The evenings were filled with dancing, masquerades, billiards, whist or parlour games. Such activities frequently degenerated under the Duchess's influence into rowdy chaos, with cushions, fruit and even candles being hurled about the rooms[3].

The guests were an eclectic mixture. Aristocrats, actors and agriculturalists rubbed shoulders. Not all the guests joined in the frivolity. Leading Whigs made Woburn a regular meeting place where their host encouraged them to gather to discuss political issues. Other guests were shocked by the atmosphere of licence.

'I am tired of the whole, and... I would not have another week of it for a hundred pounds... They are never cool, and have no time for reading or thought... It is a sin and ought to be repented to go into such company'[4] declared one guest, and Frances, Lady Shelley wrote of 'the languor created by the dearth of intellectual amusement.'[5] She complained, too, of the ease with which guests could slip in and out of each other's bedrooms.

Georgiana was a devoted mother to her own large family, playing an unusually full part in their lives for a woman in her position at the time: She and the Duke travelled extensively. The Duke was considerably older than Georgiana, a devoted husband who enjoyed his comfortable lifestyle. His travels proved a rich source of treasures for the Abbey: he brought back from Europe many fine works of art, including Canova's Three Graces. Despite his initial deep unhappiness, he showed remarkable resilience when, after some 20 years of marriage and probably not long after he had suffered a minor stroke, Georgiana started a passionate affair with the young artist Edwin Landseer, more than twenty years her junior. Although the relationship continued for the rest of her life, and Landseer was almost certainly the father of her youngest child, the Duke gradually came to accept the situation, even developing a close friendship himself with the artist.

After Georgiana, life became quieter at Woburn. The chief claim to fame of her successor, Anna Maria, wife of the 7th Duke, was her invention of afternoon tea. Her son remained a bachelor, and neither of the next two Duchesses were particularly strong characters. Then came the 11th Duke and his Duchess, Mary.

CHAPTER 1

CHILDHOOD

The Victorian age was a time of contrasts. Crippling poverty co-existed with immense wealth. For the first time, opportunities for young families opened up all over the world, yet many people chose to spend their whole lives in the same place, just as their forebears had done. A handful of women achieved remarkable success in professional careers. The vast majority used such education as they were given only for social purposes.

Mary du Caurroy Tribe's parents built a new life for themselves in India, leaving her and her sister to be brought up by a devoted aunt, who lived all her life within three miles of the house where she was born. Mary never knew real poverty, though as a girl she was fully conscious of the restrictions imposed on their lifestyle by the limited means of her family. After her marriage, she entered a privileged world of wealth on a scale unimaginable to subsequent generations. Whilst her lifestyle became that of an age long gone, her dedicated approach to her career, and the sacrifices she made for it, are typical of women born a century later than she was. Her exceptional success in a remarkably diverse group of hobbies and interests, is attributable, in part, to her own ability and single-minded determination and, in part, to the support she received from the husband who admired her so much.

Mary's father, Walter Harry Tribe, was born in 1832, the youngest of the ten children of John and Harriet Tribe, at least one of whom died in infancy. Walter was very much the baby of the family, and probably spoilt accordingly. There were twenty years between him and his oldest sister and he was four years younger than his nearest sibling, Emily. His closest bonds were forged with Fanny, who ranked one senior to Emily. Fanny was seven or eight when her little brother was born, a kind, motherly soul who even then perhaps took over much of his care: certainly it was to Fanny that he later turned, in total confidence that he could leave everything to her and

Mary as a small child

she would see that it was all right. When he grew up and needed someone dependable to whom he could entrust his own children, he knew exactly where to turn.

British families living in India in the nineteenth and early twentieth centuries knew that, as each child reached the age of five or six, separation was inevitable. The child must return 'Home' to England to be educated, although, in truth, for the vast majority of these children, England was in no sense home. It was a cold, distant land, bereft of familiar faces, familiar sights or sounds or smells, where they had nothing in common even with the other children, and they would be sent to live with total strangers. They were subjected to this shattering experience some two or three years before their British born contemporaries first went away to boarding school, and, in their case, this was not just for a term but for what must have seemed to them a lifetime. For, if either, or both, parents succeeded in visiting them more than once before they completed their education and returned to India, they were fortunate indeed. Their only link with home was likely to be through the siblings, who in turn joined them. Such children were totally at the mercy of those in whose care they were placed, as the young Rudyard Kipling (an exact contemporary of Mary) and his sister found, when sent to a cruel foster family.

The Tribe children were more fortunate. There is no evidence that they met with anything other than kindness. The three boys, Charles, born in 1868, and the twins, Jack and Willie, who were two years younger, followed a path well trodden at the time by the children of English parents living in India. They spent the first five or six years of their lives

Mary's mother, Sophie Tribe

in India, cared for by ayahs, immersed in the heat and dust and disease and beauty of that country, the atmosphere soaking into their beings in a way which they would never forget, so that India became part of the very essence of their existence, in a manner vividly described by Kipling in so much of his writing.

The two older Tribe children, the sisters Zoë and Mary du Caurroy, born in 1862 and 1865 respectively, spent their early childhood in England, not in India. The break with their parents came even earlier for them than for their brothers. Their parents did not go out to India until 1867, when Zoë was four and Mary two years old. Walter Tribe had become a clergyman in the Church of England. He spent some time at Stockbridge in Hampshire, where both the girls were born, then in 1867 he accepted a position as Junior Chaplain in Bengal. His wife Sophie was used to prolonged service overseas: her father, Charles Lander, had been Consul-General of the Dardanelles during the Crimean War in the fifties. Sophie's mother, Adèle du Caurroy, was French: Mary was given her surname as a middle name.

No doubt Walter was, in part, inspired by the sense of duty which was such a strong feature of service in India in the 19th century, in the army, the Civil Service, the Church or any of the other organisations, but his motives were predominantly financial. Walter was convinced throughout his life that he was in desperate financial straits. At this early stage in his career, with a wife and growing family to provide for, his anxiety was justified. India offered an opportunity to enjoy a higher standard of living than was possible in Britain, whilst still saving money. In common with most of the British families in India, they made constant efforts to save for a future rendered the more uncertain by the increased health risks and the high mortality rate. No economies were ever made on the most important investment of all for the future, the children's education.

When Walter and Sophie Tribe sailed for India, they decided against introducing their daughters to a new and strange environment for what would of necessity be a relatively short time. Neither girl set foot in India until she reached her mid teens and completed her education. Thus India remained, for both of them, the country where their parents lived and where they enjoyed some happy years, essentially as visitors, between leaving school and marriage.

Rudyard Kipling, on the other hand, was born within a few weeks of Mary. He too, in company with his sister, was educated in England, travelling out to India on leaving school, and, remarkably, to those familiar with his work, spending only a few more months of his adult life in India than Mary did. Yet he has come to be regarded as the personification of the British Raj in India. For at least two generations, for English-speaking people throughout the world, the popular conception of life in India under the British Raj was based, consciously or unconsciously, on the work of Kipling. Children brought up, as so many were, on *The Jungle Book*, *Kim* and *Plain Tales from the Hills* visualised India and the way of life of the British settled there through the eyes of the characters Kipling created.

In contrast, Mary remains the quintessentially English Duchess. Whilst there are other factors, such as Kipling's early success with his writing, these perceptions probably reflect their own images of themselves. Those childhood years were all-important in establishing identity. Early childhood, as St. Ignatius Loyola had pointed out centuries before, was the key to the man or woman.

More importantly for Mary, she can have had no memory at all of her parents before she settled in with Aunt Fanny. She, alone of her family, never knew the traumatic moment of separation which so devastated many of those who have been described as 'Orphans of the Raj'. Nor, unlike Kipling, did she have unhappy memories of her years in England. She and Zoë were fortunate, not only in having each other, but in being taken in by their devoted Aunt Fanny. Fanny was married to another Walter, Walter Sanders. Sanders was land agent to Sir Walter Barttelot, a Conservative politician. Walter Sanders and Fanny, childless themselves, became parents in all but name to Zoë and Mary and provided them with a happy home at Pulborough in Sussex. Aunt Fanny took the two little girls to her kind and loving heart. A great letter writer, she was still sending pages of largely illegible local gossip to 'My own darling Minnie' from 'your loving old aunt' long after Mary had grown up and the childhood version of her name had been dropped by everyone else in the family. September 26th never passed, even when they were on opposite sides of the world, without Aunt Fanny remembering Mary's birthday. She benefited quite as much from the arrangement as did the girls and their parents. While their mother liked to feel that she retained the ultimate authority, ('Tell Auntie we don't object to the boys skating' she wrote to the girls), in fact all the responsibility and almost all the mutual affection was vested in Aunt Fanny.

It was sad that ill health prevented her from enjoying an equally close relationship with Mary's three little brothers. Charles and the twins lived at Pulborough when they first arrived in England. When it was time for them to start their serious education, they shared a house in Cheltenham with their sisters, by then at school in that town, and were taught by a governess. Soon it was no longer possible even for school holidays to be spent with Aunt Fanny and Uncle Walter in the warm cocoon at Pulborough. 'I wish I was well enough to have one of the boys even at a time, but that is quite out of the question,' she wrote to Mary, who had just gone out to India, in 1882, when Charles was fourteen and the twins twelve. For several years before that, alternative arrangements were frequently made for their holidays, although she was obviously extremely fond of all three of them.

Whether their Uncle Walter was as enthusiastic as his wife about the arrangement for the girls is unclear. He appears to have been fond of the girls but to have had considerable reservations about his brother-in-law and namesake, their father. He wrote to Mary at school enthusing about the hunter ('Such a grand horse') his wife had given him, but telling Mary 'We don't hear from India. What queer people they are. I think they belong to the "Peculiar People."' This seems strong language to their daughter in an otherwise friendly and affectionate letter, unless he knew that Mary would sympathise with or at least understand his point of view. Perhaps his chest problems were making him irritable and only two years later Aunt Fanny was confiding to Mary that, 'Walter is got so fat and heavy'. But it is also possible that the girls' parents abused the generosity of the English couple and that Zoë and Mary were aware of this and supported their aunt and uncle. Certainly Zoë wrote to Mary at around this time, saying, 'I really can't understand why Father is so poor just now... (he) hasn't paid Aunt Fanny for the gun yet.' Presumably the gun had been bought for Charles or the twins.

When she first set sail for India, leaving her two small children behind, Sophie Tribe was as heart-broken and sentimental as might have been expected. She was also remarkably optimistic. She gave a rapturous reception to locks of hair, letters from Zoë and Aunt Fanny and photographs of Mary, too young to write, 'but what we should like far better would be to have our darling Zoë and Minnie's own precious little selves near us and then shouldn't we just hug and kiss them! Well Papa and Mama will do all they can to save money for their little girls and then go back to them.' It was an oft repeated theme. Perhaps Sophie at least had convinced herself that life in India was just a short term solution to a financial problem.

In fact it was to be six years before the family was reunited, and then only for a brief spell when Walter Tribe accepted a position as a locum at Bramber, some twelve miles from Pulborough. The family spent some months together there, leaving them with many happy memories. A sketch of Bramber Castle done by Mary cannot be the work of an eight year old: she must have completed it later to send to her parents as a memento. Charles was now five and it was time for him to leave India and start his education in England. The time spent at Bramber allowed him to get to know the sisters he had never previously met before he was separated from his parents and younger brothers. After they returned to India, Zoë, Mary and Charles settled down happily together with Aunt Fanny and Uncle Walter in the house at Pulborough. Life was comfortable (there were two young girls living in the house as servants[1]) but not grand. They probably shared a governess.

One important decision confronted the Reverend Walter Tribe for his daughters: the question of their education. Here once again Zoë and Mary were fortunate. In 1858, five years before Zoë was born, Miss Dorothea Beale was appointed Principal of the Cheltenham Young Ladies' College (the word 'Young' was dropped from its name a year later on the arrival of a seventeen year old pupil). Miss Beale, just twenty-seven at the time of her appointment, was to become the pre-eminent figure in the development of girls' education in the nineteenth century. She remained Principal until her death in 1906 and also founded St. Hilda's College, Oxford. She worked tirelessly, in parallel with a few friends, notably Miss Buss, principal of the North London Collegiate School, not only to provide girls with an education comparable to that expected for boys, but also to persuade Victorian society that mathematics, the classics, science and history were quite as worthwhile as the more traditional subjects such as art, music and needlework. They encountered considerable cynicism and mockery. Some was light-hearted, as exemplified by the famous jingle:

Miss Buss and Miss Beale
Cupid's darts do not feel;
How different from us,
Miss Beale and Miss Buss!

Complaints from parents were a more serious issue, threatening as they could the school's very existence. A Commissioner, reporting into girls' education generally, commented that 'the greatest obstacle to the improvement of girls' schools lay in the parents' indifference. Most assumed their daughters would marry and could not see any use for any education beyond the rudiments; they desired accomplishments designed to increase attractiveness before marriage rather than happiness or usefulness thereafter.'[2] Most girls' schools accordingly took the easy course of continuing to provide what parents wanted. The founders of the Cheltenham Ladies' College showed courage from the start in their determination to go beyond this. The first Principal, Miss Beale's predecessor, Miss Procter, suffered from complaints by parents about details of the manner in which needlework and art were taught and seemingly little or no appreciation of the much broader curriculum she offered. Numbers decreased: perhaps this was not surprising in a society where Miss Beale 'had to listen to a clergyman advising a father not to allow his five girls to teach because "their prospects would be injured."'[3] One father declined to send his daughters because arithmetic was included in the curriculum and it was not his intention that they should become bankers. Even Ruskin, passionate advocate of women's education, up to a point, declared that 'Speaking broadly, a man ought to know any language or science he learns, thoroughly – while a woman ought to know the same language or science, only so far as may enable her to sympathise in her husband's pleasures, and in those of his best friends.'[4]

Despite the opposition, a combination of Miss Beale's brilliance as a Principal and the business skills of a far-sighted new member of Council, who had moved to Cheltenham for the benefit of his six daughters, meant that the founder who had gladly sold his £10 shares in the school for £5 soon had reason to regret his decision. Another factor in the College's turnaround may have been Miss Beale's approach to the type of pupil she wished to accept. When the Cheltenham Ladies' College was described as an 'upper school' and the North London Collegiate presided over by Miss Buss as a 'middle school', this had nothing to do with the age or academic standing of the pupils. It related only to their social class. Miss Beale, when asked by the Schools Inquiry Commissioners

"Do you mean that you would refuse to admit a girl who was in a lower class of society?" had no hesitation in replying

"Yes. You will see by the form of nomination that she would not be admissible."

"In short, the object of the whole institution is that girls only of a certain class of life should be admissible to the school?"

"Yes."[5]

This, unlike her academic priorities, won her the support of the parents.

Despite any suggestions to the contrary, Cheltenham pupils were not the progeny of the nobility and aristocracy. Daughters of these families were almost invariably educated at home by governesses. However the Ladies' College gradually metamorphosed into a school of international standing by increasing the proportion of boarders. In the 1870s most of the fathers came from the professional classes or were employed in the civil or diplomatic services, the army or the Church. Walter and Sophie would have had many friends, in England but more especially in India, who had sent their daughters to Cheltenham.

Walter was keen for his two girls to take advantage of their opportunities. As her mother wrote to Mary, in a theme which surfaces constantly in their letters, Mary's father was 'very anxious about your making the most of it.' He had sent them to a first class school and had no intention of allowing them to waste their chance. A man of his time, his aspirations for them centred on marriage (though neither he nor his wife could, even in their wildest dreams, have imagined the social brilliance of the match that their younger daughter was destined to make). Walter's main interest was in drawing and painting. Both parents were always begging them to send out any sketches or paintings that could be spared, and showed enthusiasm for those they received. 'Papa I must tell you is very pleased indeed with yours & Zoë's paintings – he is particularly anxious that you should learn to sketch from nature,' wrote her mother in December, 1879, fearing that at school they would mostly be painting 'only objects in a room.' When Zoë joined her parents in India she incurred much criticism for her failure to find sufficient time for painting. 'Zoë has not taken a single sketch since she has been out. I hope she will make up for lost time when she goes to Kashmir,' he wrote. Their father was keen too that they should continue to read widely, but was mocking of what he saw as the more abstruse academic attainments of girls educated at Cheltenham.

'We have a good many Cheltenham College young ladies out here,' he wrote to Mary at Cheltenham. 'They may be very learned and be able to explain how it is a lobster turns red when he is boiled or why all animals who chew the cud get up on their hind legs first, but as a rule they don't shine in Society. Pray don't tell any of your friends what I say otherwise they will never forgive me and then I should die of a broken heart. What have you done with the little red bird you painted? If you don't want it you can send it to me.'

Despite any such initial reservations, the decision was taken for both girls to go to the Ladies' College in 1876, around the time of Mary's eleventh birthday, when Zoë was thirteen.[6] In their second term at the school, both became boarders in Miss Hopkins' house, but this was a short-lived arrangement. The following term, in the summer, the school was originally expecting both girls to continue this arrangement, but the boarding element of Zoë's school fees has been crossed out in the accounts book, though Mary's remains in pencil. By the start of the winter term, neither girl was boarding.

This change in arrangements may have been made because their brothers had now joined them in Cheltenham, enabling all the siblings to live under the same roof. Their address was given as 23 Cambray. This was the result of a private arrangement made by the family, not an official boarding house. Although the Ladies' College was seen as a boarding school, such boarding houses as existed were a perpetual source of conflict for Miss Beale. Perhaps their one or two terms as boarders enabled them to make friends in the early stages. This was certainly not easy for them once they were staying in a separate house. A rule was introduced by the first Principal, and retained for many years, enforcing silence throughout school hours, even in the changing rooms and during break times. Miss Beale thought this admirable, feeling the rule 'has done so much to give all the habit of conscientiousness in little things, and the quietness which minimises irritability.'[7] The girls were probably less impressed. During lessons the rule was reasonable, particularly since all but the youngest children were taught in one big hall simultaneously, so that there could be up to nine separate lessons being taught at any point in time, but during breaks it was excessively restrictive. The message the restriction was intended to convey was one of self-restraint, discipline and not a moment being wasted, but it must have been hard for a group of giggly twelve year olds and did nothing to help them develop their social skills. Mary had her chance to comment many years later when she returned to the school to make a speech, and pointed out that this was one thing her education had not equipped her to do. Perhaps Mary benefited more in later life from what the rule taught her than her contemporaries did. When she later suffered from deafness, she was at least used to making her own world for herself within her head.

After two years at Cheltenham, Zoë at fifteen was coming close to the end of her formal education. Their parents decided to send both girls to Zurich for a year. Virtually nothing survives to show how they spent their time in that city. In itself this is perhaps an indication that Mary was not altogether happy during this year, for she loved to keep mementoes of all the happier times in her life, both before and after this period. There is no evidence either as to Zoë's feelings. Perhaps the two year gap between them, which had hitherto seemed so little, became too great as the thirteen-year-old struggled to cope with life in a foreign city and the fifteen-year-old gloried in whatever scope there was for spreading her wings and flying away from her little sister.

Mary did enjoy some aspects of her life in Zurich. Always a great animal lover and keen rider, she had the opportunity to learn to ride well, a chance she embraced with enthusiasm. The two girls had riding lessons with an outstanding instructor, a cavalry officer, and both attributed their lifelong skill as riders to his teaching.

Hitherto the two girls had been very close and when they were reunited in India after Mary left school the old bond between them was soon as strong as ever, But at thirteen, in a foreign country where she struggled to

Mary aged about thirteen

understand a word of the language, cut off from all her family and friends except for her sister, she longed for the comforting form of Aunt Fanny and was miserably homesick. Fifteen year old girls are frequently more sensitive to their own feelings than the feelings of those around them. Just when Mary needed to be loved and cherished, Zoë suddenly discovered that her little sister was a tiresome embarrassment. It is hardly surprising if Mary lived only for the riding lessons. At least here she could excel. She found too that it is easier to love an animal than a person; the relationship is less complicated, the animal's love unconditional.

At the end of the year the sisters were separated for the first time in their lives. Their mother came over to escort Zoë to India and Mary and her three brothers had to settle down once more to school life in Cheltenham, made the more difficult by returning in the middle of the autumn term. Even if Mary had begun to feel that a break from Zoë was overdue, Zoë's letters, full of the excitement and freedom of her new life, must have made the younger girl feel somewhat bitter. Zoë's interest in the school news was genuine enough – 'I want very much to know what class you are in I suppose Miss Andrews'es. Mind you write and tell me <u>all about everything</u>,' but it was hardly tactful of her sister to add condescendingly to Mary 'and if you get a prize I will send you something pretty.'

Her father was more understanding. 'You must all miss your dear Mama and Zoë very much, at the same time you must feel much happier with your brothers and many old friends around you than you did at Zurich,' he wrote in November, conscious that the previous year had not been a success for Mary. He was kind too when the first batch of exams after her return did not go as well as she had hoped: 'You must have found them rather difficult to answer as you did not join the class at the beginning of term – next time you will have a better chance of doing well.'

As Zoë settled into her new life in India, the sisters once more became close confidantes. She was aware of how envious Mary must be feeling ('How funny it must have seemed to you to go back to College') and Mary was quite capable of defending herself.

'My sweet infant,' Zoë responded to one such remonstrance, 'I am so truly grieved to think that my letters have been so insulting that you cannot write to me any more.' Despite Zoë's promise to 'be more guarded,' one of the attractive features of the correspondence between all the siblings is its light hearted directness. Zoë's letters are full of the excitements of life at Simla (she had been invited to join another family there), the riding (she wished 'Polly' was there to join her), the parties and her art classes, which were much more fun than the German classes. She was taught art by Mr. Kipling: Rudyard's father was Principal of the School of Art in Lahore. Soon she was again sharing confidences with her sister:

'Don't you breathe a word… and you must not imagine that I am in love with him.'

Meanwhile Mary had her three brothers for company in Cheltenham. All three were doing well at school: exams never worried them and their hand writing put all her adult correspondents to shame. Charlie was trying for a scholarship to Marlborough. Charterhouse was the family's reserve choice but it was not needed. He was not in awe of his sister. After Mary too left for India he wrote to her:

'My dear Cheeky,

….Advice… which however I am afraid will be cast away on you… you talk of my being honoured by a letter from you which is a state of things. Zoë can keep you pretty well in check – easy enough when near but when out of range…'

Perhaps he missed her, though he was certainly not going to admit to any such feeling. 'I can just remember an insignificant little creature who used to live in this house who used to be the torment of everyone's life.'

The twins too were good letter writers, enthusing over a half holiday specially requested by the Queen herself. Despite having to spend some of their holidays in London because of Aunt Fanny's ill health, they were country boys at heart, both hoping to grow up to be farmers, though Willie, who was writing this particular letter, conceded that, if his mother would much prefer it, he was prepared to be a doctor instead. Sadly he was never to realise either ambition, for he died of typhoid at the age of twenty-two. His twin Jack became a tea planter and lived until 1947, when he was seventy-seven. Health was always a source of major concern to every family: there was considerable anxiety over Jack when he contracted scarlet fever at Cheltenham, although the Cheltenham schools had an excellent record for the time on health.

Charlie went into the army and served on the North West Frontier in India and in the Boxer Rebellion in China. During the First World War, Colonel Charles Walter Tribe fought first in France and then in Mesopotamia, where he was killed in January 1916 while commanding his brigade. He is buried at Amara in modern Iraq.

Once Mary had settled back into life at the Ladies' College, she enjoyed herself. Miss Beale's regime of constant activity and mental stimulation was well suited to her temperament. Although finding suitable female teachers still presented problems, because of the lack of higher education facilities for women, Miss Beale preferred them, particularly for the younger pupils. Individual teachers were required to cover a wide range of subjects, one woman teaching both Geography and Science, another combining Mathematics and Chemistry with Latin 'etc.' Miss Beale's options were limited, but she liked the fact that this enabled a particular teacher, known as a class governess, to get to know a group of pupils exceptionally well and, the headmistress hoped, exert a powerful influence over them. Moral guidance and leadership were as important as academic education.

The timetable for the older girls was filled with activities covering a fourteen hour period, but the school day must have seemed even longer. The enforced silences during breaks meant that girls continued turning the pages of their books as they drank their milk. Exercise was limited to walking in the garden or long marches, two by two in 'crocodiles'. Miss Beale eventually reluctantly permitted the playing of organised games, but that was not until after Mary had left. Despite the importance Miss Beale attached to academic work, independent examiners brought in to conduct internal exams found that pupils sometimes struggled to attain the same standards as their brothers. There was a worrying shortage of text books, for example, and the need to satisfy parents by keeping up the hours devoted to the traditional girls' subjects, such as painting, music and needlework, for all pupils took its toll.

Miss Beale herself regarded the late '70s and early '80s as the most depressing time of her life. Her health was not good, her mother died at this time and she was suffering above all from a loss of religious faith which rendered her temporarily incapable of offering her pupils the level of support they deserved. Perhaps something of this affected Mary herself. It is remarkable that Mary, the daughter of a successful clergyman, living in an age when religion played such a large part in so many people's lives, should have been an agnostic devoid of faith throughout her adult life.

However her relationship with Miss Beale may never have been close enough to have any such influence on her. Miss Beale taught the top class in the school and, as Mary left before reaching it, she was probably never taught by her. Her main teacher, who continued to write to her after she left school, was Miss Andrews. Alice Andrews was only slightly older than Mary herself and remained for many years as a teacher at the school where she had been a pupil, later taking responsibility for preparing the most senior girls for their exams. She wrote to tell Mary of the academic triumphs of her contemporaries ('See what you missed by not staying at College!'), the books they were reading and once to ask for money for an organ installed in the Great Hall in 1883 to celebrate the 'Silver Anniversary' of Miss Beale's accession to the headship.. A more entertaining account came from Mary's school friend May Blackader. Even such great headmistresses as Miss Beale were not exempt from the mockery of their pupils.

'I think Miss Beale gets dowdier and dowdier, a new little dodge of hers is to pick up her dress in front so that we can see all her legs up to her knees (NB she wears white stockings.)'

Yet in some ways it was a vintage time to be at the Ladies' College. The insecurity of the early days was a distant memory and there was a vitality in the school atmosphere which was never to be equalled as Miss Beale became older. A pupil who arrived two years after Mary left recalled years later: ' "Its most rapid and vigorous growth was just beginning." (She) remembered it as intensely alive and marvellously well organised. "The busy hive hummed with work…" '

Another old girl recalled, '…a feeling of spaciousness, of liberty – liberty without licence – of ordered freedom, of elasticity and adaptability, of vitality.'[8]

External as well as internal examinations had recently been introduced. London, Oxford, Cambridge and St. Andrews all set different exams; girls being selected for different papers according to their interests and abilities. The year Mary spent in Zurich, thirty girls passed the London, Oxford or Cambridge Higher Examinations, though these do not seem to have been exact equivalents. Miss Beale thought the Cambridge Higher and University of London exams the most useful. The Oxford class was for 'younger and generally well trained but not advanced pupils.'[9] After Mary had left school and travelled out to India, her school friend May Blackader wrote to tell her of her contemporaries 'who passed the London first class –see what you missed by not staying at College.' May herself passed the Oxford, as did all but one in the class.

For many of Mary's contemporaries, the new vista opened up by an education which would enable them to become doctors or headmistresses, to take on challenging work anywhere in the world, was a thrilling prospect. They were otherwise faced with the depressing prospect of remaining at home with their parents, awaiting a proposal of marriage from the restricted circle of family friends. Leaving school without the new qualifications was not an opportunity to broaden their horizons but a return to a narrower, more restricted existence. For the most intelligent, the attraction of new worlds to conquer, combined with the chance to satisfy their intellectual curiosity and develop their full potential, gave higher education an appeal which no 21st century girl can know.

For Mary, no exams were required for her to spread her wings and fly out to a new and exciting world. All her life she had looked forward to experiencing for herself the magic, mystery and excitement of life in India, which had come through vividly in her parents', and in particular her father's, letters. More recently, the anticipation had been intensified by Zoë's letters too, for Zoë was not only endorsing the existence of this strange, attractive country, but telling of the way in which it enabled the dreams of a teenage girl to be fulfilled: the parties, the boyfriends, the social life, the opportunities for sport, all more than living up to Zoë's own expectations.

Nor was there any parental pressure to offset these feelings. Neither of her parents harboured any academic ambitions on her behalf: on the contrary, her father made plain his disapproval and mockery of the Cheltenham bluestockings he had encountered. He declared that she should ideally have stayed for one further year at school, but his reasons were related more to conditions in India than to any wish for her to prolong her education. Both parents were naturally keen to have their younger daughter living with them for the first time in her life, and there was the additional issue of the financial strain of keeping her at Cheltenham: she could certainly live much more cheaply with them in India.

Although she had no wish to continue her education in a formal sense, her contemporaries at school would have been amazed to learn that fifty-five years later, a few months before her death, Mary would explain to her son how the fire which was to inflame her whole life was first lit as she sat at her desk in a Cheltenham classroom.

'Dear Hastings', she wrote, 'My interest in matters medical began at Cheltenham College where my desk was next to an open door of a room where lectures on Anatomy were given to which I attended instead of the business on hand.'

Scientific subjects had a particular appeal for Mary, and Cheltenham was almost the only girls' school of the time to take the subject seriously. The first Chemistry laboratory had been opened in the year before her arrival at the school, and outside lecturers taught the girls such topics as Elementary

Mechanics and Hydrostatics. Mary did not complain of exclusion from the lectures which so interested her. The school curriculum, most unusually for the time, at least included discussion of such subjects.

Whatever the attractions of scientific lectures, Mary had had enough of the restrictions of school. Despite having spent so little time with her parents, she knew exactly how to handle her father, saw an opportunity for escape and was soon on her way to India. The long separation from her parents spared them from becoming the target for adolescent revolt. All feelings of teenage rebellion were directed instead against the limitations of boarding school life. Mary, despite her refusal to continue her education, was, by the standards of her time, an exceptionally well educated sixteen year old girl. No doubt many of her school friends and teachers were shocked and saddened by her casual rejection of the opportunity to benefit from the higher education which they prized so highly. The more perceptive amongst them perhaps realised that the opportunity was not completely lost, that the challenging academic environment, the half-heard lectures, had had their effect. The seed lying dormant in Mary's active brain had been stirred into germination, even if the time for swift growth was still far off.

As she packed her trunk to leave Cheltenham for the last time, she looked forward to the joy of being reunited with Zoë, once more on almost equal terms as Mary herself took her place in society, no longer the tiresome little sister of their last year together in Zurich. She was excited by the anticipation of the wonderful new life awaiting her half a world away: the thrill of travelling, the dazzling prospect of spending her days riding and playing tennis, going to parties and dancing, giggling with friends of her own sex and, for the first time in her life, making friends with members of the opposite sex. All her life, from before the dawn of conscious thought, she had been brought up to dream of the day when she would live all the time with her parents.

There were griefs and anxieties too. The pain of separation from her beloved aunt was real enough, even though she was now used to living most of her life away from her at Cheltenham. Aunt Fanny's failing health caused her pangs of guilt, though she could tell herself in all honesty that there was little she could do to help the suffering woman, other than write her long letters which would be much more interesting if describing life in India rather than life at Cheltenham. The sad truth had probably already dawned that ill health and pain frequently make people less entertaining as companions than they were in their more active, happier days. She was sorry, too, to be leaving her three brothers, but their lives were already filling with their own preoccupations. All in all, the excitement of the new life opening up before her left little space for regrets, particularly for the rigours of the institutionalised life of Cheltenham.

Mary

CHAPTER 2

CARPY

The Reverend Walter Tribe did not take much persuading to allow his daughter to leave school and come out to India at the age of sixteen in 1881. He put up a token show of resistance ('Shouldn't you like to go back to the college once more? I thought your Mamma intended sending you there') but after such an extended separation he longed to have her with him. It would also save him money. As he wrote to her in April 1881 after the decision had been taken:

'So you are glad that you are coming out so soon – I scarcely need tell you that we shall all be delighted to welcome you after such a long absence. I think you are coming out a year too soon but we shall find it less expensive to keep you out here than at home and hope you will keep up your reading after you come out though I must tell you that it is rather difficult to settle down quietly and work during the winter months when so much is going on.'

Zoë had also come out to India at sixteen. This did not necessarily strengthen Mary's case, for, apart from the educational issues, there was also a health risk and Zoë had contracted typhoid in Lahore. Their parents were agreed that India was 'not a healthy place for young people.' Although they were keen for Mary to keep up her reading, there is no indication that they regretted her failure to stay on at Cheltenham to take further exams. The possibility of her later wishing to pursue a professional career never occurred to either of her parents. Had it done so, the idea would have appalled them. Their only thought was that perhaps an additional year of supervised reading, study of modern languages and above all more art lessons could have made her an even more attractive girl. If Mary herself later had any regrets about missing the chance to qualify as a doctor, she was sufficiently pragmatic to keep such reflections to herself.

At last everything was agreed. Mary left Cheltenham late in November

1881 and sailed early in December. Charlie's letter covered up any sadness he may have felt with teasing, but Aunt Fanny's long, rambling, illegible epistle showed what a gap Mary's departure would leave in her life. 'I never knew such a wandering Tribe as yours,' she declared.

For Mary this was the moment she had been dreaming of for years. Perhaps she was allowed to go to the Army and Navy Stores to buy a trunk and suitable clothing, both for the journey, when she would be expected to dress for dinner every night, and for use in India. The P & O ships were particularly full at this time of year with those travelling out for Christmas and especially with 'the Fishing Fleet.' 'The Fishing Fleet was… made up of the "highly eligible, beautiful daughters of wealthy people living in India. This was the only way in which they could come out under the protection of their parents, to meet eligible young men and marry." Those who failed returned to England in the spring and were known as the Returned Empties.'[1] Mary, who had only just had her sixteenth birthday, must have found it interesting to watch from the sidelines the whirlwind of shipboard romances; the anxieties of those coming out, already engaged to marry men whom they may belatedly have reflected they hardly knew; the sorrowful mothers returning from leaving young children in England; the young men on their way to their first posting overseas.

The origin of the word POSH as meaning Port Out, Starboard Home, to define the cabins least affected by the heat of the sun and with the best views, is mythical. All the same, the refinements of travel on the steamship gave Mary her first introduction to the protocol of Indian life. With her quick intelligence, she soon learned to distinguish the status of the different passengers, clearly defined in the seating arrangements for meals and adhered to throughout. Her energy and enthusiasm made her a boon to those responsible for organising a constant round of activities, deck games, parties, fancy dress balls and so on. As they journeyed further, every port brought new experiences of the east: the hawkers crowding round the ship in small boats, selling fruit, bangles, brightly coloured materials or anything else likely to appeal to a gullible traveller; the young children performing tricks in the hope of earning a few coins; the beggars.

The journey was as exciting and romantic as she had imagined. Yet it is sometimes better to travel hopefully than to arrive. She had probably only left England once before in her life, and that journey, to Zurich, had brought her little happiness. Now she was coming to a strange continent, several weeks away from England, where in reality she knew no-one but her sister Zoë, and her most recent recollections of their time together were not encouraging. Her parents were virtual strangers. She knew that conditions were not considered conducive to good health. Her youth had given her a special standing on board, sufficiently distanced from the social politics of the other passengers to watch, as it were, with amusement from the wings. Once she reached India her age would become a handicap. Not yet old enough to 'come out', her mother would keep a strict eye on the invitations she was allowed to accept as well as the company she was allowed to keep. She had never been taught to dance. Her dress sense depended on her innate good taste: Aunt Fanny had hardly been an icon of fashion. School life had offered no training in the niceties of small talk. It was a daunting prospect.

Zoë wrote a description of Mary at this time:

The bat, in India, probably responded to Mary as well as this otter, in England

'She seems to be very little changed in face, but tremendously grown, and such a lovely *figure*! She is very quiet and subdued in manner, but I daresay she will very soon find her tongue and be more at ease. We took her to the Hall last night, and Mother got Colonel Medley to dance with her. She was terribly frightened at first, and didn't like to begin, but I am quite sure she will dance very well indeed with a very little practice. Mother is going to allow her to dance at the Hall before dinner but not afterwards, that is to say, she is not to go to balls and dinner parties. It is so nice having her…'[2]

In one respect, everyone's worst anxieties were realised when, soon after her arrival in Lahore, Mary contracted typhoid fever. The consequences for her were more serious than anything suffered by her sister, for this illness was the cause of the serious deafness which afflicted her for the rest of her life. It became progressively more severe and was later exacerbated by tinnitus. The disabling effect this had upon her had profound consequences in everything that she did in later life, and in the way in which her character developed.

Soon after her recovery from the fever, her father was moved to Dharmsala in the Punjab. The Punjab was perhaps the most fashionable and popular of all the fourteen Indian provinces.[3] Walter Tribe's work required him to spend much of his time travelling the country on horseback, and Mary now joined him on many of his tours, covering immense distances on their travels, through the Kangra and Kulu Valleys and over the 13,000 feet high Rohtang Pass into Lahoul. She also had some taste for solitary study: after her father's next transfer, to Sialkot, she would study Persian history and literature in an old church: the primary attraction of this setting was a bat, living in the steeple, which she befriended.

Towards the end of her life, in the Sahara, she recalled those days:

'The life in these outlying stations, the Officers and their polo ponies and syces, the bungalows and native servants all bring back to me, with a touch of sadness, my girlhood days in India. Those were happy times. We each had our ponies, there were no horrid motors, our very faithful servants loved us, and there were no Gandhi revolutions. Father and I travelled much together, and as I look back upon it I see what a gloriously happy time it was for those last six years of my unwedded life. The girl of today, with her cocktails, smoking and motors may be as happy, but cannot have as good a time as we had. The time spent over drinking cocktails, etc., sitting and sipping them for hours, cannot be conducive to the health we enjoyed; and as it is now thirty-eight years since I spent a whole day indoors, and then only on account of a carriage accident, I have a right to have my say. Only in the matter of dress has the modern girl the advantage over us. What would I not have given for the ride-astride habit, the short skirt, or even the absence of it. But even in those days I rode astride with my father when there were no Europeans looking on. We shared a pony on some of our trips and also his saddle. Later I was the first woman to ask Busvine, the London tailor, to make me a ride-astride habit, though not of course the first woman to ride that way in London. I shocked my relations by what were then regarded as very short skirts for shooting, in which I now marvel that I could ever have walked the moors, seeing that they were down to my ankles! Short hair is another boon of today which we were denied; and certainly the girl of to-day, with her slim figure and loose, scanty clothing, is an infinitely more graceful being.'[4]

It did not take Mary long to find her feet. As she got older, she was encouraged to play an increasingly active part in the social life. Even for the older generation there were always parties. Her father had written to Mary at Cheltenham commenting that 'She (Mary's mother) has, I have no doubt, told you how often she has dined out of late. I am pleased to say that we have only one dinner party in view at present and that a public one given in honour of... one of the judges.' For the young, the activities were never-ending. Once Mary started going to dances regularly she fulfilled her sister's prophecy and was in her element on the dance floor. She kept the attractive little cards from the more formal occasions, in which she recorded her partners for each dance of the evening.

Mary first started keeping a diary, a habit she was to retain for the rest of her life, in 1885. The two girls were living in Sialkot with their father. Their mother had returned to England in the previous year: since Aunt Fanny was no longer able to cope, the boys needed her help. Mary and Zoë both led an active social life, with Zoë frequently away from home for social events, and Mary, despite her reservations about the fashions of her time, had always enjoyed being smartly turned-out. Zoë wrote when Mary first came out to India:

'She has such pretty things and everything so nice; as to her boots and shoes, they are perfectly 'ravissant'; for best she has such a lovely blue velvet trimmed with satin, and it suits her so well.'[5]

Mary however preferred a more energetic outdoor life, playing tennis, riding or both almost every day. Her companion for much of the time, lending her his pony, playing tennis, joining her on visits to neighbours and having lunch or tea or both with the family two or three times a week, was a young man she referred to as 'Carpy.'

William Maxwell Carpendale was three years older than Mary. The family came from Ireland: Willie's grandfather, like Mary's father, was in the Church. His father was a Colonel in the Royal Engineers who served for most of his life in India, becoming in effect Commanding Officer of the Public Works Department in Madras. Willie was the sixth of eight children (seven of whom survived) and the only one except the oldest to be born in India, in Madras. All the others were born in Ireland, so it is probable that that is where he spent most of his childhood.

In 1872, his father was on his way home from India on the P & O ship the '*Khedive*' having been invalided out of India. Sadly, he died on board ship, just ten days before Willie's tenth birthday. Ten years later, Willie's mother too died, in London, not long after her son had passed out from Sandhurst. The fun-loving young man with a strong sense of humour who had grown up surrounded by a large family was lonely when first sent out to India and was delighted to be made so much a part of the Tribe family. It was not long before he fell deeply in love with Mary.

She at first regarded him rather as an older brother. Even her name for him, somewhat facetious and based on his surname, is more indicative of schoolboy humour than romance. But by February 1885 she was caught up in the excitement of a secret romance. Rides and walks with him are highlighted in her diary with mysterious asterisks. An occasional comment is transcribed into Greek letters which, when read, relates to remarkably innocent-sounding gifts of pictures. Later, perhaps finding that Greek characters were not sufficiently effective at keeping her secrets, whether from inquisitive servants or from her father and Zoë, she resorted to a more secret code, based on her study of Persian. When separated from each other even for brief periods, the young lovers wrote letters.

In April Mary accompanied her father to the magnificent Durbar given at Rawalpindi in the Punjab by the new Viceroy, the future Marquess of Dufferin and Ava, for his conference with the Amir of Afghanistan. The Durbar was not only a splendid occasion but also a professional triumph for the Viceroy, who demonstrated considerable diplomatic skill in his handling of the ramifications of the recent so-called Panjdeh incident, when Russian and Afghan forces had come into conflict on the Frontier. Amongst the A.D.C.s whom Mary may have met in attendance on the Viceroy, though she does not mention him in her diary, was a young Grenadier Guards officer, Lord Herbrand Russell, the second son of the ninth Duke of Bedford. Mary, now nineteen, tall, with quick intelligence and a strong personality, was always surrounded by young men, mostly officers in the regiments stationed in the Punjab or members of the elite Indian Civil Service. But she remained more interested in the spectacle, watching wide-eyed as the Viceroy's magnificent procession passed from the station through the streets lined with troops, the bodyguard mounted, she noted, on splendid horses. Only the weather spoilt the occasion, with rain falling heavily day after day. Even this gave her cause for amusement: on the 1st April, appropriately, she recorded in her diary, 'Could not drive up to our tents so had to be carried to be carried (*sic*) across the ploughed (?) field on driver's – syce's back. My man is small for me consequently I was deposited in the worst of the mud (Tableau!)'

Soon after their arrival in Pindi 'Mr. P. Carpendale' called. Perhaps this was Willie's older brother Percy. At all events, Carpy himself joined them for Easter weekend and the grand parade on Easter Monday of 80,000 troops before the Amir and the Viceroy. Mary was invited to attend the evening entertainment at the Viceroy's. She shook hands with and spoke to Lord Dufferin, the Duke and Duchess of Connaught were present and everyone danced around a huge bonfire. Next day, however, she found the Viceroy's garden party 'very slow'. Perhaps this was because Carpy was no longer in Pindi.

Back in Sialkot, and noting that it was just a year since her mother left for England, life returned to normality. The Maharajah of Kashmir passed through the town, Mary was given a kitten, rode Carpy's pony and Carpy came to tea, lunch and breakfast and sometimes dined with them. There were earthquakes too, but these were of less interest than Carpy riding in a nominated race for her at the gymkhana. Increasing coded symbols, asterisks and Greek and Persian letters, punctuate the diary.

Zoë too fell in love that summer. Fred Beaver was eleven years Zoë's senior, and known as Beefsteaks: he later became a General. An attractive and amusing young man, he was somewhat wild and irresponsible at that time. More worrying in her father's eyes, he was also impecunious. This did not worry Fred in the slightest:

'I am afraid he is rather careless about money matters,' declared his loved one. She did not mind being poor, she told Mary, she just hoped that Fred would not regret it.

Their father's attitude to them and to financial issues perplexed both girls. In some ways Zoë found his concern about Fred's poverty reassuring. At least he was not desperate for her to accept the first offer made to her. 'I really and truly think we have been unjust to Father in thinking he wants to get rid of us at any price,' she wrote to Mary. But after Fred and Zoë became engaged in December 1885 and plans for their wedding progressed, Zoë was in regular communication with many members of the extended family. She found that her father was the subject of much criticism. Aunt Flo, she told Mary, 'speaks in anything but flattering terms about Father, and so does Uncle in his less emphatic way.' She was worried too about the impression her father's meanness was making on Fred. 'Fred should think me meanly set up especially after the way he was treated at first. I really can't understand why Father is so very poor just now.'

Walter Tribe, Archdeacon of Lahore,
Mary's father

For most of that long, hot summer of 1885 the sisters were enjoying themselves too much to concern themselves with such issues. They rode and swam and went for drives; they watched the young men playing polo and racquets. Fred broke his arm on the polo field and a colonel had his eye knocked out at racquets. They wrote long letters to their mother and Aunt Fanny in England and heard that their brothers had gone to Brussels.

At the end of September Mary's birthday celebrations covered several days. On the 27th Carpy received a telegram ordering him to join his regiment at Allahabad. He stayed for her birthday dinner on the 29th and on the 30th he came to say goodbye. At 1.15 next morning Mary was still sitting up on the roof singing *For he's a Jolly Good Fellow* and *Auld Lang Syne*. Next morning he left for Allahabad. For the next month letters were constantly flying between Sialkot and Allahabad, or Calcutta when he was moved there. Mary's father too wrote to the young man, and Mary and her mother wrote long letters to each other.

The Viceroy was equally preoccupied with the movements of British troops, following the imposition of an impossible fine on the Bombay-Burma Trading Company by the bellicose young king of Burma. King Thibaw threatened that if the fine was not paid he would confiscate all the company's rights and property. The British responded on the 22nd October with an ultimatum which was rejected. By the 9th November the Viceroy had resolved to occupy Mandalay and dethrone the king. This was the start of the Third Burmese War.

Before the rejection of the ultimatum, Carpendale's regiment was ordered to Burma. Before leaving, he wrote again to Mary. When she received his letter on 2nd November, their engagement was announced. From then on she no longer refers to him as Carpy, but always as Willie, or sometimes Billie. Both had been forced to grow up almost overnight. The boy Carpy, her old playmate, was gone, his place taken by an army officer, responsible for leading his men into battle, fighting for Queen and Empire. For Mary, too, the time had come to put away childish things and prepare to become a wife.

Less than three weeks after he left Calcutta, Willie was indeed under fire. There was heavy fighting at Minhla. The British victory was not achieved without considerable loss of life, including casualties from Willie's regiment. Unfortunately for Mary, at this worrying time, she lost the support of her father, who was sent to Lahore to take over from the Archdeacon there, a position which he officially accepted early in the following year. As for Zoë, her mind was on other things: her engagement to Beefsteaks was announced on the 5th December.

Mary decided to join her father in Lahore. She attempted to fill her time with dances and cricket matches. She was busy too with arrangements for her wedding, writing to a number of relations. She was planning to return to England in preparation for her wedding and stay with her cousin Edith Tribe at Westward Ho! Edith was a point of contact between many of the family members. She was in touch with Mary's brothers and passed on news of them and of Mary's mother, who by now had taken over many of Aunt Fanny's responsibilities. The net of relations spread all over the globe: Edith also had a married sister, Blanche, living in Canada. Edith was even sent a picture of Willie and showed suitable enthusiasm. 'I like the look of Mr. Carpendale's picture very much. I should say he had a good deal of fun about him,' she wrote in November, anticipating the day when he would come to England to fetch Mary. 'And now dear Mary,' she concluded, 'Hoping the course of true love will run very smoothly in your case.'

Communications with Burma became more difficult. Zoë told her in mid December 'There is no letter for you this week. I wonder why, I suppose something has gone wrong with the post or he is perhaps on the march.'

On New Year's Day 1886 Burma was officially annexed by the British. Mary by then had returned to Sialkot. Letters were less frequent than they had been, though she instantly responded when she heard from her fiancé. A few days later, for the first time in months, she confided her thoughts to her diary using her secret code. On the 11th February she received a telegram from Willie, again responding immediately. Just a week later Willie wrote to Mary's mother:

'Pagan
Upper Burmah
18th Feb 86
My dear Mrs. Tribe

I have just heard from my darling Mary this morning saying that our engagement had been broken off. I am very grieved and broken down at the news, but must say that the fault is <u>entirely mine</u>. Would you kindly forgive me for having treated poor Mary a little unkindly. I never meant it in earnest and am very sorry for I love her most dearly. My mind is quiet (*sic*) upset, so much so, that I hardly know what I am about. I never wanted her to give me up. I have tried hard for a whole year to win her, and having done so it seems hard to lose her. It is a blow I can scarcely bear. Would you my dear Mrs Tribe, <u>persuade</u> Mary to change her mind and take me back again.

I have nothing left in life now to live for, nothing to work for. Please write to me again and give me a few words of encouragement & hope, and believe me

Ever yours affectionately

W.M.Carpendale

Address

W.M.Carpendale Esq,

11th B

Field F

Burmah

I would like to write more to you, but I have not the power. I don't know what I am saying'

We will never know why Mary changed her mind. Her diary gives no clue. Willie's letter shows a willingness to shoulder all blame. Whether he really felt that the breakdown was his fault, or this was simply the natural reaction of a conscientious young man still deeply in love, is not clear. Perhaps he had been teasing her in some way. But Mary was not usually lacking in a sense of humour. Nor was she otherwise cruel or insensitive, but it seems a hard time to deal him such a blow. Perhaps she had begun to realise that she did not love him sufficiently deeply, that her emotions without him were not as strong as they should have been, or her own sudden growing up had revealed to her that he had not sufficient depth of character or maturity to satisfy her for the rest of her life. She may then have believed that it was no true kindness to allow his illusions to continue; indeed with her honest, forthright nature she would have found it almost impossible not to tell him her decision immediately. It is possible that all the pressures of the months since he sailed, when she had no-one in whom to confide, had become too much for her, but there is no indication that she ever regretted or attempted to reverse her decision. Nor is there any suggestion that she had met anybody else at that time.

A flurry of telegrams and letters passed between them throughout March and April, then there is no further mention of the young man who had played such an important part in her life throughout the previous year. No letters, dance cards or other souvenirs remain, only the record in her diary and the devastated letter he wrote to her mother. No doubt she destroyed everything at the time, except for the letter, which probably only came into her possession many years later, long after the wound had healed, perhaps on her mother's death. Even so, the bottom half of the final page has been cut off and destroyed.

As for Carpy himself, it is pleasant to record that he did not die, either in battle in Burma or of a broken heart. He remained in the British army, becoming a Colonel, and in 1890, four years after his first engagement was broken off, he married Caroline Mary St. John in Bengal. Caroline herself had been born in Calcutta. They had four sons, three of whom survived, and at least one grandson. All three sons had distinguished military careers, becoming respectively a Colonel (Honorary Brigadier) in the Indian Army; a Squadron Leader in the R.A.F.; and a Colonel in the Indian Army who won an MC at the end of the First World War. Eventually Willie and his wife returned to Ireland, where he had been brought up, and he died there having reached three score years and ten. Ireland must have been his choice of home, for Caroline returned to London before her death five years later, just five weeks before Mary's own death. Mary's decision, whatever prompted it, was proved right for both of them, although it certainly did not seem like that to Carpy at the time.

For Mary, the break-up with Carpy marked a beginning as well as an end. When she first came out to India, she was very young, emotionally as well as physically. Despite the glamorous image of India she had built up in her mind, she preferred to spend her time riding, swimming, playing tennis and walking in the company of either her father or her closest friend, William Carpendale. Since Carpy happened to be a young man, and since this was clearly how he wished their relationship to progress, it was the most natural thing in the world for her to see him as a boyfriend and build up the excitement of a romantic novel with secret codes, hidden messages and thrilling adventures together. Such stories always culminated in a fairytale marriage.

Her enjoyment of outdoor activities and country life was to remain an important part of her character. Her life at this time fully satisfied that side of her nature in a way that had been impossible at school and with Aunt Fanny. But, as she matured, other needs asserted themselves. For the rest of her life she needed to be active in a wider sense, achieving objectives, overcoming obstacles. At Cheltenham there had always been challenges to rise to. Life since she came out to India had been too easy. When Carpy was away fighting and she had time to reflect, she probably began to realise that the sort of everyday, practical challenges she would have to meet were not sufficient for her. The role of devoted wife, left at home to wait and weep, powerless to influence her fate, was not for her.

This feeling owed more to her education than she realised. Most Victorian girls took it for granted that man took the active role in life and woman was his passive companion. This was the central tenet of their

Mary, by Lady Abercromby

upbringing. It was not an approach which was accepted at Cheltenham. Mary's contemporaries there went on to become eminent doctors and headmistresses. Dr. Lilias Hamilton was a pioneer woman doctor in India and Afghanistan, Annie McCall founded a maternity hospital which bore her name, Mary Wolseley-Lewis founded the girls' public school North Foreland Lodge, and other contemporaries or slightly older girls became headmistresses of schools from Vancouver to Tasmania, from South Africa to India, or were the first to achieve various academic distinctions.[6]

Mary was possessed of an exceptionally capable brain, as she was to demonstrate throughout her life in her ability to absorb almost any topic which caught her attention, usually soon demonstrating a remarkable command of it. Carpy was not a stupid man but he was more interested in practical matters than anything intellectual. Mary started to realise that such outlets as studying Persian and attending occasional medical lectures were not sufficient. Her mind as well as her body demanded constant exercise. She began to realise that as Carpy's wife she would eventually become very bored.

Mary's collection of Dance cards

CHAPTER 3

LORD HERBRAND

Mary's father's next career move was well timed for her. Early in 1886 he was appointed Archdeacon of Lahore. This meant that the family was in future to be based at Simla. Social life for British families living in India was always hectic. The most social time of all was in the summer, when the women and those of the men whose work was not tied to the plains moved to the hill stations to avoid the excessive heat. Of all the hill stations, the most glorious and glamorous was Simla. The Viceroy moved the seat of government there every year. Balanced precariously on a series of ledges high in the hills (which meant that it retained its Victorian character throughout the British Raj, for it was inaccessible to motor cars), it was the ultimate in Indian society.

'The facilities which Simla offers are startling. There are garden-parties, and tennis-parties, and picnics, and luncheons at Annandale, and rifle-matches, and dinners and balls; besides rides and walks, which are matters of private arrangement,'[1] wrote Rudyard Kipling.

In her diary, Mary mentions his mother, sister and Kipling himself amongst her fellow guests at different functions. Zoë had been lucky enough to be invited to join another family at Simla in her first summer in India. From April 1886, when their father was appointed Archdeacon of Lahore, summers at Simla, with regular invitations to dances at Viceregal Lodge, were taken for granted by the Tribe family.

This was the perfect atmosphere for Mary's recovery. Even though she had instigated the break, she was deeply affected. Communications with Carpy continued throughout March and April, after the move to Simla was complete. At first she had difficulty in taking her part in the social round. 'Dress rehearsal for tableau shockingly mismanaged' she complained to her diary just before the move, and, as she rarely concealed her feelings, no doubt those around her were well aware of her state of mind. She was in urgent need of a change of environment. The move to Simla averted any need for this to be artificially contrived. Soon she was enjoying musical parties, fancy dress balls (she attended one as a Girton girl), racing, Lady Dufferin's fête, lectures (topics ranged from the medical subjects she had long found so interesting to the fall of the Moghul Empire), dancing and dinners at Peterhof, as Viceregal Lodge was then called. There was usually dancing after dinner, when Mary danced with the Viceroy himself, as well as other members of his establishment.

Although a constant round of parties never appealed to Mary, she threw herself into the social whirl, for she no longer had anyone with whom to share her everyday activities. Early in the summer, Zoë left India for England, to join her mother in Pulborough and prepare for her wedding there on the 18th September. It must have been sad for the sisters, who had always been so close, to be separated on this occasion, one of very few events to be recorded in capital letters in Mary's diary. The following day's entry was equally significant: 'Went for a ride with Lord Herbrand Russel (*sic*) on his pony.' Four days earlier on the 15th she had described a dance at Government House as a 'very jolly dance. Danced 4 with Lord H.' She celebrated her twenty-first birthday on the 26th September with another ride with Lord Herbrand and from then on they rode out together two or three times a week, once going to visit his foxhounds, until he left Simla on the 19th October.

Lord Herbrand Russell was one of several young men serving on the Viceroy's staff at this time. Twenty-seven years old, he was the second son, and youngest child, of the 9th Duke of Bedford and had joined the Grenadier Guards when he was twenty, seven years previously. He had served in the Egyptian campaign in 1882 and was now one of the Viceroy's ADCs.

Herbrand's father, a nephew of Lord John Russell, the Prime Minister, inherited the Dukedom when Herbrand was thirteen years old. While he acquired a lifelong attachment to the family home at Woburn Abbey, with a reverence for its traditions and the magnificence of daily life there, he had no expectation of inheriting it, at least in the foreseeable future. At the time when he first met Mary, in 1886, his parents, in their mid sixties, were flourishing. His older brother George, some six years his senior, was a qualified barrister who, following in their father's footsteps, served as a Liberal Member of Parliament for a decade and took an active part in Bedfordshire affairs, although after almost ten years of marriage George remained childless.

Lord Herbrand as ADC

George was the more intellectual of the two brothers. He graduated from Balliol College, Oxford where he was taught by and subsequently became close friends with the great Dr. Benjamin Jowett[2], as did their father and George's wife. Herbrand, too, was at Balliol before joining the army. He was a soldier by inclination as well as profession, though his passionate interest in mammals, and deer in particular, later developed along academic as well as practical lines.

Herbrand first met Mary at a dinner given at Peterhof by the Viceroy soon after the Tribe family moved to Simla in 1886. They were introduced by Herbrand's friend Lord William Beresford, who was also serving at the time on the Viceroy's staff; Lord William was some ten years older than Herbrand and had won the V.C. in the Zulu War nearly a decade before. This first meeting was remembered by Herbrand for the rest of his life, though for Mary, new to Simla and still unable quite to forget Carpy, the novelty and glamour of such occasions made a deeper impression than the individuals she met.

Herbrand at this time was somewhat shy and diffident, lacking in self confidence but with an ability to laugh at himself which would have astonished his grandson Ian, the 13th Duke. (Ian declared in his own autobiography *A Silver-Plated Spoon* that he had only ever heard of one joke attributed to Herbrand, when Herbrand, speaking to the Zoological Society, quoted a letter from his agent: 'I beg to inform Your Lordship that the emus have laid an egg. In Your Lordship's absence I have obtained the biggest goose I could to sit on it.')

Even his own name struck Herbrand as farcical. He later told Mary that he cursed his Godfathers and Godmothers: 'Why they could not have called me Samuel or Jeremiah I can't think. Any decent well known name would do.'

Nor did he have any delusions about his position in India. The Viceroy's two eldest daughters were aged twenty-two and eighteen. Both were unmarried at this time. After his engagement to Mary, Herbrand wrote to her to explain the need for particular tact in dealing with the Viceroy and his wife.

'Because, dear girl, if you insist on knowing the truth, Lord and Lady Dufferin always meant me to marry somebody else and not your own dear little self at all. This parental plan you have entirely upset. It was this idea that kept me on the staff, otherwise, being the worst of ADCs, I should have been sent away with several fleas in my ear long ago.'

Herbrand was far from the only young man to be taking an interest in the new arrival. Mary was not only one of the best looking girls at Simla, she was also different from the others. In England at this time, a girl who excelled at sport and was constantly becoming involved in sometimes dangerous adventures would have been regarded as shockingly boisterous, causing the older generation at least to raise disapproving eyebrows at her antics. Mary had long since learnt to shoot and the skirts she frequently wore, short enough to reveal her ankles, were regarded by some as scandalous. But the atmosphere at Simla was sufficiently relaxed for her tomboy nature to be widely admired.

An elderly General (Major-General Nigel Woodyatt of the Gurkhas) told in his memoirs *Under Ten Viceroys* of an episode when, for some reason, he was transporting jackals by train. One got loose. Mary and her father happened to be on the station and Mary was soon crouching in the doorway holding the railway van door ajar to let in sufficient light for the General to attempt to catch the jackal in a blanket, while she prevented it from making a bid for freedom through the gap.[3]

She had nerves of iron. Riding with Herbrand on a narrow mountain track, her pony shied and lost his footing on a slope just above a sheer precipice. Mary kept her cool, sitting absolutely still, and miraculously the pony managed to stop just before they both went over the edge. Talking of the episode years later, she recalled

"You remember when I came down from the Kud on the pony. Do you know, when you came down to help me you had turned as white as a sheet?"[4]

Mary was an excellent horsewoman, the only benefit she derived from the year in Zurich which cut into her time at Cheltenham. Herbrand shared neither her love of nor her skill with horses.

She also had a tremendous sense of fun, enjoying such activities as captaining the Lahore Ladies at cricket against the 5th Fusiliers and Lahore in a match commemorated in a Kipling poem. The game was not played totally in accordance with the rules of cricket: 'The Ladies were to play as they liked. This they certainly did...' While the Ladies used cricket bats, the men had broom sticks and could only bowl and field with the left hand or foot. Miss Tribe was singled out for particular praise, not only for her bowling but also because, when she perceived that 'the batsman at her end had backed up too far, she dexterously ran him out.'[5]

Mary as Joan of Arc for the Viceroy's fancy dress ball

A highlight of that summer was the Viceroy's fancy dress ball. Mary appeared, to the admiration of Herbrand, as Joan of Arc. Lord William Beresford was a Chelsea Pensioner: no record remains of Herbrand's own dress. The Viceroy received his guests in formal attire then caused consternation by reappearing as a tiresome elderly Arab Sheik, whom nobody recognised. At a similar occasion the following year, the correspondent of an English newspaper recorded the event, commenting 'I should certainly recommend the wearer of a costume à la Watteau to adopt that dress in every-day life, for it was decidedly becoming.' The person in question was Mary.

Her older grandson Ian, the future 13th Duke of Bedford, had a somewhat different impression of his grandmother's early life. In *A Silver Plated Spoon* he writes:

'There' (in India) 'she compounded her frustrations by retiring at frequent intervals to the top of the steeple in her father's church, where she learnt Indian dialects and made friends with a bat. One of the military heroes of the time, Lord William Beresford, V.C., who was military secretary to the Viceroy, persuaded her to come down from the belfry long enough to attend a viceregal ball, where she was introduced to her future husband.'[6]

The autumn was quieter as the men returned to their work in the plains. Mary and her father remained in Simla for Christmas, then came back to Lahore in January. In addition to the ever popular amateur theatricals and tennis, Mary once more pursued her own interest in medicine. She was soon attending regular classes and lectures and recorded with glee in February 1887 that she had just bandaged her first real patient.

Herbrand had three main interests in life. His enthusiasm for matters military persisted for the rest of his life, long after he ceased to be a professional soldier. His loyalty and devotion to Queen and country, particularly as represented by the army, was much to his credit. It was unfortunate that this was also the principal reason, many years later, for his bitter disillusionment with his only son.

The other two abiding passions of his life flourished only after he inherited Woburn. The estate itself, the house, the land and the whole way in which it was managed was of absorbing interest to him. His ownership of it also enabled him to develop his fascination with and deep knowledge of natural history in a remarkable way. He set out to collect at Woburn representatives of every species of deer in the world. Although he did not succeed in this, he did have some extremely rare ones, successfully establishing a breeding herd of Père David deer, which were close to extinction, so that eventually healthy specimens were sent back to China, where they originated, to re-establish themselves. Mary too had a keen interest in natural history. Although she gave no indication at this time that she would later become one of the leading ornithologists of her age, this shared interest undoubtedly made a major contribution to the early bond between them.

Most of the Russell family are tall and thin, sometimes with a slight stoop, with sallow complexions and dark straight hair. Herbrand was quite different. He was short, relatively thickset, with gingery hair and moustache. His younger grandson, Lord Hugh Russell, described him as 'a very short man with a temper to match, a little man with a little man's personality.' But he was also usually kind with a keen sense of responsibility. He took the duties which went with his position seriously, sometimes excessively so. This could make him appear more pompous than he might otherwise have done. It was also evidence of a strong philanthropic streak in his nature. The manner in which this manifested itself later in Herbrand's life may appear to modern eyes paternalistic and even somewhat patronising. But the way in which he cared for all his staff at Woburn was not seen in that light on the estate at the time. He was popular with his army of employees. Hugh recalled standing by a window at Woburn in the 1930s with his grandfather and a cousin. As they watched they could see six men, side by side, scything the lawn. At every third stroke they stopped to sharpen their scythes. This had continued for most of the morning. Finally Sheila asked,

"Herbrand, why don't you buy a motor mower?"

He looked at her and said

"Sheila, that takes six men. If I bought a motor mower it would take one."

He never sacked anybody on the estate. They all had houses to which they retired. His quiet generosity during and after the First World War to the men who had fought, and to their families, far exceeded that shown elsewhere.

This spirit struck a chord with Mary, who had a deeply philanthropic nature. She probably already had some conception of the ways in which Herbrand's position and money could open doors. Perhaps she had a vision of how much could be achieved by allying his generous nature and his wealth with her energy and the ability she already knew that she possessed. She can have had no concept of the hospitals she was eventually to establish and run so successfully for the benefit of so many people, entirely financed by Herbrand: had he not inherited Woburn much sooner than anyone could have anticipated, achievements would inevitably have been on a much smaller scale. But her imagination could have been fired by dreams such as these.

If she was already thinking of what could be achieved for others with his money, then it might be suggested that the whole basis of their relationship on her side was mercenary: that she planned to marry him for his money. If she thought about it at all, which she must have done, she would certainly have been conscious of what money could do, not just for the wider community but more specifically for her family and perhaps herself. None of her papers in any way indicates an avaricious streak, though after their marriage her financial position undoubtedly enabled her to achieve personal as well as philanthropic goals. But she had never complained about the lack of money, never seemed other than content with her lot. Discussions between Mary and Zoë about family finances tended to revolve around what they perceived as their father's mercenary streak and how mean he could be, usually in relation to Aunt Fanny or to one of their brothers. One letter Zoë wrote to Mary expostulates at length on how difficult it was for Charles when he stayed with friends in England and had to be dependent on other people 'treating' him, although he had reached an age when he needed some financial independence and to be able sometimes to 'treat' his friends. With Herbrand's money, Mary would be able to right so many such injustices, and indeed later did so. But an appreciation of the benefits which money can confer is very different from an intention to marry for money. Mary's direct, forthright nature would not only have made any such idea utterly repugnant to her, it would also have made it impossible. Concealing her emotions did not come naturally to her.

It is unlikely too that Mary derived satisfaction from the idea that she was 'marrying well', although her father, much more socially ambitious than either of his daughters, felt that all his hopes and dreams, all his plans and the investment he had made in Mary's education, had reached fruition in a remarkable way. Mary probably saw the new life opening up before her as offering new challenges and new opportunities on a hitherto undreamed of scale. She always relished a new challenge. Later she became increasingly averse to social life as her hearing deteriorated, but at this stage she had shown since her move to Simla how willing she was to conquer new worlds socially.

At first, however, she was shyly conscious of the yawning social gap between them. She worried a great deal about Herbrand throwing himself away by marrying her, despite his constant assurances that this was arrant nonsense.

Herbrand was soon deeply in love with her. His devotion was in itself a most attractive quality. They had many interests in common, in particular their burgeoning passion for natural history. From the start, they enjoyed each other's company: Mary found him a congenial companion. Fifty years later, they still found time every day when they were both at home to enjoy a walk together. In the early days in India they had so much to talk about, so many shared interests, so many totally different experiences.

On the other hand, her diary no longer contained all the cryptic passages in secret code which with Carpy surely indicated the sharing of greater excitements than mutual delight in the animals and birds of India. Perhaps Mary had learned discretion in the keeping of her journal: accurate though it is as a record, never again does it show quite the ingenuous sparkle of those early years. But even those coded diary entries from the time of her romance with Carpy which are easily interpreted are generally totally innocent, typical of a young girl in love for the first time. Putting them into code was just part of the romance and the fun. All the evidence suggests that Mary was not a highly sexed woman, that physical passion played little part in her life at any stage. Her grandson wrote that after the birth of her son 'I very much doubt whether she and my grandfather ever lived together again as man and wife.'[7] Unreliable as so many of his writings are, it is possible, as will emerge later, that in this case the 13th Duke was correct. If this was so, it probably had nothing to do with her feelings for Herbrand himself. In later life she had ample opportunity to find someone more attractive to her. There is no suggestion that she ever showed the slightest inclination to do so. From the start, this was the only characteristic of Mary which worried Herbrand, as he openly told her, in as light hearted a way as possible. After their engagement, he teased her gently in his letters.

'I could count on the fingers of my hand the number of prim little, cold little, short little kisses which were given me under great pressure. I once knew a gilded youth who, when he went to meet the young lady to whom he was engaged, left the Guards Club swearing that if she attempted to kiss him he would break off his engagement. I think he would have suited Miss Mary du Caurroy Tribe better than her present lover...'

He teased her too about a pain in her ribs; presumably this had been an excuse for avoiding close embraces. He also assured her that he would never so much as touch her against her will. No doubt he hoped that a combination of patience and gentle teasing would, with the passing of time, resolve the problem, attributing it in his mind to the modesty of an inexperienced young girl. Yet, even had he realised that no such outcome would ever occur, passionate as he was, Herbrand would still not have hesitated.

At the time of their engagement, Mary knew very little about sex.

Victorian girls were kept in total ignorance of the subject. Since all her contemporaries at school shared her innocence, any discussion amongst them was likely to disseminate more false information than factual truth. However, Mary's interest in medical matters and her travels with her father to remote villages where Victorian ideals of modesty had not been adopted may in practice have given her a greater knowledge than her friends in England.

Women at the time were generally believed to be incapable of experiencing physical pleasure or desire. The traditional advice to young brides was to 'shut your eyes and think of England.' Herbrand's own knowledge and experience was probably relatively limited. Yet these limitations applied to almost all the young men and women of the time. Herbrand's letters reveal considerable sympathy and understanding for the feelings of his future wife, which should have boded well for their long-term relationship. But it is also clear from his letters that Mary was already showing considerable reluctance, and that Herbrand was keen to bring her anxieties into the open between them. Even mentioning the issue at all before their marriage was unusually open on the part of the bridegroom, and reveals Herbrand as a very different character from the insensitive reactionary later portrayed by his grandson.

Mary's relationship with Herbrand was quite different from her relationship with Carpy. Carpy was the archetypal 'boy-next-door', her best friend and playmate, sharer of a thousand jokes and games, who inevitably soon started to see her in a different light. It took her longer but soon, like teenagers and students the world over, the young couple fell in love. We do not know what caused Mary to change her mind. It was not a physical issue, for the change in her feelings occurred while they were hundreds of miles apart. Perhaps she simply felt that they were growing away from each other, though this would have been less likely to happen in Mary's world than with a similar young couple today. The girls coming over with the 'Fishing Fleet' expected to have made a match for life after a single season. Mary's engagement to Carpy must have seemed perfect to onlookers. They knew each other very well and had been close friends long before they fell in love. They enjoyed each other's company, shared many interests and Mary had a much clearer understanding of life in India than the girls coming over for the season. Mary had all the qualities required for an army officer's wife and Carpy was an attractive young man, fun, kind and a capable soldier, likely to make an excellent husband and father. Most likely, she realised that she wanted more out of life than this, that she had more to put into it than most of her contemporaries, and the vision of life as a wife and mother in a remote corner of the Empire seemed frustrating and depressing.

Herbrand by comparison must have seemed an exciting and exotic figure. If part of Carpy's attraction had lain in the similarity of their backgrounds and experience, Herbrand's appeal was that he had seen and done so much. He was older than Carpy and the England of his childhood was a world away from hers. Herbrand was an ordinary man, possessed of no exceptional qualities, of average intelligence, kind and loyal with a strong sense of duty, but he came from an extraordinary background. For his part, he immediately recognised in Mary, before others were aware of them, a strength of character, intelligence and capability which were most unusual. He was flattered and delighted by her interest in him and his devotion to her never wavered.

In some ways the relationship between the couple altered amazingly little in the fifty years of their courtship and marriage. From start to finish they enjoyed each other's company and shared many interests and objectives while retaining large parts of their lives independent of each other. Theirs was never a passionate love affair, yet Herbrand loved her deeply all his life. She was unable to respond in the same way, but repaid his devotion with consideration, kindliness and a sense of appreciation which rarely faltered. They developed their own ways of dealing with the tensions inevitably created by the position. Each had a price to pay, but ultimately both thought it had all been worthwhile.

In the spring they returned to Simla. The enduring magic of the place probably helped Lord Herbrand. Generations later another young girl was to recall 'It's difficult to convey how enormously romantic the atmosphere was in Simla,… the warm starlit nights and bright, huge moon, those towering hills and mountains stretching away, silence and strange exotic smells.'[8] At all events, from their return, Mary's collection of dance cards features Lord Herbrand with increasing frequency. At one such occasion in June the name of her original proposed dinner partner is crossed out and that of Lord Herbrand substituted.

He knew then that he had found the girl of his dreams and longed to propose immediately. The ideal would have been a midsummer engagement with a wedding at Simla in November, surrounded by all their friends, before the inevitable return to the plains. No separation would then have been necessary. There was just one problem, as he afterwards explained to Mary.

'Of course I ought to have married you in November at Simla, but dear girl if you throw your lot in with that of a poor younger son you must remember that he can't disregard his relations and consultations with them take a very long time when conducted by letter from India.'

This was prudent and sensible. If he had failed to carry his parents with him, the young couple could well have found themselves cut off without a penny. As it was, Mary and Herbrand's older grandson Ian (the 13th Duke) maintained in his biography of Mary that the reaction was somewhat chilly. Not only, he tells us, were the 9th Duke and his Duchess known as 'The Icebergs', but they were dismayed by the news of Herbrand's marriage.

"'You don't mean to say", said the Duke, "that he's going to marry a barmaid or a native woman!"

And the Duchess is said to have answered: "Not quite that – she's European at least, though only an Archdeacon's daughter!"[9]

Eventually Herbrand succeeded in winning them round sufficiently to obtain official sanction, though neither his father nor brother (the 9th and 10th Dukes respectively) was prepared to travel out to India for the ceremony, both pleading ill health. Herbrand was not concerned. Despite his reverence for his family in the abstract, no love was lost between him and the individual members of it. He may have left England on bad terms with his father. He told Mary that it was only through her that he was able to return. As a married man he would be able to live independently in his own establishment.

On several occasions he told Mary how much he disliked his family, characteristically including himself in his condemnation.

'I don't want you to become a Russell in more than in name. They are a cold, cynical, selfish, hard-hearted race. You, my darling, are the opposite to these attributes and I want you to remain unchanged... I have had thirty years' experience of them. As you have probably found out, a Russell is a very disagreeable beast indeed.'

Having overcome the first obstacle, the opposition of his parents, he had now to confront the second: Mary herself. At last he was in a position to propose to her. Her response was more chilling and demoralising even than that of his family

"Really, Lord Herbrand, I could not."

The uncharacteristically icy pomposity of the reply was probably caused by her consciousness of the social chasm between them rather than by any reluctance on her part. Certainly, Herbrand teased her unmercifully about her reply in the months that followed. By the time that he proposed for the second time, she was ready to accept.

Their friends seem to have been unaware of the problems. Few of them were surprised when they arrived for yet another Viceregal Ball in October 1887 to find the young couple standing on a dais beside Lord and Lady Dufferin.

'Before we were told, we could all guess what had happened,' one of them later recalled. 'The natural and striking beauty of Miss Tribe was enhanced by happiness, and we all of us, for the most part serving and living in India, rejoiced in her happiness and felt proud of her.'

The Viceroy's letter to Mary paid tribute to Herbrand. 'I am very much attached to your future husband, and have the highest opinion of his abilities and of his character. He is one of the kindest, sweetest-tempered, and most high-minded men I ever knew – and in marrying him I am sure your future happiness in assured.' In fact, just the sort of man he would have chosen for his own daughter to marry.

Still Herbrand himself continued to worry right up to the day of the wedding. He had no doubts at all that he had taken the right decision. He was only afraid that Mary would change her mind. Knowing how she had jilted Carpy after they were engaged, he was in constant fear that she would treat him in the same way.

'You see, dearest Mary, I can't help being suspicious of a young lady who has jilted several lovers.' (Presumably this is mock exaggeration: there is no evidence of a third romance.) 'It is like a buck jumping horse. You never know when they won't do it again.'

He goes on to remind her that there is only one thing which is worse.

'Please remember that it is much easier to throw a man away before marriage. (Afterwards) there are legal complications and you are not free.'

The young couple were separated for the last two months of their engagement but wrote to each other every day. Herbrand's letters were often four pages or more in length and are delightful, reflecting a dry sense of humour. The pompous, cold image held by later generations is stripped away, 'especially as he (referring to himself) happens to love you more than you probably think him capable of.'

He teases her constantly, about her Cheltenham education (particularly if she happens to make a spelling mistake), about showing some of his letters to 'the archidiaconal father', about the arrangements for all her boxes of possessions, about the failings of her horse and about her reluctance to accept presents from him. He grows a beard, sends her a photograph and, when she expresses revulsion, shaves it off again.

He guides her through the minefield of relations with his family and with the Viceroy, giving her hints on the letters to be written and does his utmost to protect her, allaying her fears by his mockery of their pomposity.

'The Dufferins are the most ridiculously 'touchy' people I have ever seen and unless you make a terrible fuss with them they howl like scalded cats.'

'I should rather like to avoid Easter in England... you see my family have a habit of going to the ancestral halls at Easter and I don't think, Mary dear, it would be fair on you to pitch you into a gathering of Russells immediately after arrival, and if you were in England you would have to go.'

He assures her that he has told his family that her Christian names are Tabitha Mary du Caurroy, because they will infer from this that she is low church and puritanical. Because of, or despite, this, his mother, at a loss as to what would give pleasure to the daughter-in-law she had never met, sent the massive sum of £500 for Mary to spend as she chooses, except, Herbrand himself puts in, she must not 'fritter it away for purposes of charity.'

He tells her tales of his everyday life:

'There is a horrid cat here which attacked me in bed this morning. I hate facing savage animals in my 'chemise de nuit.' You say you love the feline tribe. I love the Mary Tribe but not the feline.'

Herbrand's own contribution to the plans for the wedding seemed always to be moving too slowly for his impatient longing for the day. They were to be married by a Mr. Orton, chaplain of Barrackpore, assisted by her father, the Archdeacon of Lahore. Herbrand was responsible for negotiations with Mr. Orton, and was soon referring to him as 'a lunatic.'

'The Barrackpore parson has not yet answered – I can't think what he is doing. I expect he knows nothing at all about how to marry people properly and is finding out from his friends how this may be accomplished.'

His personal preparations included selling a horse and his pack of hounds in readiness for returning home 'with one wife (more not being allowed), one maid, one manservant, three arab horses, one white pony Jessamine with a maid of her own and probably two sweet little one-year-old wild boars... it is just as well not to go home with too many things when one is married.'

Wedding – standing behind Mary are (l to r)
the Viceroy (in black top hat), her father and Herbrand (hatless).
Next to Herbrand in grey top hat is the best man, Lord William Beresford

The wedding took place very quietly on 30th January 1888 at eight o'clock in the morning (despite Lady Dufferin pointing out the disadvantages of weddings held on an empty stomach, such as brides fainting and other disasters) at St Bartholomew's Church, Barrackpore, in what Mary later described as 'the record time of 15 minutes.' Lord William Beresford was Best Man and lent them his bungalow at Barrackpore for the first part of their honeymoon. The wedding breakfast took place under the banyan tree in the garden there.

Their extended honeymoon was passed in magnificent style. After a stay at Darjeeling, they left Bombay for England, stopping on the way in Cairo, where Herbrand had served during the Egyptian campaign. They stayed at the world famous Shepherd's Hotel, but Mary's chief recollection of it in later life was of the bedbugs. She next returned to the city forty-two years later, on her record-breaking flight to the Cape, and insisted on finding a different hotel. In Europe they visited Cannes and Berlin. On the Riviera they met Herbrand's unmarried sister Ela and his first cousin Lady Margaret Cecil. In Berlin they stayed at the British Embassy with his other sister Lady Ermyntrude Malet and her husband Sir Edward. Lady Ermyntrude kindly offered them the use of her Eaton Square house for their final port of call, London.

It was all a far cry from the Europe Mary had previously known: Aunt Fanny's house in Pulborough, lodgings in Cheltenham and in Zurich. Despite the happiness and enthusiasm surrounding her in the weeks leading up to her wedding, Mary needed all her courage to confront the changes which lay before her. She realised that she would be entirely dependent on her own inner resources and on the support of her husband. In some ways she knew him less well than she had known Carpy, for their courtship had been a more public affair, taking place in the full glare of Simla society.

Perhaps it was fortunate that Mary was less impressed with the change in her social position brought about by her marriage than were many of her friends and family. This probably helped her to approach her first meeting with her parents-in-law with some equanimity. Even at this time, she had a self confidence and composure unusual for a girl of her age. Despite all this, it was undoubtedly an ordeal. Her meetings with her two sisters-in-law did little to reduce her anxiety. Neither was ever to become close to her. She later expressively described Ela as writing and speaking 'with a thump. And I always thought she administered her charity with a mailed fist.'[10] Later, Herbrand himself used to refer to his married sister, Lady Ermyntrude Malet, as 'Aunt Vermin' when talking to his son Hastings, though the nervous small boy found her unfailingly kind.[11]

Despite this inauspicious start, when the Russell family met Mary, her dignity, poise and strength of character won them over. Although relations between mother-in-law and daughter-in-law remained strictly formal for the rest of the older woman's life, the Duke and Duchess both realised that their son had made a wise choice.

The months leading up to and following her marriage had brought Mary the challenges and changes her nature craved. Now she became aware that her life was about to change again. She had already achieved what her parents-in-law saw as her most important duty. She was pregnant. The relief of knowing that she had done what was expected of her probably did more than any delight in the prospect of forthcoming motherhood to compensate for the discomforts of pregnancy. Not a naturally maternal woman, she was an extremely dutiful one. She knew that, in marrying her, Herbrand was hoping for a wife whom he loved, a loyal friend and a son and heir. Mary always believed in keeping her side of any bargain.

Dance cards with
Lord Herbrand's name predominating

CHAPTER 4

HASTINGS AND JEMIMA

Mary, taken at Dublin 1901

To Mary's delight, Herbrand now proposed that they should settle in Scotland. Already she had learned that, in England, families like her husband's were expected to entertain and be entertained, and to put in occasional appearances at court. Social life in Simla was fun for a young girl, but she had no wish to devote endless evenings, in Bedfordshire or London, to people with whom she had little in common. Mary lacked patience with those who bored her. She was becoming increasingly aware, too, that she had difficulty sometimes in hearing what strangers were saying to her. Although not yet a serious problem, her hearing had been deteriorating ever since her illness when first she arrived in India. This made her reluctant to risk situations where she might feel that she had made a fool of herself.

At heart she always preferred life away from the city. This was probably her first experience of Scotland. She came to love the country deeply, and, as she awaited the birth of her baby, the hills, moors, bird and animal life and above all space, to be alone, or with only Herbrand for company, was what she most desired. She was relieved, too, not to be expected to live in close proximity either to her parents-in-law or to her brother- and sister-in-law.

If Herbrand was responsible for the decision, he displayed exceptional sympathy and understanding. Despite the number of houses owned by the family at Woburn, in London, at Endsleigh in Devon and elsewhere, the house they moved into was rented. The Cairnsmore estate in Galloway (which plays a prominent part in John Buchan's book *The Thirty-Nine Steps*) was to be their Scottish home for the rest of their lives. It remained on a long lease and was never bought by the family. Houses meant little to Mary: the countryside in which they were situated was important.

Fortunately Herbrand's parents approved of the move. Mary dutifully sent regular reports on all that was happening at Cairnsmore to her mother-in-law, though the correspondence remained stiff and formal. The Duchess continued to address her daughter-in-law by her title. Letters between the different members of the Tribe family are warm, affectionate and direct. They sparkle with merriment, shared intimacies and open criticisms of the correspondent or other family members. The Duchess addressed Mary, if not, as Queen Victoria complained of Gladstone, as if she were a public meeting, at least as a Duchess addressing a member of society of slightly lower rank.

'Oct 29 1888

Dear Lady Herbrand

I thank you for your letter received on the 16 of October and for the photograph of Cairnsmore, where I am glad to think that you have, happily, spent your earliest married days. That you may make Herbrand a good, and a very good, wife is what I ask. If you can do this, I shall indeed be grateful

Yours affectionately

Bedford'

A year later there was no relaxation.

'Nov 5 1889

Dear Lady Herbrand

Until you see your Teypore Shield, hanging in my writing room, with its inscription, you can have no idea of its splendid effect.

In no other place could it have been seen, every day, to such advantage

Yours affectionately

Bedford'

Mary was left in no doubt that her present from India was honoured indeed by being hung on the wall at Woburn. This was the closest to an expression of gratitude which she was likely to receive for her gift.

As Mary's pregnancy progressed and activities inevitably became restricted, she was delighted to have her sister Zoë to stay. Zoë had had two little daughters, both of whom tragically died in India in a cholera epidemic. She never forgot them and still had a box with her containing two babies' dresses and locks of hair when she died in her late nineties. By the time of Mary's pregnancy, she also had a year old son, Philip. Her second son, Noel, was born in 1892. Zoë stayed with her sister until mid December, leaving Mary to prepare for a quiet Christmas with Herbrand. The baby was due in the New Year. Whatever plans Mary had made for the birth of her baby were pre-empted on the 20th and 21st December. Her grandson gave the following account in *A Silver-Plated Spoon*:

'It was here' (at Cairnsmoor - *sic*) 'that my father was born, and I cannot help feeling that the circumstances of his arrival had a direct influence on the personal relationships we all later had to suffer. My grandfather and grandmother were walking together alone across the moors one bitter winter morning, only four days before the Christmas of 1888, when she suddenly realised that her child was about to be born. With an icy wind whistling round them and the cries of wild birds as their only company, they had to seek shelter in a derelict shepherd's cottage, the only building in sight. There was no doctor, no midwife, only a couple of hurriedly summoned farm servants. My father was born on a rough couch of heather, something which our hardy ancestors of Tudor days might have survived better, but which was certainly a cause of lasting shock and distress to my grandmother. She never had another child and I very much doubt whether she and my grandfather ever lived together again as man and wife. He had always wanted a large family and for the rest of his life remained a withdrawn and disappointed man.'[1]

Cairnsmore

When the 13th Duke came to write another book, a biography of his grandmother, nine years later, this story was totally omitted. There is only a simple statement of the date of his father's birth in the text[2]. A revised assessment by John Gore, Mary's first biographer, of her life and character, written with less constraint since Herbrand was no longer alive, is included as an Appendix. John Gore had unique access, not only to the relevant documents, but also to the personal recollections of Herbrand and many others alive at the time. His original biography gave no details of the birth of Hastings at all[3], suggesting that this was not an occasion which Herbrand recalled with any pleasure. In the Appendix[4] Gore states: 'There at Cairnsmore, their only child Hastings (afterwards 12th Duke) was born before he was expected in December 1888 (and not, as local tradition had it, in a shepherd's hut on a lonely moor without expert assistance).' Gore evidently felt that the 13th Duke's original account required correction in content as well as in spelling.

Even if the precise circumstances were later exaggerated, there is no doubt that the birth of her only son, named Hastings after his grandfather, was a deeply distressing event for Mary. It is widely recognised that a traumatic birth can cause a mother to have difficulty in bonding with her baby and she appears to have suffered from post-natal depression.

Throughout her life, however, from the time when her pony fell down the Kud near Simla to her flying adventures in old age, Mary was renowned for her physical courage and resilience. Her grandson Ian's conclusion that she maintained a lifelong grudge against the unwitting cause of her suffering, the baby, seems somewhat implausible. Nor is his suggestion convincing that she resolved never to have another child and ensured that she did not by refusing ever again to share her husband's bed, if this is based solely on her experience of the actual birth. Any such deep-seated resentment would surely have extended to the countryside where it happened, but there is ample evidence that she loved Cairnsmore deeply for the rest of her life. Nor was it in her character to react in such a way. Mary had a quick temper but a forgiving nature, as Herbrand himself wrote after her death:

'Her wrath was highly disconcerting to its object; but it passed, leaving no sting behind. And, though I never heard of a formal apology coming from her lips, her friends were made aware by some special little act of kindliness that the crisis was over! …as I myself can testify, the resentment and impatience were short lived.'[5]

Mary on the moors near Cairnsmore on a pony

Yet the facts remain that Mary did not become pregnant again and that her relationship with her son was never good. There is no evidence as to whether she resumed full marital relations with her husband. There was no reliable form of contraception available at the time and Mary had done her duty: she had presented Herbrand with the obligatory male heir, if not with the traditional 'spare'. Any explanation of these matters must be sought beyond a single winter's day on the Scottish moors.

Nearly fifty years after the birth of Hastings, Mary responded to a letter from her oldest grandson Ian:

'You ask why I did not give my son the education I recommend for you 'if I think it is so good'. I had nothing whatever to do with your father's education; it was taken entirely out of my hands. At the age of one month his grandparents altered all the arrangements I made for him and continued to preside till they died, after which your grandfather and Miss Greene' (Flora Green, spelt without a final 'e', arrived originally as governess to Hastings, and remained at Woburn for the rest of her life; she was always known to the family as Jemima, although she remained Miss Green to Hastings and his children) 'entirely ruled matters and I was not permitted even to know what was being done. I was entertained for a night in Africa during one of my flights by the Governor of a province who told me that he had been tutor to my son for a time. I had never even heard of him!...'[6]

This seems a much more likely reason for Mary to lose interest in her son, or in having any further children. She blames both her parents-in-law, though the tone of the letters written by the old Duchess at this time is neither dictatorial nor indicative of anything but the most bemused and distantly polite interest:

'Oct 21 1889

I forget when babies begin to crawl? When will the small boy begin?'

'7 Sept 1890

No wonder the little boy likes the use of his legs. They are a great delight, while they last... Mine are wearing out fast. God grant he may turn out well. Bring him up as well as you can. It is a first duty.'

Unfortunately Ian does not indicate what she was recommending as a desirable form of education. The chief complaint of Hastings later in his life was that he hated his time at Eton. He consequently refused to send any of his own children to public school. Mary is unlikely to have shared this opinion. She had enjoyed her own time at boarding school. Perhaps the plans, which she felt were so wantonly disregarded, related rather to his early education, though it is hard to imagine why these should have come up in discussions with a grandson in his late teens.

Mary may have planned to start her son's education herself. She was an intelligent woman who had not at that time found an outlet for her immense energy and ability. A rebuff on this front would have hurt and angered her bitterly, particularly coming within a month of the ordeal she had endured to bring Hastings into the world. Nor would it have crossed the minds of her husband or his father, the old Duke, that a young girl like Mary could have any worthwhile opinion on the education of a boy, the heir to one of the greatest families in the land. This, they would have argued, was a matter for themselves, with their knowledge of their own education and that of their forebears, and for professionals, for trained, qualified and experienced tutors and governesses.

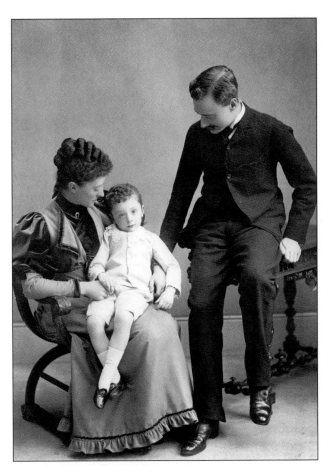

Mary and Herbrand with Hastings

If such a battle did take place, and Mary's letter to Ian makes it clear that there was some such clash of wills, it would explain much that followed. With her husband and parents-in-law united against her, there was nothing that Mary could do or say to alter the situation. Her father-in-law was described by Benjamin Disraeli as having 'a lower opinion of human nature than any man', which does not make him sound an easy character to deal with. On the other hand his official papers show that he was involved in a wide range of interests and activities and clearly commanded affection as well as respect from many people. Perhaps his wife was more deserving of the somewhat cruel nickname, 'the Icebergs', than the 9th Duke.

Just after his grandson's second birthday, in January 1891, the Duke contracted pneumonia. He became feverish, running a very high temperature. Tragically, while he was delirious, with his mind unbalanced by his illness, he shot himself. Herbrand's older brother George became the 10th Duke of Bedford.

George was thirty-eight years old. He was a barrister and had been a Liberal Member of Parliament for ten years until the abolition of his Bedfordshire constituency. At the time of his father's death, he had been married for fourteen years, but the marriage was childless. Only two years later, on the 23rd March 1893, George died of diabetes. Herbrand became the 11th Duke of Bedford.

The early 1890s were a sad time for Mary and Herbrand. In 1892, after the death of Herbrand's father but before the death of his brother, Mary's own younger brother Willie, who was only twenty-two, died of typhoid. She grieved for the wasted life of the little boy who had dreamed, with his twin, of becoming a farmer, but had been willing, if their mother so wished, to become a doctor instead. Mary's only consolation was that she had been able to help all three of her brothers, paying for their further education.

If Mary shed tears only for her brother, perhaps on the death of her brother-in-law she wept for herself. Cairnsmore, henceforward, was only a holiday home and a retreat. The young family moved to Woburn Abbey to take up their formal position. The glamour of becoming a duchess had scant appeal for her. On the other hand, she was always looking for new challenges. Cairnsmore offered little scope for her to expand her horizons, restricted as she was in the part she was allowed to play in the life of her son. At this time in her life, she had a wide range of interests which she pursued in turn with indefatigable energy, almost always excelling, whatever skills the favoured activity demanded. She did not have any set purpose or overriding interest. That was to come later. If she was consciously looking for such a cause, she may even have imagined that she would find it in the administration of Woburn. If so, she was to be bitterly disappointed.

For Herbrand, despite the sad family circumstances, this was the opportunity of his dreams. Although he had spent so much time away from Woburn, his heritage and his home meant everything to him He passionately believed that it must continue to be run as it always had been, and made it his life's work to ensure that this continued. We do not know whether Mary at first wished to take over any part of the empire: whatever her original intentions, she soon accepted that there was no place for her on the managerial side. For the next fifty years, Herbrand supervised everything. Probably Mary had no interest even in such details as discussing the meals each day with the cook. With the management skills she was later to demonstrate, providing back-up support held no attraction for her. Herbrand wished to take sole command. As soon as Mary accepted that this was the way her husband wished to run their lives, she stepped back and found her own interests elsewhere. Herbrand, in return, gave her full support, moral and financial, in whatever she chose to do.

We do not know either whether this agreement was reached smoothly and spontaneously or whether it was the outcome of a prolonged and bitter struggle. For Mary, who retained virtually every letter she received as a child and young adult, has left no personal correspondence whatever, except for a handful of letters from Hastings towards the end of her life. It is true that, from correspondence with Carpy before her marriage, only his last sad letter remains. She kept safe all the letters which she received from Herbrand, when they were separated during the months of their engagement, as well as a few after their marriage. Perhaps she later decided that it was best to destroy everything as soon as she had replied to it. Perhaps, late on in life, she decided to burn everything, but this seems unlikely, since not only her childhood letters but also the diaries which she had kept throughout her life, as well as Herbrand's letters, survived. Perhaps Herbrand decided after her death that the correspondence she had received, including presumably all his own later letters, should be destroyed, but that the diary which she had written herself should be preserved, This he provided as the main source for John Gore's biography. Herbrand, too, left no private papers of his own. Mary was a very private person without close confidantes, unless she continued to confide in Zoë. Her voice can only speak to future generations through her actions and through the memories of those who knew her and recorded what they remembered.

Everyone at Woburn knew that all decisions relating to the house and estate were outside Mary's sphere of influence. If this applied equally to issues concerning her son, Hastings himself was not aware of this. When he came to write his own autobiography, he held his mother responsible for everything which happened to him which caused him unhappiness. The first such event was the departure of his beloved nurse 'Teetums'. So upset was he that the timid child plucked up courage to beg his father to let her stay, but to no avail. Whatever the merits of the case, the impression it made on the young boy was lasting: he spoke of the 'awful hopeless grief of childhood'[7] and one of his greatest concerns for his own children was to avoid them suffering a similar trauma. When a nurse did leave and he found that her departure was not a source of grief to his children, Hastings was shocked by their heartlessness. Hastings described Teetums as buxom and kindly but conceded that she drank. He attributed her departure to his mother's disapproval. She was followed in quick succession by another nurse, then a governess, inexperienced and bad tempered, who once nearly strangled him. When the child was six, this dismal sequence came to an end with the arrival of the next governess, Miss Green.

Flora Green (known to Mary and Herbrand as Jemima) was a remarkable person. She arrived with impeccable credentials. Her father, Sir George Green, had fought with General Gordon at Khartoum. Brought up in Bedfordshire, she had attended a boarding school, possibly at Peterborough, although a lady's maid who later worked for both Miss Green and the Duchess was under the impression that both had been at Cheltenham Ladies College, but was not sure whether they had known each other there. Her curriculum vitae included a spell as governess to the children of the German Emperor. Even so, no-one anticipated that she would remain at Woburn for the rest of her life, becoming, some fifty years later, the only person who was not a Russell to be buried in the family vault. Her first triumph, appropriately, was with her young pupil.

'While I don't think we *always* hit it off perfectly in early days,' he recollected later, 'with the passage of time the bond of affection between us deepened and strengthened and she became, and long remained one of my dearest and most devoted friends.'[8]

As a child, Hastings enjoyed a good relationship with his father: it was only after he grew up and started to assert opinions at variance with those held by the Duke that they fell out so bitterly. The timid small boy would spend time with him every morning and every evening,

'...before dinner, when he read to me in the winter time, while I cooked chestnuts or Indian corn on a shovel on the study fire.' 'Relations between us were always happy and affectionate.'

Even after all that happened later, Hastings' childhood memories of his father were not bitter.

'Though normally kindly and even-tempered, he resented intensely anything which seemed to him to be unreasonable opposition, and the punishment which he visited upon the offender was sometimes out of all proportion to the offence.'

A generation later, Hastings' younger son, Hugh, whilst acknowledging his grandfather's occasional fierce reactions, bore tribute to the kindliness and consideration with which his grandfather always treated him.

Although Hastings was able to recall so much that was endearing about the father with whom he was later to quarrel so deeply, his recollections of his mother were darker.

'Relations with my Mother were not so easy...' he wrote.

He pays tribute to her many achievements, but concludes:

'Unfortunately, however, her rather hasty temper and impatience with any form of incompetence, coupled with the fact that she sometimes punished me severely for things I did not even know were wrong, made me afraid of her, and though I was readily touched by the rather infrequent occasions on which she showed me affection, my response was too timid for her to perceive it, and she considered me a cold and unloving little creature'.

In contrast with the disintegration of his relationship with his father, mother and son came to understand each other better in later life. But this unhappy description of how his mother appeared to him in childhood contrasts sharply with his memories of Miss Green. Hastings admired his parents, and his mother in particular. He wrote of canoeing in the Tamar when staying at their house at Endsleigh,

'My Mother, always brilliant at every sport or more serious enterprise she turned her hand to, was hardly ever unshipped. And my Father was also very good in a canoe. The rest of us were not so fortunate.'[9]

He goes on to tell of an occasion when Miss Green inadvertently caused his canoe to turn over and him to be washed downstream, bruising himself badly on the rocks. Yet his love was reserved for Miss Green.

Mary enjoyed children. She liked to pass on her skills and enthusiasms to them. She formed a bird-watching club for boys from the village, encouraging them to attend with such practical inducements as cream teas. She took a deep interest in a young boy who was a patient in her hospital. She delighted in teaching her grandson Hugh about anything in which he showed an interest, encouraging his love of birds, his knowledge of mechanics or his skill with a shotgun.

But somehow with Hastings she would always lose patience. She drove him from Woburn to Scotland, hoping to show him objects and places of interest on the journey: his attention never left the flies on the windscreen.[10] Years later she wrote to a friend who wanted to interest his own daughter in bird watching,

'I do not believe it is a bit of use your forcing your hobbies on her. As quite a small boy Lord Tavistock filled me with despair; he cared about nothing but insects.'

She took him with her on her yacht to Norway: he was seasick throughout the journey.[11]   He was, as he himself emphasised, a nervous child totally lacking in self confidence. But, a generation later, it was the quiet, gentle, younger boy, Hugh, who developed a good relationship with her, not his flamboyant, opinionated older brother, Ian. In the long term, Hastings, like his mother, had a passionate enthusiasm for, and knowledge of, ornithology. Despite this common interest, they were unable to share this or anything else.

Later, Mary seemed, like so many modern career women, to find her work more absorbing than her son. But, although she had many intense interests throughout his childhood, her life's work did not begin, with the opening of the cottage hospital in Woburn, until Hastings was almost ten. Naturally she was working on her plans long before this, but, had she truly enjoyed spending time with him, she would have made her arrangements in such a way that he had a space in her life. At this time too, as she later recognised, her commitment to the hospital was on a part-time basis, a few 'polite little visits' totally different from the absolute dedication of 1914 and beyond. Her hearing difficulties made Hastings' high pitched child's voice difficult to hear, but she overcame this difficulty with the bird watching boys and with Hugh.

Whatever the reason for Hastings' failure to hold her attention while other boys succeeded, there seemed little point in fighting it, for her husband and father-in-law had decided long ago that decisions concerning Hastings rested with them and not with her. When Miss Green entered the equation, the position was exacerbated. Hastings, already wary of his own mother, found in Miss Green a substitute mother. By then, Mary did not care enough to resist.

Hastings was not the only member of the family to be impressed by Miss Green. His father soon found that the new governess made a very able assistant, willingly providing the back-up support which Mary found so tedious. She gladly took over all the little details which in most large establishments would have been the preserve of the wife. It was Jemima who planned the menus and supervised the details. Many years later, Ian described her as 'the power behind the throne'.

Herbrand started to turn to her more and more frequently, for help, for the day to day care of Hastings and, gradually, for companionship. Soon it was taken for granted that if the Duke was travelling to Cairnsmore or to Endsleigh, Jemima would go with him.

There is no evidence that Mary in any way resented this. The two women seem to have had, superficially at least, an excellent relationship. They shared a love of dogs and each supported the other in dealing with any canine problem. References to Jemima in Mary's diary are either neutral or friendly and considerate. Had Herbrand predeceased Mary, Jemima was appointed her Executrix. Mary seemed content to allow the governess to take her place in the details of everyday life and in the affections of her son. There were never half measures with Mary. She was either committed to something with all her heart and mind and soul or it became a chore. If Jemima was willing to take on minor duties at Woburn, which Mary might otherwise have been expected to perform, then she was happy to delegate them to her. Her tragedy, and the family's, was that, through a combination of circumstances, she seems to have seen the care of her only child in a similar light.

It was widely believed at Woburn that Jemima took over Mary's role also in another way. The position she held in the family for so many years and the fact that she eventually became the only non-member of the family to be buried in the mausoleum at Chenies certainly indicate that she was more than a governess, housekeeper, secretary or even family friend. If the suspicions were justified, Mary's apparent calm acceptance of the position is remarkable. Neither John Gore in his later appreciation of Mary nor the 13th Duke in *A Silver-Plated Spoon* or in his biography of his grandmother even hints at any such relationship, but Ian wished to portray his grandfather as an unhappy, frustrated, lonely recluse. A mistress who remained with him for a lifetime, without occasioning scandal, did not tie in with this scenario.

There are no corresponding rumours about any man in Mary's life. Perhaps she simply decided that sharing the Duke's bed was another duty she was only too glad to delegate. Not only is there no evidence of any resentment; she went so far, when writing to her sister Zoë, as to describe Jemima as 'such an excessively loyal person'[12]. Mary is writing here about the dilemma facing Jemima as the former governess to the Hohenzollern family, in England, in September 1914, at the outbreak of war, but her tone shows genuine sympathy and these are hardly the words she would have selected if she bore her any resentment.

A rare picture of Miss Green (Jemima) –
(l to r) Herbrand, Sheila Russell, Marjorie Russell, Jemima and Mary

The advent of Jemima in their lives allowed the relationship between Mary and Herbrand to move into a different phase, one which in essence remained constant for the rest of their lives. From her first arrival in Europe as Herbrand's bride, his family and friends had in their different ways made clear to her that they were not meeting Mary Tribe, a young girl of independent mindset who enjoyed walking, riding and a host of other tomboyish activities, who was interested in lectures on medicine and other unladylike subjects, and who was exceptionally capable at almost anything she undertook. The originality of all this had attracted Herbrand himself. But, as he introduced her to his circle in England, she knew that they were wondering how soon she was likely to produce an heir to the Dukedom, how the new Lady Herbrand would comport herself in society and how fittingly she would take her place, should fate decree that she became a duchess.

Before her marriage, she had generally found it easy to live up to expectations. At school she made friends easily and had no difficulty in coping with the academic work. If her teachers were disappointed with her decision to conclude her education as early as possible, that in itself was a form of compliment. There was no sense of failure. In India, she was secure in the love and admiration of William Carpendale. When she moved on to the wider stage at Simla, once again she found that she was sought after: people came to her easily on her own terms. When she accepted the proposal of the young man of highest social standing in India at the time, it in no way went to her head, but, once again, she was confident in the admiration of her peers.

Back in England as a young bride, she suddenly realised that everything about her was being questioned. Her family was socially inferior, her desire for an active life must be curbed, her opinions were sometimes outrageous. She was different from the simpering misses who filled the drawing rooms of the time. Unconventionality was not viewed as a desirably quality.

Herbrand did his best to protect her, taking her to Scotland to live away from prying eyes and gossiping tongues. But she felt that she was being viewed like a new brood mare: was she yet pregnant, if not why not, if so was she living the restricted life-style expected of a Victorian wife expecting her first baby and above all was she the right type to produce the sort of offspring that was needed?

Now at last, for the first time since her marriage, the pressure was off. She had, despite difficulties, fulfilled her perceived role in life. She had produced a healthy son. His education was in safe hands: he was being brought up in the same way as countless generations of his family. Mary accepted this with fewer qualms than a more maternal girl would have felt. Her duty as a mother was complete.

As the Duke's wife, other duties remained to her. Most chatelaines of great houses were expected to play a minor, subsidiary role as hostess and mistress of the house. Herbrand was seen as somewhat eccentric in his desire to take much of that commitment on his own shoulders, but it is a Duke's prerogative to be eccentric and if he was happy to take charge, with his son's governess to assist him, no-one saw any reason to criticise.

It remained of vital importance that all his needs were satisfied. Not only had he every right to expect a full private life, but if he was not getting it and started to look elsewhere, the dread vision of scandal raised its ugly head. Mary, on the other hand, had never seen sex as an important part of her life and the early years of marriage had done nothing to change her mind. For a twenty-first century couple, this might be seen as disastrous. In Victorian times there was an expectation that the marriage would continue. For Mary and Herbrand, there was no hypocrisy in coming to an arrangement, whether tacitly or after private discussion, which enabled their marriage to continue for the rest of their lives. They loved each other even though they were not in love – perhaps they never had been; they had a child together, shared many interests and enjoyed each other's company; both had everything to lose and nothing to gain by a separation. Both became not only more relaxed and contented but also infinitely more appreciative of the other.

It was almost as if each was able to stand back and appreciate all the good qualities of the other, for each was deeply grateful for the way in which the other ensured that the system operated for their mutual benefit. They often argued, for both were quick tempered. Mary did not suffer fools gladly and Herbrand could be amazingly tactless, as Mary explained to Hastings in a letter in the last year of her life:

'Your Father is not a good hand at writing tactful letters when he wishes to convey a gentle reproof. He does at times write the most forbidding letters when there is absolutely no call for it. I laugh at them in his presence but they are very chilling when one is away from home.

'After his illness his sight was for a time very much worse and also as he was very feeble I suggested his occupying the scarlet rooms (as he had voluntarily done before) to avoid our crooked dark stair case.' (Probably they normally had adjoining suites of rooms.) 'He consented quite readily as much the best arrangement.

'I certainly never opposed his returning to his own rooms but one day received an intimation by letter "I have today been to see my doctor in London. He says my heart is in no way the worse for my illness. I am therefore going to return to my rooms upstairs as there is no reason whatever why I should not do so and I have ordered my things to be removed."

'I was at home and all this might have been said without the letter which was put on my table.'

Despite such incidents, Herbrand had a profound admiration for his wife, for all that she achieved and her whole approach to life, which was probably stronger on the day she died than on the day he married her. The instructions he gave when he commissioned her biography are evidence of that. He delighted in her company and begrudged any diminution in the time they spent together. Mary on her side was deeply appreciative of all that he did for her, a theme to which she frequently returned. He allowed her to spend as much money as she wished on any of her projects and he gave her his public and private approbation and support in all that she undertook. Even though he had a dread of her flying, which was to be tragically justified by events, he still made it possible for her to continue precisely as she wished. She strove to reciprocate in any way she could. In another letter to Hastings, written at around the same time, in 1936, she explained:

'He attaches so much importance to my walking out with him that I feel quite guilty when I miss it & if anything happened to him feel that I should reproach myself for not giving him all that I could in return for all that he has done for me.'

Amongst Mary's legendary list of achievements, it is sad that the only conspicuous failure was in her relationship with her only child. Her lack of patience and what seems to have been almost a clash of personalities were root causes, for where one of the two personalities is that of a child, it is incumbent on the adult and not the child to build the necessary bridges. Like many a modern career woman, she found, at that time in her life, that her work and other commitments held her interest in a way that few children, and certainly not Hastings, were capable of doing. Today it is becoming acceptable for mothers to acknowledge this. At the time, such an admission was inconceivable. In her defence, her attention was held by much more worthwhile occupations than those of her contemporaries who feigned a devotion to their children which they did not feel, and preferred to spend their time on frivolous pursuits. Unlike these other mothers, it is possible that, left to her own devices, she would have been able to develop a worthwhile relationship with her son, had her husband and father-in-law not placed an embargo on her plans.

If she failed as a parent, her marriage was not the failure that her oldest grandson imagined. It was not true that his 'grandfather and grandmother lived isolated lives of their own, at least by the time I met them, and this had been true for many years.'[13] His conclusion that 'there was no emotion between them at all'[14] could only have been written by a young man who had not learned to distinguish passion from emotion. Theirs was a marriage built on friendship, affection, mutual admiration and appreciation, some shared interests and some individual pursuits, consideration for each other and loyalty. Ian was perhaps misled by watching them sit or walk together in silence. He forgot that her deafness made conversation difficult. Mary's personal maid, more perceptive, remembered years later how very fond they clearly were of each other as they spent the evening quietly together in the Canaletto Room, which they used as their drawing room, sitting round the fire, reading.

Mary canoeing on the Tamar

CHAPTER 5

WOBURN

Herbrand, Mary and Hastings out shooting

From the time of her first meeting with Herbrand, Mary had been aware of the shadow of Woburn Abbey, providing, as it were, a backdrop to her husband's life. Woburn (always pronounced Woo-burn by Herbrand and Mary in the traditional style: today the modernised pronunciation Woe-burn is used) had an almost disproportionately strong hold on the young man's imagination. He did not move there until he was fourteen years old, when his father succeeded to the Dukedom, and he had spent most of his adult life away from home, much of it serving abroad. His parents were both alive and in good health and he had an older married brother: there was no reason for either of them to anticipate that he would ever live at Woburn. Yet, despite all this, Mary probably had a vivid image of the place long before they left India.

By the time that Mary became a duchess, she had sufficient self confidence to seek no role model in the way she developed her position. Many of her predecessors came from aristocratic backgrounds, which made them familiar with the lifestyle of ducal establishments. Aunt Fanny's house in Pulborough gave Mary no such understanding. She lived her life in her own unique way, yet, paradoxically, by doing so, she was herself upholding a family tradition. Herbrand was neither the first nor the last of his family to marry a woman of strong character and independent outlook. He had none of the reservations of many men of his generation about accepting a strong-minded woman into the family. He liked and admired determination and personality in a woman: this was the key to much of Mary's attraction for him. He also accepted without question her right to lead an independent life and pursue her own interests.

Herbrand, with his overpowering sense of the need for continuity, found the way in which Woburn had been organised by his predecessors a fascinating subject. His main concern was that nothing should be allowed to lapse: each generation could bring in the innovations of the age but the standards and traditions of the past must never slip. To him, this showed that he was keeping the best of the past whilst introducing the best of the present. To others, and to Mary in particular, this must frequently have seemed stiflingly claustrophobic.

Ever since the time of the 1st Duke, William, who had moved there at the age of ten to escape the Plague in 1626 and remained for the rest of his long life, Woburn had been the family home. Then it was customary for various members of the family to make extended visits, bringing large households of their own and paying their share of the expenses. Hawks and beagles as well as horses would frequently be brought too.

The Second Duke, Wriothesley, and his family spent most of their time at Southampton House (later known as Bedford House) in Bloomsbury. The music, books and pictures which he collected were taken to London and only moved to Woburn many years later.

With the Fourth Duke, John, the 'Merry Little Duke', who succeeded in 1732, Woburn once more became the hub of activity. Building work, with Henry Flitcroft employed as architect, new furniture and a redesigning of the garden: all received much attention, while, at the same time, John was using the Abbey to entertain his friends and political colleagues. The Duke was also, like so many of his forebears and successors, a true countryman. He showed a deep interest in the estate, and extended all the new ideas with which he experimented successfully at Woburn to his other properties also. As well as agricultural developments, he introduced many new comforts, including hot water, improved heating arrangements, water closets and wallpaper.

The wallpaper, incidentally, and other items, were supplied by John Spinnage of the firm of Crompton & Spinnage. It is possible that some reference to this in Mary's time within the hearing of her small son could have amused the little boy. Perhaps he kept repeating the name, linking it to the nursery rhyme phrase *Gammon and Spinach,* and so acquired the nickname of Spinach, which later so mystified even Hastings himself.

The Fourth Duke was able to combine London and country life in a way which had been impossible for earlier generations because of the improvements in travel. The heavy, elaborate coaches which had taken sixteen hours to lumber up from London to Woburn were reserved for state

Woburn Abbey as it was in Mary's time

occasions. Regular travel was undertaken in light, well sprung post chaises which, combined with much improved road surfaces, reduced the travelling time by half. Many more servants were employed than in earlier times. The more senior ones had livery coats with velvet collars, trimmed with gold lace and gilt buttons.

John continued the policy of his great grandfather, the first Duke, of enlarging the estate by buying adjacent land whenever it became available. John was an extremely capable manager and combined the two traditional family pursuits of politics and agriculture in a way which none of his forebears had equalled and increasing pressures of life made impossible for later generations. His energy, enthusiasm and ability gave new life to the Abbey.

After his death in 1771, the long minority of the 5th Duke and widowhood of Gertrude led to quieter times at Woburn. When the 5th Duke took over from his grandmother and introduced his somewhat rackety lifestyle under the direction of his ageing mistress, a different atmosphere prevailed in the house. Men servants were no longer liveried and powdered: they were paid to do a job.

Outside, however, the 5th Duke maintained the agricultural traditions of the family, introducing a model farm and various experiments for improving the soil. His enthusiasm for his sheep made the annual shearing week an event which bore some resemblance to a modern agricultural show. In addition to farmers and tenants, leading agriculturalists came from all over Britain, a wide range of competitions in various relevant skills, such as ploughing, was held and the week culminated in a banquet for several hundred guests.

It was left to the 6th Duke, John, and his Duchess Georgiana to bring the house back to life. In some ways, the atmosphere became more respectable: the Duke's three sons from his first marriage made it a family home immediately he inherited from his brother in 1802, and the boys were soon joined in the nursery by the oldest of the ten children of his second marriage. Entertainment, in the early days of the marriage of the 6th Duke and his second wife, was on a scale unequalled in the history of the Abbey, before or since. One visitor wrote of 'the magnificent yet well-regulated style of living'[1] and prayers were said daily. Despite this, many of the more traditional guests found the behaviour shocking. An endless succession of riotous parties, with every comfort provided, all ultimately presided over by the Duchess herself, sparkling, dynamic and bursting with energy, and determined to deprive neither herself nor her guests of any conceivable luxury, ensured a hedonistic but dazzling environment.

Woburn continued to provide a meeting place for the leading Whig politicians. A very young Lord John Russell, the future Prime Minister, stared in bemusement at the immense, corpulent, figure of Charles James Fox draped across a chair, sunk in heavy slumber. The small boy was commissioned, no doubt by his stepmother or one of her friends, to creep up and tickle the silk stockinged legs into wakefulness and thus silence the deafening snores.

Everything was done in splendid, if flamboyant, style. Liveried servants were evident in large numbers. Breakfast was served at ten each morning. A century later, when Herbrand insisted on retaining all the ancient traditions of the house, he continued to ensure that every guest was provided with his or her own gold teapot: these were introduced by Georgiana in 1803 to replace the ancient china ones first brought from China by the East India Company. But the timing of meals reflected Herbrand's obsession with punctuality and Mary's commitment to her work: breakfast was three hours earlier, at seven in the morning.

As the bawdy Georgian age gave way to the prim, genteel respectability of Victorian Britain, the change was reflected at Woburn too. The seventh Duke succeeded his father in 1839, two years after Victoria came to the throne. His Duchess, Anna Maria, replaced the night-long drinking and gambling parties hosted by Georgiana in her younger days with the invention of that great British institution, afternoon tea at five o'clock. Anna Maria would entertain her friends with tea, sandwiches and cakes in the afternoon.

As Marchioness of Tavistock, Anna Maria attended Queen Victoria at her Coronation in 1837 and, as Duchess of Bedford two years later, she attended her again, this time at her wedding. In the same year, the Queen and Prince Albert visited Woburn. They arrived by coach, although the railways were already becoming the more usual method of travel, accompanied by a huge retinue including the Duke of Wellington, Lord Melbourne and Lord and Lady Palmerston.[2]

The 7th Duke and his successors, his bachelor son William, the 8th Duke, and Herbrand's father and brother, the 9th and 10th Dukes respectively, continued to maintain and improve the house and land. But, after the deaths of Francis and Anna Maria, in 1861 and 1857 respectively, the sparkle and glamour of earlier days fast faded. None of the next three Dukes, the first two both in their fifties before they inherited, showed any inclination to revive the hectic social life of previous generations.

So when Herbrand and Mary first moved into Woburn in 1893, there were no expectations that they would create a dazzling social world or constantly entertain half the crowned heads of Europe, eminent statesmen and other dukes and duchesses. Few if anyone on the estate or in the neighbourhood could remember when that had last happened, half a century before. Perhaps some of the oldest ones secretly hoped those days would come again now that they had a young Duke and Duchess. Perhaps some of the younger ones dreamed that they would suddenly find themselves at the hub of the social universe. However it was not something which was expected of them.

As for Herbrand and Mary themselves, the Duke believed in maintaining the status quo and for him that had never included large scale entertaining at Woburn. He regarded the house and estate as an administrative enterprise, which his training had admirably equipped him to undertake, not a setting for the family's social life. There was no cause to which he was more ready to devote his life. He knew, too, that there were many functions which he and his family were expected to fulfil and he was confident that he could play his part.

Ironically, the two areas which he was most reluctant to allow Mary to take charge of were the very two in which, in most other households, she might have expected to exercise control: the running of the household and the care of her son. In both these areas, Herbrand subconsciously felt that the guidelines had been established over generations of his family and that these must be matters about which he knew more than Mary, but, in any other arena she might choose to enter, he would encourage and support her independence. This gave Mary a strong base from which to exercise her independence. Herbrand accepted her wish to plough her own furrow. Individualistic, frequently unconventional, women in his family had been doing this for hundreds of years.

Many a young woman in Mary's position might have seen this as her chance to undertake a brilliant role in society. She had, after all, been one of the stars of the Viceroy's court. By the time of her marriage, she had gained considerable self confidence. She was good looking, intelligent, quick witted, charming and succeeded at everything to which she turned her hand. Now she had the position, the money and the base from which to conquer the social world. Yet this was one of the few challenges to which she never attempted to rise.

Had she wished to take on this role, there was one impediment with which she would have had to contend: her deafness. Sometimes she seemed to find this a more serious handicap in her relationship with other people than it appeared to be to them. For example, she spent a day in London at the start of the First World War, racing through a series of meetings to obtain the necessary consents for the establishment of her hospital. All who knew her were amazed at how much she achieved in one day: a remarkable series of successes in an incredibly short period of time by any standards. Yet she herself felt that her efforts had been seriously handicapped by her deafness. Perhaps her handicap became, in her mind, the scapegoat for her impatience with other people in such circumstances.

Had she not suffered from this debilitating condition, it is interesting to speculate whether she would have developed into a society hostess. She enjoyed those royal occasions in which she did participate, two in her first year as Duchess, the first when she was presented to the Queen and, a few weeks later, a visit to Windsor Castle. She later attended two Coronations, King George V and Queen Mary's Silver Jubilee and other events. She also fulfilled her local duties with charm and dignity, but she had few if any close friendships. Probably, even if her hearing had been unimpaired, social life would have seemed unimportant to her in comparison with her other interests and in particular her hospital work. If she was 'always too busy' for her own son[3], it is unlikely that she would have found time for social life.

The diverse interests of generations of the family had combined to create a rare collection of treasures of many kinds, inside the Abbey and in the park. As had happened in almost every previous generation, Mary and Herbrand delighted in some of these, added to some and showed inadequate appreciation of a few. The park was their chief delight. Herbrand developed the small group of animals and birds which he inherited into a collection of world renown and took immense pleasure in doing so. This was also his way of fulfilling what he saw as his hereditary obligation to build up some particular aspect of his inheritance as well as maintaining the whole (at least at Woburn: there were different considerations where his other properties were concerned). Here was something which deeply interested them both, and Mary gave Herbrand her full and active support.

Mary and Herbrand showed less appreciation for the fabulous contents of the Abbey. The collection had been brilliantly started by the Second Duke

Mary in Coronation robes, by Miss Smith

and built up over the centuries by successive generations, particularly by young men making the Grand Tour. Mary's grandson Ian later maintained that Mary was guilty of appalling acts of vandalism, including having some of the 'superb Louis XIV and Louis XV chairs they had inherited well scrubbed and painted white.'[4] This allegation is unsubstantiated and Mary's collection of books reveals a keen interest in art, but the collection was not a part of his inheritance which was developed by Herbrand or his Duchess.

Herbrand did not despise modern inventions, welcoming them wherever they could be used to enhance the traditional methods. His grandson Hugh later recalled that he:

'…made the transition from horse drawn transport to motors in 1908 before many people had begun to think of motor vehicles as a permanent means of transport, and with dramatic suddenness, immediately getting rid of all the horses and carriages. He summoned the steward who looked after the house and grounds.

"We will change from carriages to cars," he informed him.

"Yes, Your Grace. How many cars shall I buy?"

"How many carriages have I got?"

"Twenty-one, Your Grace."

"Well, buy twenty-one cars."

Twenty-two chauffeurs were employed to enable one to have a day off.'[5]

With his cars, Herbrand applied his usual principle of utilising modern improvements whilst retaining all those elements of the past which he saw as superior. His grandson recalled:

'My grandfather was small and did not like bending. When the design of the Rolls was changed from its original carriage-like shape to a more modern but lower outline, he continued to have his built identical in body to the 1910 and 1911 models, but incorporating the most up-to-date engine.'

The motor cars may have had modern engines, but the system remained reminiscent of an earlier age. The London cars, which were all Wolseleys, were kept quite separate from the Woburn cars, which were Rolls Royces. On Hugh's first visit to Woburn when he left London:

'I was put into the front car with a chauffeur and a man on the box. My suitcase was put into the second car, also with two men in charge. We drove to Hendon where I was transferred with my luggage to the Woburn country vehicles, a crowd gathering, fascinated by the sight of eight chauffeurs and four cars transporting one very small boy and his suitcase.

'While we were standing there, an MG Midget, the sports car of the moment, passed and all the passengers pointed mockingly at the assembled cars and chauffeurs. I was now being driven by my grandfather's chauffeur, one of the youngest men. As we approached the Barnet by-pass, the first big by-pass ever built, I sat glued to the edge of my seat, my eyes wider and wider as the speedometer moved from 30 through 35, 40, 45, 50, 55, 60, 65, 70, 75, 80… we had just touched 80 mph, a remarkable speed for the time, when we passed the Midget, a smile on the chauffeur's face. The Midget's driver had not bargained on the most up-to-date engine possible under the old-fashioned bonnet.'[6]

Employing as many people as possible on the estate was a duty as well as a pleasure to the Duke. His refusal to buy a motor mower because it would leave five men without work was typical. Even in the Thirties, 'there were fifty-two indoor staff at Woburn, as well as at least thirty gardeners, thirty game keepers, numerous foresters, park keepers, farm workers, gate keepers, chauffeurs and suchlike. There were so many estate staff that they had their own football and cricket leagues and played inter-departmental matches.'[7] In fact seventy Household staff (a somewhat wider definition) were listed at the time of Mary's death in 1937. By way of comparison, at Burghley, a house of similar size, there were thirty indoor staff in 1901 and just seventeen by the early Thirties.[8] At Wentworth Woodhouse in 1902 there were sixty-three indoor staff and over three hundred outdoor staff[9], similar to Woburn thirty years later. The Managing Director of this enterprise, running his empire with military precision and attending to every detail personally, was the Duke himself.

'He never sacked anybody on the estate. They all had houses which they retired to.'

Every morning he discussed the menus for the day in detail with the cook. In most households at the time, where a cook was employed, it was the responsibility of the wife to discuss the menus and supervise the other domestic staff. Although Woburn was on a different scale from other households, Herbrand was well aware that his wife was a woman of outstanding ability, fully capable of administering the household. Yet the decision was taken that Herbrand and not Mary should undertake this responsibility. Perhaps he openly admitted to her the pleasure it gave him: certainly his administrative work in the army had been excellent training. Perhaps he doubted whether either Aunt Fanny's house at Pulborough or the Archdeacon of Lahore's official residence provided sufficient experience.

Whatever his reasoning, there is no evidence that Mary felt slighted by her exclusion. The grandeur of the lifestyle repelled her. She had little sense of history or tradition, though she was probably the first Duchess to make use of the Abbey roof for studying astronomy. She derived no pleasure from having a man standing behind the chair of every family member and every guest in the dining room, and was relieved that Herbrand, like herself, preferred the footmen to leave as soon as the meal was served so that at least they could talk during the meal without being overheard. However, in later life at least, Herbrand would eat in silence, and consequently was always the first to finish. The moment he had done so, he rang a hand bell and everybody's plate would be removed instantaneously, the table cleared in seconds and the next course presented. This selfish behaviour was thoughtless rather than intentionally malicious. When his young grandson became a regular visitor, Hugh found that the food was 'always absolutely wonderful, quite delicious,' and complained to a cousin. She explained his predicament:

"Herbrand, Hugh never gets time for a second helping."

Thereafter his grandfather never failed as he finished eating to turn to the boy and ask, with kindly solicitude,

"Does Hugh require a second helping?"[10]

Mary made no effort to change or influence her husband's behaviour on such minor issues. She was probably oblivious to the impression he made, for it was to a cousin and not to his adored grandmother that Hugh turned for support. The minutiae of daily life held little interest for her. It was all part of the background scenery over which she had no influence, nor any wish for any.

Guests, in later years almost invariably cousins, came and went. Their visits became less and less frequent (though only Bertrand Russell, a close friend of Hastings, was *persona non grata*), their impact on the routine of the house minimal. On arrival, they were met by the grooms of the chamber who took them to their rooms, then afterwards, but never before, to see their host and hostess. The only change made was that the daily late afternoon walk always shared by Herbrand and Mary was replaced by a drive. Hugh recalled one rare occasion when sixteen cousins were staying at the same time.

'Sixteen chauffeurs and eight cars were assembled, most of them Model C Fords which were open tourers, so wiser guests dressed appropriately for the weather. If possible no more than two guests were allowed in the same car, although my grandfather's V8 Ford did take three passengers. The chauffeurs were never told in advance where we were going, but my grandfather led the procession round the estate roads issuing instructions. There were gates everywhere, locked with a single master key, one copy of which was issued to the man on the box of the front car in the procession and one to his counterpart on the back car. The pace of the drive seldom exceeded 10 mph – a chauffeur who reached 12 mph received a peremptory tap on the shoulder and was instructed to slow down – but even this must have seemed quite fast enough for the poor men with the keys as the procession never waited for them. Having unlocked or locked each gate, they were expected to run to catch up and jump back on.

'My grandparents were always looking out for interesting birds and animals which were regularly being introduced to the estate. When red breasted geese were close to extinction, a large flock of them was established on the eight large ponds, which were also home to trumpeter swans and every sort of duck you can think of. These subsequently provided Peter Scott with his foundation birds at Slimbridge. My grandfather was interested too in experimental farming and in forestry. There were 6000 acres of woodland with our own sawmill. To make everything more accessible and to provide employment in the depression of the Thirties, he was an enthusiastic builder of roads, not only at Woburn but also at Endsleigh and even at Cairnsmore in Scotland, although this was only a rented property: he retained the tenancy for forty years. I was particularly appreciative of the road building policy since it meant that I could drive for miles and miles.'[11]

Herbrand had many idiosyncrasies. When the 13th Duke (Ian) enquired why the electric wiring had been so badly installed, the estate electrician told him that the 11th Duke (Herbrand) never allowed workmen to be seen in his presence. Thus it had been necessary for two look-outs to be posted while they were working. Whenever the Duke approached, the whole team hid in a cupboard.[12]

Central heating was only installed in corridors. Every room in use had a blazing fire made up in the grate. Oil lamps also continued in regular use for much longer than elsewhere when part of the wiring caught fire on the first attempt to install electricity.

In the circumstances, Herbrand's dread of fire seems reasonable and sensible. Most of the pictures were loose in their frames so that they could be removed easily, There were fire hydrants all round the house, outside and in. Every night, someone went round to put all the standpipes in position and hang a lantern on each. The Duke always had his own fire engine. In the Thirties, when Hugh was visiting regularly, this function was still being fulfilled by a 1908 Napier. It was not easy to start and required two men swinging on the handle to get it going.[13] At Hatfield, the 'Summary of Livery Men's Duties, etc., etc.' concluded with the admonition in bold type 'For the Prevention of Fire it is particularly requested that every person be most careful with matches, candles etc.'[14]

Despite a widely held perception that such magnificence and large scale employment in country houses came to an end with the outbreak of the First World War, in fact Woburn was not unique in continuing to be run in this way right up to the start of the Second World War. At Chatsworth, for example, seat of the Duke of Devonshire, the footmen continued to powder their hair when there was a party until 1924, and to wear full livery if there were more than six for dinner until 1938.[15] But there was one major difference. Chatsworth was always filled with people.

In the time of the 8th Duke of Devonshire, who died in 1908 and who was famously married, at a somewhat advanced age, to Louise Von Alten, widow of the Duke of Manchester and accordingly known, inevitably, as the Double Duchess, 'all the rooms were opened, and huge numbers of people came to stay, usually in the winter for pheasant shooting on a grand scale. The preparations for the house parties were long and complicated, as the hostesses vied with one another to put on a yet more splendid show, and arranged pleasures and surprises for their guests, who were accustomed to the best of everything.'[16] Entertainment on a similar scale continued at Chatsworth with the next Duke between the Wars. In addition there was now a large family to include: with a son and five daughters, all married, and twenty-two grandchildren, occasions such as Christmas required all the staff available. At Woburn, on the other hand, the only son visited the house just once in twenty years. The one grandchild who did spend an appreciable amount of time there later recalled that there were seldom many guests and those who did come to stay were mostly cousins.

At Chatsworth, and probably most of the other houses where an enormous staff was retained up to the outbreak of the Second World War, the staff was needed to support a way of life which, extravagant as it may appear today, was providing pleasure to some and employment to many. At Woburn, the position was almost reversed. Neither the Duke nor Duchess had any wish to entertain, although they spent as much money in other ways as their hospitable peers. The scale of the establishment was not necessary for maintaining the estate, as was demonstrated by the example of the lawn mower.

For Herbrand, the pleasure was not in what could be achieved by his small 'private army': he took pleasure in administering his empire because he had been trained to be an administrator in a greater empire. He was good at his job, and he took satisfaction in knowing that a high standard was being maintained, that his staff was kept in employment and their needs attended to and, above all, that he could look the portraits of his ancestors in the eye, confident that Woburn remained the great house which he had inherited. Life behind the green baize door was in full flow: the tragedy of Woburn at this time was that in front of the green baize door there were just three lone figures, the Duke, the Duchess and Miss Green, supported by a shadowy group of mostly elderly cousins.

Herbrand in uniform

Mary stood aside and left her husband in charge of his empire, never considering that her own approach to her hospitals was not dissimilar. She worked unceasingly to ensure that they were efficiently administered, that the staff fulfilled their duties to the highest possible standards and were themselves properly cared for, and that a hospital under her control was recognised as a model of its kind. But, if the function of a hospital is to heal the sick, and of a great house to provide a home for the family and hospitality and entertainment for their friends, then Mary's work was more successful than that of her husband. It was symptomatic of the state of affairs that shooting was the central feature of entertainment at Chatsworth and on many other large estates. Woburn is a top-class shoot and Herbrand did everything to maintain it as such. Yet few guests, except an occasional cousin, were ever invited to shoot there.

Socially, the late Victorian period, in the large country houses, in fact bore a closer resemblance to what is now generally thought of as the Edwardian era than to our image of the Victorians. As Mark Girouard has written, 'A late-Victorian household with its troop of bachelors retiring to talk ritual smut in the male preserves, its animated house-party seated at separate tables in the dining room, and a certain amount of discreet adultery along the bedroom corridors, had moved a long way from the domesticity, earnestness and godliness of a typical mid-Victorian house.'[17] Neither of these images bears much resemblance to the way of life at Woburn. Herbrand was not conspicuously religious, and Mary an avowed agnostic. She certainly showed no inclination to be restricted by all the rigorous conventions of Victorian religion. But neither the wilder aspects of Edwardian England nor the relaxed pleasures of social life enjoyed by so many of those with both time and money to spare attracted her. Mary's boundless energy and determination never to waste a moment was more characteristic of the hectic pace of life in the 21st century than of the leisured age in which she lived.

With Herbrand's constant attention to every last detail in the management of house and estate (to take a car from the garage, Mary was required to produce a chit signed by her husband[18]), Mary was relieved to find that there was no role for her. Her husband's assistant in every aspect of household management was Jemima. Cousins preparing to visit Woburn would write to Jemima, not to Mary. Any issue not personally supervised by Herbrand himself would be delegated to Jemima. Mary felt no jealousy, at least in this regard, but delighted instead in the position of honour which she came to occupy. Her every whim became the Duke's command. She certainly used his fabulous wealth, in the early days especially, to take up a succession of interests, repaying his generosity by excelling at each. Soon, however, her interest in matters medical started to take pride of place. In consequence, much of the Duke's income came to be spent for the benefit of the sick.

First, though, Mary demonstrated her remarkable ability to take up almost any interest, sport or hobby and glide, seemingly effortlessly, into the highest echelons of many, and rather more than a basic competence in the remainder of them. In their early days at the Abbey, she used the estate as a playground: within five years of moving there, she opened the first Cottage Hospital at Woburn. For Herbrand, Woburn was his home, his heritage and his life's work. For Mary, it was a springboard to achieving so many ambitions.

Herbrand aged two

CHAPTER 6

SUCCESS ON MANY FRONTS

Photography at Magdalena Bay,
Spitzbergen July 1901

When people met Mary for the first time, they often made the mistake, as Jemima herself did when she first arrived at Woburn, of thinking her exceptionally gifted and determined in one particular skill or hobby. Jemima, arriving during the shooting season and finding the Duchess 'absorbed in the sport, to the exclusion of all other interests and occupations', later wrote, 'I am afraid I did her the injustice of thinking her certainly a first-class shot, but with a rather limited outlook on life'.[1]

In fact, as the governess soon appreciated, Mary possessed an unusual combination of skills. She could devote herself single-mindedly with absolute concentration to a particular interest. Shooting happened to be the subject occupying her attention at the time when Jemima first arrived. But her interest could be captured by sports as varied as ice skating, shooting, mountaineering, canoeing, riding, yachting, fishing and flying aeroplanes. Every corner of the globe attracted her, whether she was exploring the mountain ranges of India on a pony with her father, watching birds on some remote Hebridean island, stalking reindeer in Spitzbergen, visiting St. Petersburg and Moscow in her yacht, climbing mountains in the Alps or completing the first non-stop flight from England to Africa. She painted natural subjects neatly and accurately and completed beautiful embroidery. Her enjoyment of photography soon encompassed all her own developing, printing and enlarging, and provided links to the skills of radiology and radiography in which she was to become an acknowledged expert. Her knowledge of ornithology was immense. Her enthusiasm for matters mechanical found expression in building her own radios or training her chauffeur in a proper understanding of the workings of the internal combustion engine. Yet all these matters were mere diversions from her real life's work in hospital administration and nursing.

Enthusiasts in any subject risk becoming narrowly obsessed with their particular interest, to the exclusion of all others. Conversely, many people with wide ranging interests spread their abilities too thinly, constantly flitting like butterflies from one attraction to the next. The level of success attained by Mary in so many of the ventures which she undertook reveals a remarkable combination of innate ability and dogged determination. She also had one further advantage shared by few others in her pursuit of excellence on so many fronts: the almost unlimited resources which her husband made available to her to enable her to achieve her goals.

She enjoyed many physically active sports. As Hastings remarked, she was more adept at preventing her canoe from capsizing than the rest of the party whenever they were staying at Endsleigh, where the Tamar ran through the estate close to the house. Even on quiet days, the rocks, pools, bends and rapids presented some interesting challenges. When the river was in full spate, even Mary, in her own words, 'shipwrecked handsomely on two occasions. The first time was rather a shock, as the water was so cold that it took all my breath away, and the current is too

Another sport for Mary: Jujitsu

strong to allow of standing, even if you are in your depth, which I was not. The second time I saw shipwreck was inevitable and was prepared, as I had already been under, head and all.'[2] Guests were always encouraged to join in the sport. Characteristically, Mary preferred a single kayak canoe, whereas Herbrand liked to share a double canoe with Jemima.

In winter, when the Tamar was too cold even for Mary, she spent time instead at the Princes Skating Club in Knightsbridge, becoming a member of the National Skating Association in 1900, passing the Third and Second Tests and allegedly winning a gold medal. Then in 1903 the owner decided to sell the Club. So devastated was the Duchess that she persuaded Herbrand to buy her an eleven year lease, thus extending the life of the Club until the outbreak of the First World War. Two full days a week were reserved exclusively for Mary's benefit. The Duke, by his generosity with his immense wealth, enabled her to excel. He provided the means for her success, she was remarkable for having the ability and the determination to make full use of every such opportunity..

The same principle applied to shooting. John Gore accepted, in his critical analysis on the centenary of her birth, that 'she came to be regarded as the finest game-shot among women, and was even mentioned as the peer of such men as Lord Ripon, Harry Stonor or Remington Wilson. Both at Woburn and Cairnsmore game was preserved in great abundance and often enough the Duke and Duchess, with perhaps one other gun, enjoyed a battue which would have provided great sport for eight guns. This rather selfish practice certainly enabled the Duchess to become a first rate shot.'[3] Once again, the Duke's money provided the opportunity and the Duchess's natural eye, her determination and her persistence enabled her to succeed.

Mary with her day's catch

Her grandson later recalled that 'she was in fact, unusually, equally proficient with a rifle and a shotgun and was rated one of the eight best shots in England, as well as being a really expert fisherwoman. She kept a detailed record all her life of what she shot and how many cartridges she used. This diary reveals, for example, that on the final day of one pheasant shooting season she shot twenty-one birds with twenty-two cartridges, and all of them were right and lefts; it was only unfortunate that she missed the very first. Another day, rough shooting on the island of Barra, she shot thirty-eight birds with her first fifty shots.'[4]

She hated to leave anything wounded. If someone less capable or less conscientious than herself had left a wounded red deer on the hill, or one had been involved in an accident, she was capable if necessary of bringing it down running. This gave her the double satisfaction of ending the animal's suffering and rising to the challenge of achieving something few were capable of.

Her grandson later recalled: 'When I first arrived at Woburn as a small boy, my grandparents were both impressed with how I shot, for my father and his gamekeeper had taught me well, and they gave me every opportunity to practise and improve. Flight Lieutenant Preston, my grandmother's pilot, used to be invited to shoot at Woburn, though he was not a great shot, poor man. On one occasion I found this man between my grandmother and myself in the line. Before we started the drive, she came to me and said

"Hugh, Preston will not hit these birds. I will take them on my side, you take them on your side, but let him have a go first."

'Between us we wiped the unfortunate man's eye about fifty times in the drive. He saw the funny side of it while she created an interesting drive. By the time he had had both barrels the bird was quite a long way away.'[5]

Mary's attitude to shooting, like that of Hastings, was somewhat ambiguous. Neither of them liked the enormous pheasant shoots at Woburn with the obscenely large bags widely favoured at the time. Hastings protested by shooting only the lowest birds, declaring that they were all diseased, but his mother would shoot only the highest, for they alone presented a worthwhile challenge.

Many of the greatest naturalists have also been fine shots. Mary saw no inconsistency in combining a passion for game shooting with equal enthusiasm for and knowledge of ornithology. Her knowledge of birds, although not quite on a par with Herbrand's knowledge of mammals, was immense. She was first introduced to the world of ornithology by Herr

F Blaauw, a Dutch friend with a collection of animals and birds on his own estate in Holland which was comparable to Herbrand's collection at Woburn. From the time of her marriage, Mary shared Herbrand's enthusiastic fascination for mammals, learning enough from him to be made a Fellow of the Zoological Society of London in 1892. Blaauw spent much time with the Duke and Duchess and, being fluent in English, French and German, attended all the conferences on Zoology and Ornithology throughout Europe. He succeeded in inspiring Mary with a passion for ornithology.

In 1905 Mary became one of the first fifteen women admitted to the Linnaean Society, responding to the toast on their behalf at the dinner in their honour. Five years later she became one of the first five Honorary Life Members of the British Ornithological Union. With Dr. Eagle Clarke, she established the eminent Fair Isle Bird Observatory. He dedicated his classic work, *Studies in Bird Migration,* to her in appreciation. She liked to spend weeks or even months at a time in the Orkneys or the Hebrides, on the island of Barra (where *Whisky Galore* was later filmed) in particular.

Bird-watching with Marjorie Russell

These remote and isolated places, with a basic lifestyle far removed from the opulence of Woburn, attracted her, but her scientific approach led to her recognition as a true professional. Her observations were scrupulously accurate and detailed. Her love of the truth meant that she never yielded to the temptation to embellish her reports in any way: indeed, she always preferred to omit a sighting altogether rather than include one where there was any question at all. Her interest became an all-consuming obsession in 1906, and her diaries from then until 1914 are filled with details of all she saw. For the next four years, her hospital work during the War left her no time to leave Woburn at all; her own personal celebration of the end of the fighting was a seven week visit to Norfolk for bird watching in 1919.

The early days of her passion for ornithology in 1906 coincided with the start of her extensive correspondence with Dr. Sydney Long of Norwich, a series of letters which was to continue until her death more than thirty years later. Dr. Long (she continued to address him as 'Dear Dr. Long' and sign her letters 'Yours sincerely, M. Bedford' for the rest of her life) shared both her interests and her attitudes. Professionally, medical issues and the administration of hospitals absorbed them both. They shared too their love of birds and of the wild, remote country where the most interesting species could be watched. Both were enthusiasts, capable alike of devoting remarkable levels of concentration to the subject under consideration and of analysing it with detached scientific powers of observation.

Their correspondence also gave Mary the opportunity to explore wider issues. 'Is it possible that this little world of ours, which is *but an atom* in the Universe, is the only inhabited planet?'[6] she wondered in September 1906. 'May there not be other beings in other worlds who have progressed much further than ourselves, and who have so completely triumphed over matter that they are nothing but minds? …At all events, I think it is presumption on our part to suppose that the Power which created the Universe made this little world the only breeding place for future spirits.'

Precisely what she thought of this Power she set out more clearly four years later. Dr. and Mrs. Long were clearly very fond of Mary, attempting to arrange bird watching holidays for her with them, although she always declined and issued no reciprocal invitations, on the grounds that her deafness prevented her from enjoying any social life at all. She does not appear ever to have asked them to join her on her yacht, so often the base for her bird watching. Despite this, after the birth of their daughter Elfreda, they asked Mary to become the child's Godmother. Mary replied saying that she normally made some excuse to turn down such requests, rather than explain her religious views, 'which would not generally be regarded as orthodox.' With Dr. and Mrs. Long she wished to explain her views more accurately.

'I am, as you know, a lover of Nature, and as such I think one is bound to believe that there is some great Power "which ordereth all things," but that that Power is the excessively human, revengeful Deity which the orthodox Protestants would have me believe is more than my faith can rise to.'

Mary declares that she 'believe(s) religion, as it is taught, is absolutely essential for keeping straight the masses whose sense of honour is not strong', but that she herself, while outwardly conforming to the faith in which she was brought up, does not care whether a man 'is a Buddhist or Roman Catholic' provided he leads a good and honourable life.

Worried only that she may have shocked them, she assures the doctor that she 'can readily understand that Mrs. Long and you may not want to have a godmother for your child who holds such unorthodox views.'

Three days later, having received their answer, she is clearly delighted. 'As you do not object to an infidel godmother, I will gladly accede to your request, and trust that your little daughter may grow up with the love of Nature which you so desire.' Thereafter, characteristically, Mary had no hesitation in expressing her views on a variety of topics linked to the child, ranging from the relative merits of boots and shoes for children's feet to disapproval of the parents' apparent wish to restrict Elfreda's excitement on Christmas Day.

She delighted in sharing her interest in birds with the young, particularly through the Woburn Boys' Ornithological Club, teaching the boys to identify every bird they saw. Ahead of her time on some conservation issues, she deplored any form of egg collecting, then popular not only with schoolboys but also with museum curators. Shooting rare birds for museum collections was accepted practice at the time and rare sightings were sometimes shot to prove that they had indeed been correctly identified. Dr. Eagle Clarke is often quoted by Mary as following this practice. She herself expressed considerable reservations but conceded that 'without our national collections bird books could not be written.'[7]   So successful was she with the Club members that, when she took one twelve year old, who had only left Woburn once before in his life when visiting a brother at Nottingham, with her to Scotland, he identified 126 species at sight.

Her correspondence with Dr. Long demonstrates Mary's forthright nature as well as her ability to laugh at herself. She expressed strong disagreement with the views on cruelty to animals of an individual who wrote under the pseudonym 'John Knowlittle' but was evidently well known both to Mary and the doctor. She did not accept that the way in which rabbits and seals were commonly killed for their fur was cruel, though she deplored the 'wearing of the plumage of rare birds' as well as the large scale netting of fish and the removal of protected status from endangered bird species. Her letter concluded:

'If you think it would be good for the morals of "John Knowlittle" to see this letter, please send it to him. I have too much respect for his motives to attack him in the public press, and too little respect for my ability to murder him neatly!' But the dark moods of depression, which could overcome her, also show through sometimes in the correspondence. In January 1914, when she was forty-eight, she wrote: 'I have been almost quite deaf lately, and I am afraid have found it hard at times to take a cheery outlook on the future.' In August of the same year she wrote 'Speaking for myself, all I fear now is a long life.'

Sanderling Cottage, Barra, built by Mary for bird-watching in the Outer Hebrides.
She sometimes spent weeks here, totally alone except for Che Foo.
"When it rains, the water pours into every room..."

Arthur Duncan, who edited Mary's bird watching diaries for publication as a third, companion, volume to Gore's two volumes of biography, summarised the real attractions of bird watching for her as 'the charm of birds and the love of solitary places.'[8] The Scottish islands and other places where she stayed offered both of these in full measure. She must have seemed a strange visitor to the inhabitants of Fair Isle. At first they all clustered round, desperate to sell her the jerseys and stockings they knitted. She resolved the situation by explaining that she would not buy items from all the different individuals who approached her but instead would pay for their 'Queen's Nurse'. There was no doctor on the island and every time one was needed a bill of £20 was incurred. The islanders were desperately poor and the nurse invaluable to them. They responded to the gesture: when next Mary returned to the island, not one attempted to beg.[9]

Mary always throve on hard work and seemed to derive considerable satisfaction from the most menial duties, perhaps in reaction to the way of life expected of a duchess. She would stay in a tiny cottage, usually accompanied by a single lady's maid.

'Billingham and I go shares in the housework, and I begin the day by cleaning the grate at 6.45 a.m. and go through the programme of floor-scrubbing, dusting, bedmaking, etc., before breakfast. After breakfast I clean my boots, chop firewood… and perform sundry other duties before my morning's bird watching.'

Later in the day she took responsibility for the care of her dog, (not, on this occasion, her beloved Pekinese, Che Foo, but a retriever named Marquis), cleaned her gun and laid the table, while Billingham was in charge of the cooking. She also arranged to take a fourteen-year-old boy back to Woburn to work, looking after the foreign birds. He was remarkably knowledgeable about all the varieties to be seen on the islands, even though he had never seen a pheasant or partridge, nor, to Mary's amusement, a 'tree, bush or train!'

Mary kept a detailed record of the birds she saw. She also wrote of the countryside.

'In the morning I walked up to the Western Cliffs, where one looks straight down to the sea from a height of 600 to 700 feet. The view is altogether beyond my powers of description, but how I longed for an artist who could paint it! Never in the whole of my travels have I seen any wild, rugged coast scenery which surpasses or even in its way equals it.'[10]

Even here Mary could not forget her deafness. She had always longed for a house where she could hear the waves breaking against a rocky shore. Here her little cottage was so placed, but her deafness meant that she could never hear the waves.

Mary seems to have been well liked by the islanders. She was a source of a certain amount of income to many of them, but all seem to have welcomed her into their homes and invited her to their functions, as well as trying to help her, for example with messages in the middle of the night if a large number of birds were spotted coming in to land. Occasionally they would ask for some small favour: her yacht remained at anchor not far from the island and on one occasion a wedding party was taken to the mainland. She often excused herself from their social gatherings, for the houses were very small and overcrowded and basic hygiene left much to be desired. Conversation too could be somewhat limited, with constant repetitions of

On the sands o' Barra - Mary's transport on the island.
"I have to go and feed my pony by early morning moonlight at 6.30 a.m.
On mornings like this, when it is raining and blowing for all it is worth,
it requires some courage." 13.11.1911

"Are ye well? Are ye well?" to which they themselves would reply "no so bad," or "Foine." Despite all this, in many ways Mary appears to have been happier in their company than in that of any visitor to Woburn. She had a profound admiration for the women, who worked extremely hard, though the men she frequently considered idle and selfish. She was conscious of their extreme poverty, for steam trawlers had destroyed the local fishing industry, leaving the islanders with little except their knitting from which to make a livelihood. Apart from her practical and characteristic sponsorship of the nurse, she makes no mention of any major initiative to ease their plight; indeed it is not easy to know in what other way she could have improved their lot.

Once, as she was about to leave the island, the factor's wife came to say goodbye, and wished her 'All God's blessings', but added in an undertone 'But what's the good of them when she's got everything and doesn't want 'em!'

Mary's priorities in life are well illustrated by her diary entry for 8th June 1907 at Egilshay, Orkney.

'I had an invitation to an evening party at Buckingham Palace for to-day, but walked over instead to visit the King of Birds, viz. the White-tailed Eagle at Water falls, North Roe. His Majesty was at home, and gave me a splendid view.'[11]

She added that the bird's mate had unfortunately been shot, probably by a man in a whaling boat, but the local expectation was that the eagle would soon replace her with a new mate from Norway. Sadly this did not happen: Mary had chosen rightly in seeing the King of Birds that day, for he was then the last of his kind to inhabit the Shetland Islands, although they have since been successfully reintroduced.

Mary's visits to the Orkneys and Shetlands in the years preceding the First World War were made possible by using her yacht, the *Sapphire*, as her base. She interspersed her bird watching with a certain amount of sightseeing. Reluctant at first to enter the Cathedral Church of St. Magnus at Kirkwall because she was accompanied by her dog, Che Foo, when she noticed a number of glass cases containing white china wreaths, she decided that the presence of the little dog constituted less of a desecration than these hideous objects. In 1913, on the Island of Papa Westray, she met an ancient inhabitant who had known the islander responsible for shooting the last Great Auk exactly one hundred years before, a melancholy link with the past which fascinated her. She had been keen to visit the island because it was the scene of the death of the last Great Auk, but had not expected to establish a connection so direct and personal.

The yacht *Sapphire* enabled Mary to reach many otherwise inaccessible places. Her travels extended beyond Scotland and the British islands to the far north, Iceland and close to the fabled island of Jan Mayen, although to her bitter disappointment she was unable to land. Her diaries throughout her travels overflow with her enthusiasm. But when Herbrand and Hastings accompanied her to Spitzbergen once in the yacht, her son at least regarded the experience as one of the nightmares of his life.[12] This was partly because he was so seasick, and Mary acknowledged many years later, when travelling on a 12,000 ton ship, that 'a good many of the passengers found (the swell) unpleasant, but after voyaging for many years on the *Sapphire*, these large boats hardly seem to move.'[13]

Fancy Dress on board Sapphire – MR is probably Marjorie Russell,
MB Mary Bedford, JG Jemima Green

Although the first *Sapphire* (Mary later had a second yacht called by the same name) was always described as a yacht, it was perhaps less smart than later generations imagined. Mary's sister Zoë later told her grandchildren of how she used to make 'a few trips with Mary round Europe in a rather damp and leaky wooden sailing boat.' Zoë would send home a great many post cards and bring back endless souvenirs, including a Swedish National costume which still survives, somewhat moth-eaten but intact.

The photograph of Mary and her friends in fancy dress on board Sapphire was captioned in her album with Banquo's description of the three witches in Macbeth:

'What are these so withered and so wild in their attire,

That look not like th' inhabitants o' th' Earth

And yet are on't?'

She frequently enlivened her albums and diaries with quotations or original little notes. One diary entry reads:

'It's sad to know

That ice and snow

Not long ago

Were H$_2$O'.

Spitzbergen, no stranger to ice and snow, was where Mary had her first day's stalking, in 1901. Their Norwegian guide was so convinced that 'the lady' would miss that he placed Herbrand where he hoped that the Duke would be able to shoot the deer his wife must inevitably fail to shoot. Mary, predictably, had not gone out stalking until she was absolutely confident of her skill with a rifle, and shot two stags from a difficult angle in a single stalk. She always wanted to learn to do things to the best of her ability, and struggled for years with fishing until she eventually found someone capable of teaching her to cast properly, enabling her to abandon 'harling', or fishing with three rods with spinning baits, and become a true, and very successful, fly fisherman.

In the 1890s, whenever Herbrand was with the 3rd Battalion Bedfordshire regiment, which he commanded, at their annual summer training, Mary took the chance to travel throughout Europe. She had a number of different travelling companions, including Zoë, but on her most memorable journey she was accompanied by Mrs. Agnes Thorndike, an old school friend whose parents also lived in India, her father being the Bishop of Lahore. After some days' travel, the two young women reached Chamonix in Switzerland, full of plans for climbing mountains. It was pouring with rain when they arrived, the cloud down low on the mountains and the guides dispirited, but they were woken at six next morning when the weather changed. Early in June, there was still so much snow that it was knee deep for most of the climb and a single false step plunged them in up to their waists. They and another small party on a different route on the same day were the first groups to make the climb that year. Starting out on mules, they were soon on their feet, roped to the guides, climbing in earnest for some five hours.

At last they reached their destination, the hut at Les Grands Mulets, a well known landmark on the most direct route to the summit of Mont Blanc from Chamonix. Snow lay a foot deep on the floors of the rooms, and only in the kitchen was it possible to make even a semblance of a fire. They

Mary on the deck of Sapphire

slept in the one room where there was only deep mud rather than snow. After a frozen night in the icy hut, they made their descent, encountering on the lower slopes a Russian princess, most unsuitably clad in silk or satin and lace, with a husband bent on reaching the same point, although the English girls later learnt that the couple had not reached even the first glacier by nightfall. Meanwhile, Mary and her friend found everyone in their hotel assembled outside to greet them with a cheer on their return. At this early point in the season, reaching Les Grands Mulets was seen as quite an achievement., acknowledged by the presentation of a certificate from the Company of Guides at Chamonix confirming their feat.

Two days later, after driving and riding as far as was possible, they walked for two hours through deep snow to the famous Hospice of the Great St. Bernard, where they had a memorable stay, enjoying playing with the St. Bernard puppies. In the twenty-four days of their holiday, there were only three days when they were not travelling for between eight and fifteen hours. The account Mary submitted to her old school newsletter showed a much greater consciousness of the discomforts of the journey than her later terse records of her flying adventures revealed, though she was quite as appreciative of the beauties of the scenery.

Mary with her hunter David at Woburn

In other years, Mary's travels included Milan and Venice; Brussels, Bonn and Geneva; Amsterdam and Bergen; Vienna and Constantinople; and, from her yacht in 1900, St. Petersburg, Moscow and Berlin. Beautiful scenery often caused Mary to lament her inability to paint the world she saw, but, although she had little success with landscapes, her paintings of flowers, butterflies and toadstools were beautiful in their neatness and accuracy. The science of photography was unfortunately still in its infancy, but the combined attraction of preserving the images which delighted her and grappling with the scientific concepts involved, soon made her a keen photographer. On the Scottish Islands, the fascination of some wise old elder's face led her to devote long hours to portrait photography.

Long before her experiments with different types of photography led her into the fields of radiology and radiography, she found more light-hearted ways of amusing herself with a camera. Her enjoyment of domestic animals and her skill at training them led her to attempt to emulate the work of Harry Whittier Frees, who became famous in Edwardian times for his photographs of cats and dogs dressed up in human clothes and taking part in tableaux, with the animals portrayed acting out a school classroom scene, for example, or a fishing party. Mary photographed her cats playing the violin, playing a game of croquet and engaged in other human activities. As so often, she enjoyed combining a range of different skills in a single challenge. She always had a number of cats, either Persian or Siamese (Goblin, a Siamese, was beautifully painted by the Belgian artist, Henriette Ronner), and she thoroughly enjoyed devising their costumes and persuading them to play their parts as she photographed them.

Several other photographs, some taken by her herself and some by other people, reveal her remarkable rapport with animals. One shows her immaculately dressed in a riding habit with a bowler hat, kneeling on the ground to talk to her hunter David. No-one is holding the horse, but he clearly has no more intention of breaking off the conversation than his mistress. Another photograph shows her Pekinese spaniel Che Foo enthroned in a tiny carriage resembling a converted wheelchair with shafts drawn by her Shetland pony Viking. On other occasions apparently Che Foo rode on Viking's back. Mary was proud of her success with both animals:

'My little pony "Viking", which I brought back from Fair Isle fourteen months ago, now follows me everywhere without leading, like a dog. He has been trained to carry Che Foo and Che Foo to ride him. All of which things my family predicted would never be accomplished. At times, when a demon of wickedness possessed him and he galloped off a mile or so in exactly the opposite direction to that which I had intended him to take, qualm filled my mind, lest my family might be right, and that he might have been too old to train (sixteen months) when I got him, but I always professed implicit confidence in him which he has since justified. He drives in the dog van, walks up- and down-stairs indoors, will follow me over the narrowest of plank or stone bridges, and is afraid of nothing.'[14]

Mary loved the animals themselves but also, as ever, delighted in the challenge of achieving something which others were convinced could not be done. Perhaps with Che Foo himself she was less successful. Although there were many other dogs at Woburn, including shooting dogs such as the retriever Marquis who went to Fair Isle with her in 1909, and a variety of dogs kept by Herbrand for taking bucks alive in the park, when a particular buck needed to be brought in for extra feeding, Che Foo, known as Wuzzy, was described by Gore as Mary's only pet dog. He was given to her by a friend for her birthday in 1905, being delivered in a basket with an enormous bow round his neck, over which he had been very sick in the train. No-one imagined for a moment that she would keep him, but Mary was adamant. For the eleven years of his life, his mistress doted on him and Jemima, who was obsessive about all dogs, provided back-up support.

He was extremely spoilt and although he rewarded both women, and Mary in particular, with his undying devotion, he had few other friends. Hastings, who readily admitted to a complete lack of rapport with both horses and dogs, described him as 'a most crotchety and aggressive little brute, and even members of the household were not immune from attack. He not only bit any servant who accidentally trod on him – which was perhaps understandable – but he made a practice of assaulting me whenever I kissed my mother good-night, and also went for the footman when he removed a cloth from the table towards the end of dinner. All visitors were anathema to him and on first arrival were attacked with fury. Mr. Findlay, an old Indian friend of my parents and, incidentally, a very kind friend to me when I was a boy, used to be much amused by Che Foo's ferocity and consequential airs. There is a quaint Chinese description of the principal attributes desirable in Pekinese, which is well known to lovers of the breed. One characteristic of a properly educated dog is that "he should never fail to bite the foreign devil". "Ah, little man," Mr. Findlay would say to Che Foo, "you never fail to bite the foreign devil, do you?" – and Che Foo, turning a baleful eye upon him, would growl an emphatic assent.'[15]

Che Foo had a particular aversion to the vet. Mary had a parrot at the same time, who could give an impressive re-enactment of encounters between the two, interspersed with would-be soothing murmurs from the Duchess and Jemima. The little dog suffered from a weak heart and, in his later life, complicated schemes had to be devised to prevent him from becoming over-excited whenever Mary returned to Woburn from any of her travels on which he was unable to accompany her, in case he had a heart attack.

Mary believed that Che Foo shared her feelings, declaring that he understood 'stalking (birds) as well as his mistress, keeping as still as a rock'[16], and, like her, dreaded the return to Woburn from Cairnsmore. 'When he took his first walk at Woburn he carried his tail down so persistently that I took his temperature in the evening, but evidently it only drooped in becoming sympathy with his Mistress's feelings. However, we both hope to carry our tails up again shortly.'[17]

Mary with Viking and a dog

Many people, especially women, spoil their dogs, yet it was remarkable that Mary, who prided herself so much on her training of animals, should have done so in this one case, yet never had another dog who occupied at all the same position in her life. Che Foo had two predecessors who did not win their mistress's heart in the same way. In 1899, she brought two Pariah puppies home from Constantinople: they proved so wild and difficult that one had swiftly to be found a new home and the other ended by living in kennels on the estate, where it was apparently devoted to the kennelman, but he confided to Jemima 'If she were mine, I would dhrown *(sic)* her!'[18]

Mary was perhaps more successful with her more unusual pets, which included a swan and two otters. But Che Foo and other dogs established a close link between the Duchess and Jemima. Tu Fu, no doubt a connection of Che Foo's, was brought by Jemima to welcome her home from her record breaking flight to the Cape in 1930. His enthusiastic greeting won him almost as much public attention as the 'Flying Duchess' herself, and he was invited to accompany her and Jemima to tea with Princess Victoria and Princess Marie Louise.

Mary's fascination for all things mechanical was infectious, particularly to small boys, although, inevitably, not to Hastings. Henry Newbury, one of the village boys who was a member of the bird watching club, proved himself such an apt pupil that he eventually became her chauffeur. He in turn, together with Mary herself, first taught her grandson Hugh about the mechanics of cars, showing the boy how to drive a Model C Ford (the next after the Model T), an open tourer with a crash gear box and nothing resembling synchromesh, where it was necessary to double-declutch with great accuracy.

Despite Newbury's ability, Mary preferred to drive herself, which in the 1920s demanded skills often possessed only by professionals. Many an undergraduate keen to have a car to drive at university would meekly accept that at the beginning of term it was delivered there by the family chauffeur, who would then return home by train, leaving the young man to cope to the best of his ability with short, local runs. Mary, aged sixty-one, cheerfully drove herself in the Rolls to Dartmoor.

'The hills are appalling & I punctured a tyre in a narrow lane where it was impossible to pass another car. In spite of the isolation of the neighbourhood, cars to the number of three collected on either side of me before I had done. It is a heating and harassing job for a single female to change a Rolls wheel under any condition but when you are keeping 3 cars waiting it is worse. However the owners seemed quite good tempered, & No. 1 tried to assist but did not understand the job.' Soon she was on her way 'with streaming hair and well greased hands and crimson face'.[19]

Her embarrassment was but momentary. There was a challenge to rise to, and she gloried in having an audience to whom she could demonstrate her skills without having to become involved in social small talk. By this time in her life, her deafness and the tinnitus from which she suffered were so acute that she was almost a recluse, enjoying only the company of those with whom she could relax totally, sharing a common purpose, where actions not words were all that counted. Whether she was contemplating the mechanics of the internal combustion engine with Henry Newbury, identifying a rare bird with Dr. Eagle Clarke, or setting up an interesting challenge with her grandson on a day's shooting, she revelled in succeeding where others would fail. She saw no point in buying a wireless set: the interest lay in building her own. Whilst appreciating congenial company, she was quite as happy pursuing her many interests on her own. No doubt it was pleasant to catch the admiring looks of an audience, but she was not looking for compliments. Her interest lay rather in the satisfaction of a job well done, a target attained against all the odds. Even when quite alone, she was perpetually setting herself challenges. She could work in a team if the situation arose, with her pilots when flying, with her grandson out shooting, with doctors and nurses in the hospital, with her friend climbing a mountain. With kindred spirits or alone, so long as there was a challenge, she would rise to it. She was not competitive in the manner of a sportsman keen to beat his opponent. She was rather of the nature of the mountaineer who must climb the mountain 'because it is there.'

Acquiring her many diverse skills was a different form of teamwork. Sometimes it was simply a matter of application: persistence with painting, for example, enabled her to increase the facility she had acquired in her school days. Sometimes her title and connections helped to open doors: without Woburn, she would never have met Herr Blaauw. In many fields, only her husband's wealth provided the opportunities she needed. Her ice skating career would have terminated with the sale of the Ice Rink more than a decade earlier had the Duke not purchased the lease for her. Woburn provided the opportunity for her to acquire the practice necessary to become a first class shot. Bird watching without her private yacht would have been more restricted, though here she showed herself willing to live the life, so different from that she normally enjoyed, of a visitor staying in a small cottage without any of the comforts of the day.

But the opportunity in every case had still to be followed up and worked at. Most of the leading shots of the day had access to similar facilities to those enjoyed by Mary to enable them to acquire a similar level of skill. None took up all her other interests with comparable determination, or became equally successful in so many diverse fields.

Each of these interests, absorbing as it was at certain times in her life, was but a hobby. In addition to these, Mary had the passion for which she is best remembered, her flying, and, far exceeding everything else in the time and commitment she devoted to it, her career in the medical world.

Che Foo and Viking

CHAPTER 7

PROFESSIONAL CAREER

Ever since Mary first strained to overhear the lectures on Anatomy in the classroom adjoining her own at Cheltenham, she had had a fascination for matters medical. During her time in India, she attended such lectures and classes as came her way, but opportunities were severely restricted. Finally on the 9th February 1887, after the break-up of her relationship with Carpy but before her marriage, she was able to record gleefully in her diary:

'Nursing lecture. Bandaged first real patient.'

She also (as she told Hastings in the year before her death[1]) 'obtained permission from the woman doctor to attend and wait upon her in outpatients' hours… such was my youth and ignorance that when ladies of doubtful character appeared as out-patients I was requested to leave the room.' After her marriage, she attended lectures at the London Hospital, Whitechapel, and elsewhere. She later told one of the doctors with whom she worked that as a young girl it had been the dream of her life to become a hospital nurse.[2]

Writing to Zoë at the outbreak of the First World War, she listed her medical qualifications as follows:

'St. John's First Aid Certificate
St. John's Nursing Certificate
St. Andrew's First-Aid Certificate
National Health Society First Aid with Honours
National Health Society Nursing ditto
A course of the nurses' lectures at the London Hospital, Whitechapel
Practical instruction under Dr. Bielby at Lahore – dressing wounds and bandaging of real patients, etc., etc.
Unqualified but highly skilled veterinary nurse, also.'[3]

Being a woman at the time made it more difficult to obtain medical qualifications. It did not make it impossible. A number of her Cheltenham contemporaries went on to become successful doctors. Much as Mary was interested and attracted by the work, at that time studying for a medical qualification was not her priority. This would have been much more difficult to do after her marriage, when Herbrand would have been unlikely to give her any encouragement.

The first outlet she found for her ambitions was perceived as more appropriate to her position. In 1898, five years after the move to Woburn, she opened a Cottage Hospital in a house in the middle of the town of Woburn. It was at this time that she attended the course of lectures at the London Hospital where she became friendly with Sydney Holland, who had recently become Chairman of the London Hospital House Committee. Holland, the future 2nd Viscount Knutsford, much encouraged Mary's interest in hospital work, and exerted a powerful influence on her career.

The satisfaction of opening her own hospital, far from causing Mary to rest on her laurels, spurred her on to greater ambitions. Not content with the restrictions imposed by the size and location of the town house, she immediately started to plan a purpose built model hospital on an attractive site in open country. She commissioned Percy Adams, then in his thirties, who went on to become an eminent architect specialising in hospitals, to bring her designs to life. When she showed the plans to Sydney Holland, he wrote across them:

Maryland

'Quite perfect, but you had much better have given your money to the "London."'[4]

This building was opened for the benefit of the local community in 1903. It contained both medical and surgical facilities at this time, though Mary was always much more interested in the surgical cases than the medical ones. The Hospital attracted considerable interest: in November 1909 the Visitors' Book was signed by Edith Cavell, who had originally undergone her own training at the London Hospital. Perhaps she had met Mary there at that time, or had later heard discussion of the Woburn Cottage Hospital and wished to see it for herself. Alternatively the first move may have come from Mary herself, who was always endeavouring to find sufficient well trained nurses to staff the hospital. For in 1909 Edith Cavell was already training nurses in Brussels, just as she was doing in 1915, when the help she gave to British and French soldiers fleeing from Mons led to her execution by the Germans.

At the time, Mary was justifiably proud of her flagship hospital. Its design was the subject of widespread admiration. It was financed through her by the generosity of the Duke. She personally selected her matrons, who 'were highly recommended by London Matrons & I believed all was well.'[5] Thirty years later, she realised that this had not been the case, as she explained in a letter to Hastings.

'Before the War as you are aware the Hospital was practically run by the local doctors & I paid polite little visits, believing all was well except that they squabbled with each other & some were not on speaking terms & they ruled my matron to her distraction. They operated themselves on cases they should not operate on and there are such entries... in the operating book as "G.O.K." (God only knows).'

In retrospect, she was convinced that the hospital was run 'by the doctors and surgeons. A Matron in her hospital training has to treat them as little gods and say nothing. They would be perfectly efficient at their own job and see the nurses did their part of it but they know nothing and cared less (about) the general running of the Hospital behind their backs and most cottage hospitals that I have seen are pig sties. The surgeons would favour paying patients and doctors who brought them. And doctors would get in the cases that it was most bother for them to visit.'

This damning verdict on her own hospital came only with the benefit of hindsight. At the time she was justifiably proud of her achievement, but her days were fully occupied with all her other interests and activities.

The hospital featured prominently but at this time she was certainly not a single-minded career woman. She gloried throughout the pre-War years in the rich variety of her interests, the diversity of her lifestyle. Any neglect of her only child can in no way be attributed to the pressing demands of a full time career. Hastings was twenty-five when War broke out, and Mary herself fast approaching fifty.

Perhaps the account she gave to Hastings is unduly modest. John Gore later wrote:

'Her work as planner, builder, organiser, and manager was signal, her experience became immense. Her record of service is even more remarkable. She served in every department in her profession, from floor-scrubber to theatre sister, and was never too busy or too proud to undertake the meanest tasks to the last year of her life.

'For thirty-four years she devoted herself to hospital work: for many of them she gave a full day's work, year in, year out, and all the year round, exactly as any professional nurse must do, to her hospitals.'[6]

This suggests something very different from the 'polite little visits' to which she herself referred, and the thirty-four years indicate that she started to work in earnest in 1903 when the new building was opened. It is probable that the truth lies somewhere in the middle. Her other interests before the War must inevitably have prevented her from working the long hours she undoubtedly undertook during the war, though at the end of her life her disciplined lifestyle enabled her to combine a serious devotion to duty with her flying exploits. Indeed the correspondence with Hastings was provoked by a suggestion from him that she should reduce or give up her hospital commitments.

On the other hand, the distinction she herself so forcefully draws between the time before the War and the later period is significant. The initial venture certainly paled into insignificance in comparison with what was to follow. Her grandson was quite unaware that there had been a hospital at all before the War: he was under the impression that the 1914 Hospital at the Abbey was opened before the Cottage Hospital.

The year 1914 is perhaps the greatest watershed in world history. For Mary, as for so many millions throughout the world, life was never to be the same again. Unlike so many others, though, for Mary the turning point was not a tragedy but an opportunity, gladly seized with both hands. In a sense, her whole life had been preparing her for this moment, inadequate though the preparation was in so many ways. Before the outbreak of War she played with life, played with as much skill and determination as any professional sportsman. From this time on, her heart and soul were in her work, and she clearly saw all her other activities as the diversions that they had become. The fact that one new hobby, as yet undreamed of, was to propel her to the front pages of every newspaper and win her the acclaim so grudgingly accorded to her true life's work, in no way detracted from her own perception. She belonged in her own hospitals.

On 4th August 1914 when War was declared, Mary was staying at Endsleigh. Next morning she went down to Plymouth where her yacht *Sapphire* was one of the few remaining vessels. The Fleet had steamed in darkness up to Scapa Flow a few days earlier and Captain Elliott of the *Sapphire* was keen to reach Southampton as soon as possible. This was Mary's second yacht named *Sapphire*. The original *Sapphire* was first hired (all the yachts she had used before this time had always been hired, not owned, by the Duke) in 1901 and subsequently bought and used by Mary for many bird watching expeditions and other adventures. In 1911, she persuaded Captain Elliott, most reluctantly, to sail the yacht within sight of the fabled island of Jan Mayen, 310 miles north-north-east of Iceland

Sapphire I off Jan Mayen

and 240 miles from the coast of Greenland, as she later recalled in an article for *Country Life*. With floating ice to one side of them and heavy surf on the other, even Mary conceded that to attempt to land would be unwise: she merely stopped the yacht a mile from the island, unable to drop anchor as they were close to the Wille Glacier, and rowed the dinghy within a few yards of the shore. As they left, the fog came down, to be driven away in its turn by an easterly gale and sea which even the Duchess described as dangerous. 'But I had seen Jan Mayen, and did not greatly care what happened.'[7]

The following year, in 1912, the first *Sapphire* was replaced by a second, specially built for her at John Brown's Shipyard on Clydebank, with a tonnage of 1,421 and a speed of 15 ½ knots, driven by twin-screw triple expansion engines. Her Captain and crew had long known that serving the Duchess was no sinecure: she wrote of Captain Elliott on his death many years later:

'He was an ideal Captain, capable, willing, and always cheerful, except when I made him follow the ice-pack up to Jan Mayen.'[8]

They knew too that they would never be asked to undertake any risk which their boss was not ready to share with them. It is unlikely, though, that they had anticipated the proposal made in August 1914. Mary proposed to the Admiralty that the *Sapphire*, her crew and the Duchess herself should be placed at the immediate disposal of the Admiralty. The offer was declined: they could not allow a woman to take war risks.

Mary never saw the *Sapphire* again after that final visit. The yacht was later requisitioned, survived the War but was then sold. The original *Sapphire* was less fortunate, being used as a patrol boat and eventually sunk.

Her first scheme for helping the War effort thus thwarted, Mary returned to Woburn. Her next move was to convert the Cottage Hospital into a Military Hospital for the wounded. She then turned the old Riding School and Tennis Court at Woburn Abbey into another, much bigger, hospital. The old Cottage Hospital had just twenty beds, the new hospital at the Abbey initially held eighty beds, with a further twenty being added soon after. The staff for the combined hospitals included twenty-four fully trained nurses. For hospital surgeon Mary was fortunate enough to secure the services of an exceptional London consultant, Mr Bryden Glendining, who was to become a lifelong friend. A total of 2,453 serving soldiers passed through the combined hospital. Yet in August 1914 her main anxiety was that her hospital would be rejected, just as her offer of the yacht had been.

Sapphire II

'If they don't send me patients, I shall ask for Germans!..'[9] she wrote to Zoë.

The speed at which she moved was remarkable. On 5th August 1914 she was in Plymouth on board the *Sapphire*. On 11th August she spent the day in London at the War Office ensuring that the Director of the Army Medical Corps did not forget the Cottage Hospital, meeting the Head Matron of the Red Cross and arranging for University College to send those patients who were 'fit to travel' to Woburn. On her return to Woburn she found that she had had 150 applications to join her corps in twenty-four hours, with double the number expected in the next twenty-four hours. By 19th August, twenty-four beds were ready, with the hospital accepted by the War Office and properly registered. On 7th September the first soldier patients were admitted.

Mary's enthusiasm and drive amused as well as impressed those about her: Herbrand remarked that he felt sorry for the first patient to arrive, for there would be such jubilation over him. But her approach had the desired effect on the officials and civil servants with whom she had to deal, even though Mary herself hated all such negotiations. Whenever possible, she refused to attend meetings or take part in discussions, claiming that her deafness made such direct communication hopeless. The success of her day in London in obtaining what she wanted from so many different authorities contradicts this, though her comment to Dr. Long that she was 'always getting hold of the wrong end of the stick' suggests that she did genuinely find her deafness a handicap on such occasions.

The declaration of War brought out all the latent feminism in her.

'I am inclined to think', she wrote to Dr. Long on 19th August, 'that for the women who have some "go" in them and would gladly go to the Front to be shot at, it is hard work sitting still and being told they may send their money and knit socks.

'You being a man will be horrified at my views, but there *are* men who do not want to go, even though they have not much to do at home. Speaking for myself, all I fear now is a long life.'

In her next letter to Dr. Long, she reassured him 'Please do not suppose I want to go to the Front and use my rifle.' Her efforts were to be devoted to nursing. Aware of her inadequacies in this role, she resolved to rectify her lack of experience by devoting from 7 a.m. to 9 a.m. every day to practical work in the hospital. Soon she was arriving daily at 5.45 a.m. Mary prided herself on undertaking every task ever required of any nurse, however menial. Thus, as well as fulfilling a managerial role, she gradually

Open Air Ward at the Abbey Hospital

trained herself to take on the other duties at which she excelled: theatre sister, radiographer and radiologist.

Even before the first patients reached the Cottage Hospital, the new Abbey Hospital was being created under the close personal supervision of the Duchess. The riding school was converted to contain eighty beds, the tennis court became the recreation room. Further buildings were erected to contain the operating theatre, X-ray room, kitchen and bathrooms.

Later extensions were made, including converting a veranda known as the Covered Way into an open-air ward. This was apparently most effective in preventing wounds from becoming septic. It seems likely that the patients were kept warm in the same way as they were in the Robert Jones and Agnes Hunt Orthopaedic Hospital in Oswestry during the Second World War. A former nurse there, Philippa Carne, recently recalled in a letter to the *Daily Mail*:

'In the winter we had to brush the snow from under the beds. The children were not cold because halfway down the bed we placed heated metal plates, which we were forever reheating in an oven at the end of the ward.'

Not long after the Abbey Hospital became operational, it was officially listed as a Base Hospital, able to take wounded men direct from the Front. The establishment received official accolades on every hand. The Military Correspondent of *The Times* concluded a glowing report with the words:

'For anyone who needs to learn how best a War Hospital should be organised and managed, a visit to Woburn is a liberal education.'[10]

The Editor of the *British Journal of Nursing* visited in February 1915. Her detailed report was equally complimentary, referring to the Abbey Hospital as 'this wonderful hospital', and the Cottage Hospital as 'a model of its kind.'[11] The officer responsible for granting official approval was similarly enthusiastic, adding a tribute to the Duchess herself:

'I was greatly impressed with her earnestness of purpose, her ability for management, and her unusual capabilities in respect of knowledge in regard to the administration of hospitals. Not only could she apply herself to such matters with extraordinary success, but she could also herself perform the duties she expected others to carry out, with accuracy and efficiency and with such interest as never fails to appeal to patients. Her work during the War was of the highest order, and the more I saw of it the greater became my admiration of her who was able to make the fullest use of the resources of Woburn Abbey.'[12]

The County Director of the Red Cross, reporting to the Chairman in 1918, concluded his report:

'This hospital has now been selected as an Orthopaedic Hospital. There are only eleven others in England. The fact of this hospital having been selected proves how efficient the military authorities must consider the management to be.'[13]

The most important single managerial decision taken by Mary in 1914 was the selection of Bryden Glendining as chief surgeon. Glendining was an eminent gynaecologist, who came to Woburn from Guy's. His health was not good, which no doubt influenced his decision to leave London, for, even though the Duke and Duchess ensured that he lost nothing financially, the move must have seemed like professional suicide.

Perhaps, even at that early stage, he and Mary recognised in each other a professional compatibility, a spark of genius, which would enable them, working together as a team, to achieve so much more than the sum of what each, working individually, could have achieved. At first, the prospect did not look bright. Glendining, a gynaecologist, was taking charge of two hospitals where all the patients would be male. He was answerable to one person, a woman, whose sole claim to supremacy was the money she could command. She had no knowledge or experience of medical matters, yet no-one doubted that she would take all the important decisions.

Probably Mary never even contemplated the problems seemingly inherent in the situation. By this time, she had sufficient self-confidence .to know that such things were unimportant. She also had sufficient modesty as well as common sense to realise that one of the objectives in persuading a man of consummate professional expertise to undertake the job was to make full use of his skill.

Whether she could in fact have brought herself to do so had Glendining not been the man he was, was never put to the test. She found in him probably the only man in her life whom she could acknowledge in her heart as a superior being, a true hero. She first came to know her father at an age when his human failings, his selfishness and his greed, were only too apparent: she loved, but did not idolise, him. Carpy, the eternal labrador puppy, had been a delightful playmate but never, in any sense, her superior. Of the three, she perhaps had most respect for Herbrand, but this was based on his generosity, both material and in a deeper sense, towards her: she never doubted her superior ability, intellectually and in almost everything they undertook. Much of her correspondence with other men, acknowledged experts in their own fields, Dr. Long for example, and a number of eminent ornithologists, reveals a certain unconscious sense of superiority, almost of arrogance. In part this was social: if she had been asked to express an opinion, she would probably have repudiated any such thoughts, but the obsequious homage paid to duchesses at the time, regardless of their abilities, inevitably left its mark. In part, too, she felt herself to be at least their intellectual equal.

In Bryden Glendining she was confronted with a man who shared her own ability to excel at almost anything to which he turned his hand, from surgery to hospital administration, from angling to poultry keeping. Nor did he, on his arrival at Woburn, show unqualified admiration for what Mary had achieved.

Bryden Glendining

Ward at the Abbey Hospital

'My London surgeon,' she told Hastings many years later, 'A very strict disciplinarian, found things very imperfect at the little hospital – the Abbey one he practically made his own way.'[14]

Above all, Mary recognised that his superiority in the field which now most interested her, that of medicine, was attributable to more than his experience and training. Had she enjoyed precisely the same professional education, Glendining, she knew, would still have been the greater surgeon.

There was never any risk that her admiration would turn to love or passion. These were not emotions which had ever held the same sway over her as they did over other women. Approaching fifty, she was not going to sacrifice professional success and one of the finest hospitals in Britain to anything so trifling. She was a close friend of Mrs. Glendining: the three holidayed happily together after the War. On the other hand, Mary's relationship with Glendining was in many ways, personally as well as professionally, the most successful and enjoyable relationship of her life. Here at last was a man whom she could genuinely admire and respect. Gore, in the biography commissioned by her husband after her death, described the relationship thus:

'His was a masterful nature. It might be expected that two such natures would clash. They rarely did so. Differences of opinion were inevitable, but harmony was never long disturbed. It is a proof of the Duchess's womanliness and of her sense that, while Mr. Glendining was in health and in charge at her hospital, he was always Master – and sometimes a harsh Master – and she would not have it otherwise.'[15]

He in his turn saw a woman dedicated to using the immense riches at her disposal for the good of humanity, a woman, moreover, who would be guided by his advice in her decisions about the most effective way in which to achieve these aims. He was immediately impressed with all that she had already achieved in making the hospital operational so fast against the full weight of bureaucracy, and with the standards which she maintained. He saw, too, how hard she was prepared to work at menial chores and how willing she was to learn her new life's work without skimping or shirking. He realised that this was a way in which he could help her and indirectly all who used her hospitals, by guiding her down the right paths to enable her to develop her career in the best possible way.

As he told Mary, her menial work seemed to him a waste of intellect. She never regarded it in the same light, feeling that it was important for the rest of her life to understand through personal experience precisely what a nurse's duties entailed. She gloried in getting up at 4.45 every morning, as she continued to do even beyond the end of the War, and combining this work with the immense secretarial load required in support of 102 beds.

Glendining saw immediately that, hard and conscientiously as she laboured to attend to the routine duties of patient care, her real interest, like his own, lay in the field of surgery. She admitted that medical, as opposed to surgical, work 'bored her to extinction.' The theatre sister in the Cottage Hospital at the time was very inefficient, so Glendining informed Mary that he would far prefer to teach her rather than have 'one with ideas of her own.' Mary did not take long to become fully capable of assisting the surgeon at operations. It is hardly surprising that such a gifted and enthusiastic pupil, working under a surgeon of the calibre of Bryden Glendining, whose brilliance in the field of surgery had been recognised for many years, should have attained the highest standards. Further 'promotion' came a few months later when Glendining needed her to take charge of the patients occupying 86 beds at the Abbey Hospital in the post operative period. To enable her to do this, she had first to train a subordinate to take on all the cleaning and preparation before surgery in the Cottage Hospital.

In 1917 the second surgeon, who had assisted Glendining in all his operations at the two hospitals, sadly died of pneumonia. Once again, it was to the Duchess that Glendining turned. He officially appointed her surgeon's assistant at the Abbey Hospital, in addition to her onerous commitments as officer-in-charge of both hospitals. Mary was now responsible for preparing for, and assisting at, around a dozen operations per week. She continued to fulfil this role, never missing a single operation performed by Glendining personally until his own death in the mid Twenties.

Other surgeons, who at various times worked with or later succeeded Bryden Glendining, did not always command the same level of respect. Mary usually developed an excellent relationship with her Matrons. They felt that it was particularly valuable to have the Duchess on duty in the absence of Glendining. One Matron explained their reasoning to her: 'I always feel happier when you are there because you tell them (the surgeons) if they do anything wrong!'[16] She not only had the authority to impose her judgement. She had reached a level of experience and knowledge where she was trusted further than the young surgeons themselves.

So skilled did she become that she was eventually capable of performing minor operations herself. In December 1919 her diary, neglected throughout the frenetic years of the War, records:

'I here place on record that I to-day amputated a toe and excised a painful scar in the sole of the foot for Leslie Coop, of 43, Arden Road, Birchfields, Handsworth, Birmingham.'[17]

While Mary was developing all these new skills at the same time as she continued to control the administration of her hospitals, she had one important further step to take in her medical career. Once again, this was initiated by Bryden Glendining, who had the vision to spot a major need for expertise, recognise that the required skill was one which the Duchess was well equipped to acquire, stimulate her interest and show her how she could learn.

After the Abbey Hospital was given up, Glendining felt that his operations were being hampered by the low standard of the X-ray department. The first X-ray was taken in 1895. An amazed world learnt, over the ensuing years, just how dangerous as well as how valuable the new technique could be. Those operating the new equipment frequently suffered serious injury and sometimes death from burns and cancer caused by the new techniques. Few people, including the scientists involved with the development of this new branch of medicine, had any understanding of the risks presented by the process, and indeed there was a concerted effort by some of those manufacturing the equipment to attempt to conceal the risks.

The First World War led to an acceleration in the comprehension of the risks together with a developing knowledge of the ways in which these risks could be counteracted and the beneficial effects utilised. By the end of the First World War, it was becoming recognised and relatively safe practice for the patient to be X-rayed before an operation was undertaken.

Few topics could have been better suited to the skills the Duchess possessed. Her scientific curiosity made such a new branch of medicine particularly interesting to her, her work in the operating theatre made her fully appreciative of the contribution the use of X-rays could make, she was quite without fear of the risks inherent in the practice, which was in any case now becoming relatively safe as the nature of the hazards was better understood, and she had long been a skilled photographer who routinely developed her own work.

As soon as Mary had mastered the rudiments of the topic from the original radiologist, Glendining characteristically arranged for Professor Russ to visit the Cottage Hospital on a weekly basis and instruct her further. Russ was one of the foremost experts of the time: when the National Radium Trust was established in 1929, he became its first Scientific Secretary. Predictably, Russ found his pupil a delight to teach. When she had mastered the details of radiography (the taking and developing of X-ray photographs, which is not considered a medical skill: she became a Life Member of the newly formed Society of Radiographers) and radiology (their interpretation, a skill in which she was highly trained and proficient, but which she modestly forbore ever to claim because of her lack of other medical qualifications), Russ asked her whether she wished to go further still and become a radiotherapist.

This was the subject which was absorbing Russ himself: the treatment of malignant disease by the use of X-rays. Mary was keen to follow this path too and soon became highly competent. Eventually, however, she realised that conditions at the Cottage Hospital did not justify the necessary equipment and other expenses to establish a centre for radiotherapy. This was one of the few paths in life which she followed, but eventually abandoned.

The outbreak of the First World War brought a complete change not only to Mary's way of life, as it did to millions of her fellow countrymen, but also to her whole approach to life. The dilettante, albeit with the highest of standards in all that she undertook, disappeared for ever, to be replaced by the dedicated professional.

The remarkable thing at the time was the speed with which she first took her decisions and then brought them to fruition. Within thirty-four days of the declaration of War, she had not only admitted failure on 'Plan A' but had already executed Plan B'. 'Plan A' was to place the *Sapphire,* under her own command, at the disposal of her country. Presumably she had anticipated the inevitable outcome and already prepared 'Plan B'.

The way in which she not only made her own arrangements but sliced through the Gordian knot of officialdom and bureaucracy which threatened to engulf her, so that, just five weeks after the declaration of War, the first soldier patients were admitted to her hospital, must rank among the most amazing achievements in the lifetime of this remarkable woman. Naturally her money and title helped. Even so, there was a yawning gulf between her initial plans and their realisation which she somehow managed to bridge in little more than a month.

Not only did she demonstrate, then and throughout the War, the determination to overcome all obstacles. She combined this with an unexpectedly high level of modesty as well as good judgement, which enabled her to select the right candidates for the most important positions. Pre-eminent among them was Glendining himself. His selection made all future decisions an easier undertaking, for his own innate good judgement, his knowledge of the main players in the medical world which Mary was now entering seriously for the first time, and his determination and resourcefulness, which matched those of the Duchess herself, all helped her to attain her goals.

Mary had never been a driven career girl, either at school or afterwards, until 1914. She had long demonstrated the will to be the best at whatever currently occupied her mind, but her devotion to the world of medicine far transcended any such qualities demonstrated hitherto. Probably the development of her own career was driven by Glendining rather than by Mary herself. Her own ambition was rather to run the best group of private War hospitals in Britain. From this aim, many of her other successes at this time emanated. She moved steadily up a career-ladder set up for her by the surgeon responsible for running her hospitals. There was no longer a great reservoir of untapped potential to cause her frustration. She happily bartered the freedom and delights of her pre-War existence for the satisfaction which came from pure hard work, expertly guided along a worthwhile route. She knew that she was doing the job for which nature intended her, to the best of her ability, in such a way that she was helping her country in the most horrendous War that had ever been fought. She was doing all this with the active support and encouragement of her husband, at the behest of a man who had all the characteristics she most admired in the opposite sex and who far outshone any man she had ever known.

The War years, so tragic for so many of her countrymen, afforded her all the opportunities for which she had been searching throughout her adult life. It was a time of immense personal achievement when she was able to put back into the world so much that she had hitherto taken out. She flourished, and the self confidence born of her success enabled her to demonstrate a modesty, a willingness to learn and an acceptance of another's right to lead her, which themselves generated even greater success.

One of Mary's book plates

CHAPTER 8

THE HOSPITALS

Mary developed and administered four separate hospitals at Woburn during her lifetime. First, in 1898, came the original Cottage Hospital at Number 1 Leighton Street, right in the centre of Woburn. Five years later that was replaced by the purpose-built hospital outside the town, which was opened on 22nd May 1903 and was later known as Maryland. When War was declared, the Abbey Hospital sprang to life for the war wounded. In 1914, Maryland and the Abbey Hospital together were officially designated Woburn Military Hospital. Between 7th September 1914 and 31st March 1920, when the Military Hospital was officially closed, 2,453 serving soldiers, non-commissioned officers and men, passed through it. They were often brought direct from the battlefields of France. In 1917 the Abbey Hospital was declared a special surgical unit for other ranks. At the end of the War the Army Council requested its conversion into one of only twelve Military Orthopaedic Hospitals in the country. The Hospital continued in operation under the name of the Woburn Surgical Hospital for the treatment of Pensioners.

The fourth hospital to be opened by the Duchess was Battlesden, in a house on the estate. During the War, this building was used as a rest home for nurses. After the closure of the Abbey Hospital, Battlesden was opened as a hospital for certain categories of people whom Mary considered to be in particular need of free medical treatment.

Other buildings on the estate were also used as hospital annexes of various descriptions at different times. One such was the Paris House, now a restaurant. This attractive half timbered building was originally built for the Paris Exhibition, then bought and brought to Woburn in pieces to be reassembled under the directions of Herbrand's father. For a while, Mary brought this building into her orbit: it was known locally as the Tonsil Hospital. Later Mary's pilot lived there and then during the Second World

War it became a part of Bletchley Park. Distinguished guests who stayed there included both Charles de Gaulle and King George VI with the Queen Mother. The expenses of all these hospitals were met by the Duke and Duchess themselves.

'Expenditure was lavish on the Woburn Hospital, and no War Office grants were ever taken,' wrote a correspondent to *The Times* after her death. 'This could not have been done without ducal means, and, as the Duchess ever acknowledged, without the generous help of the Duke. But highly qualified surgeons, fully trained nurses and other competent members of the staff with the most up-to-date equipment for hygiene, nursing treatments, operations and X-raying, with no stint in feeding or in general means of comfort for patients and for staff, were not provided without sacrifices. These were not grudged.'[1]

Mary later declared that it had 'always been the wish of my life to have a hospital for the impecunious upper classes who could pay little or nothing.' This was not snobbery: frequently, the very poor had better access to medical treatment through various charitable institutions than those higher up the social scale who were still unable to afford the going rate for treatment of any sort. Battlesden was opened after the War with this in view. Mr. Glendining 'met me more than half way and charged little or no fees and I as a rule charged none. They were treated as I would a guest.'[2]

Unfortunately, when Mr. Glendining was succeeded by Mr. Ogilvie, everything changed. He was paid a salary of £1200 by the Duchess, but he had four children to educate and a career to establish. When Mary found that he was charging up to fifty guineas or even more, she felt bound to pay his fees, over and above his salary, on behalf of patients whom she was particularly keen to help.

'This became more than I could do, and with decreasing dividends and ever increasing expenses, I had to give up Battlesden,' she later told Hastings.

The personality clash between Mary and Mr. Ogilvie led to divided loyalties amongst the other staff. Miss Livesey in particular, who, in Mary's words, was 'a little too loyal to me', and had been trained by Bryden Glendining, found difficulty in working with his successor (although she later worked happily with Mary's third and final surgeon, Mr. Massey, who succeeded Mr. Ogilivie in 1936). This in turn created problems for Mary for the rest of her life, since Miss Livesey was one of the few people capable of standing in for the Duchess to act as theatre sister to the surgeon on operating days.

Surgical work required more staff than would have been necessary for medical work and, even after the closure of Battlesden, Mary was spending two thirds of her annual income on the hospital. After the death of Mr. Glendining, she became increasingly disillusioned with the medical profession. Her comment to Hastings in February 1936 draws a somewhat depressing conclusion:

'I am sorry to say my long experience of doctors & surgeons makes me hope but not expect that I shall die without them.'

Bryden Glendining was the one exception to this. Sadly he did not enjoy good health. Although he succeeded in keeping the hospital running until 1925, he had been a sick man for some time before that and eventually died in May 1927. Although his successor Mr. Ogilvie never had anything approaching the same relationship with the Duchess which Glendining had enjoyed, he wrote an excellent appreciation of her in *The Times* after her death, pointing out that she had assisted at all the operations done at her hospital and nursing home in the last twenty years. There were more than 5,000 such operations.

Between 1914 and 1920 in particular, Mary was in effect combining two careers in the medical world. She had her nursing career, in which she progressed from basic nursing to become a theatre sister and eventually a radiographer and radiologist. She was also heavily committed to hospital management. She hated some aspects of hospital management. She disliked working through committees, finding them slow, ineffective and a waste of time. She believed, with reason, that she could achieve much more by working on her own in collaboration with those colleagues in whom she had confidence.

She wrote to Dr. Long in August 1914, 'On all sides I am asked to attend Committees, or "Can I come over and see you?" "Will you come and see 'So-and-So' at the War Office?" etc., etc., and to everyone I have to answer that I am too deaf.'

It was true, but it also provided the perfect excuse. She would have been quite as reluctant to participate even if her hearing had been normal. This was the one recompense which her hearing problems could provide for all the misery which they caused her. She concluded pessimistically:

'The line I *can* take, which is to offer skilled nursing and make my hospital useful, will probably be of no use.'

Her fear of being useless was unfounded. Her declaration of what she had to offer was true, and would have been equally true had she enjoyed full health. Her suffering, on the other hand, was real enough. She wrote to Dr. Long in 1917:

'I am too deaf to stay with people now... I have had a blessed and unexpected respite this summer from the bad deafness of last winter, but I never know from day to day how long I shall retain the present amount of hearing, and though it (the hearing) is good, for me, I should not like to inflict myself upon strangers.'

On Boxing Day in the same year, she outlined to Dr. Long what her commitments entailed:

'As the Cottage Hospital used to get empty before the Abbey Hospital was ready for a convoy, we started taking in nerve suture, bone grafting, and other interesting cases from the Command Depot, with the result that we are operating there every second or third day. This keeps me there from 6.30 a.m. to 4 or 5 p.m., and as I assist both my surgeons in any private cases they have as well, my work, plus the writing, saves me at least from deserving the title of one of the "idle rich".'[3]

An independent report in 1920 states:

'The Duchess of Bedford worked as a sister in the hospital from its commencement in September 1914. From January 1915 she was absent for three weeks, when necessary repairs were being carried out, since which time she has been continuously present and on duty.

'There were 45 convoys of wounded, who arrived at the main-line station eight miles distant. The Duchess met each convoy, and arranged for their transport by Motor Ambulance.'[4]

As if the hospital work was not enough during the War, Mary converted Battlesden, later to become the hospital for the impecunious upper classes, into a rest home for London nurses in need of a break during the long years of war. She paid their travelling expenses and charged them nothing. They were allowed to stay for not more than two weeks and there were never more than three there at a time, to ensure that it had the atmosphere of a family home, not a hospital or other institution. While they were there, the lucky nurses enjoyed every luxury, from breakfast in bed to the best entertainment the Duchess could provide. For the first two years all went as Mary had planned: towards the end of the War a more demanding group of nurses showed inadequate appreciation, wanting to stay for longer than the permitted fortnight and complaining about details. Mary was not sorry

Mary in nurse's uniform.

to close it down as soon as the war was over. By then, 224 nurses had been able to rest there.

Mary generally succeeded in creating an excellent atmosphere in her domains. Her word was law, she had a quick temper and she could be terrifying, but the thunderclouds were often followed by a burst of sunshine, particularly if, upon reflection, she felt her attack had been unjustified. Keen to correct the injustice, her charm rarely failed to win round anyone whom she had inadvertently upset. Her kind heart and strong sense of humour, combined with a fund of entertaining stories, enabled her to delight and amuse any gathering, provided she did not feel constrained by the shyness her deafness induced, and she allowed the nurses to tease her gently about her little 'fads', such as her obsession with fresh air. The nurses admired the way in which she worked as hard as any of them, and maintained standards as high as anything expected of them. Her three successive matrons, and the redoubtable Miss Livesey, did not feel that she interfered with them. She was proud that each of her three matrons had made the same remark: 'I can't bear the days when you are not here. It does not seem right.'

This was partly explained by the fact that, in other hospitals at the time, even matrons were expected to give way to the wishes and sometimes the whims of the doctors. At Woburn they knew that they could count on the support of the Duchess if necessary against the doctors, with the inevitable exception of Mr. Glendining: fortunately, he appears to have been as popular with the rest of the team as he was with his employer. Mary delighted in telling of the occasion when her Matron wrote: 'I don't know what we are going to do with a thyroidectomy on Monday, and you not here,' even though she had arranged for Miss Livesey to take her place.

The relationship Mary enjoyed with the senior nursing staff was well summed up in a letter she wrote to Miss Livesey towards the end of the War:

'There have been some very difficult times in the past as well as some very pleasant ones, and I have wondered whether you would or could hold out. But we came through "smiling", and I have always realised how entirely the success of my hospital hung on you... Though I am an amateur, you have never *let me know* you were professional, and you have always been so ready to fall in with any suggestion...'[5]

Sometimes she treated them in a manner which they could well have resented had the relationship been less close. A visiting Matron was shocked when Mary opened all the store cupboards to show her how tidily they were kept, seeing this as interference. The Woburn nurses accepted this because they accepted her as part of the team: they worked with her, they did not work for her.

Mary was as solicitous for the wellbeing and happiness of the patients as she was for the staff, but, because most of them were not there for as long, she found the relationship more difficult. On the wards, the patients knew her as Sister Mary, although the majority must have been well aware that she was in fact the Duchess. Most of them would have been amazed to learn that the reason she seemed so austere and remote was that she was afraid of them, afraid that her deafness would cause her to make some mistake in conversation with them, to create some embarrassing misunderstanding. Her deafness made her dread talking to strangers.

Mary was always concerned with making the physical environment as comfortable and pleasant as possible. She was shocked when, after the War, a nursing home, which she had built at Woburn Sands for around twenty patients, had to be sold because Mr. Glendining was too ill to do the work. The London organisation which bought it crammed eighty-two patients into the same space. She chose bright, light, clean paint and fabrics and appreciated that people's tastes and preferences differed. Fanatically keen on fresh air herself, when one distinguished visitor commented 'Well I don't mind dying but I always say let me die warm!' Mary immediately started to visualise the sort of facilities which would appeal to patients with this approach, 'a small cheery bed & sitting room, common library and dining room, the doctor of their choice, a lovely garden with shelters'[6] as well as the usual hospital fitments.

She did her best, too, to provide entertainment for the patients. The Duchess laid on film shows, concerts, plays and professional entertainers. Patients physically capable of doing so could play tennis, go for drives and enjoy walking in the 40 acres of garden. A particularly popular sport amongst those who had been in residence for some time was to trick the unwise into exploring the Labyrinth, preferably just before the next meal was served.

War-time Christmases always presented a challenge.

'I took in 60 patients two days before Christmas, altering my dinner party from 18 to nearly 80, but I do not expect the authorities to consult my convenience. The Abbey Hospital chef was called up for service without a day's warning, the day before, but here again I do not expect the French government to consult me, and I still hope to "keep smiling"'[7] wrote Mary in 1915.

The following year was no better. This time the hospital was full, with three secondary haemorrhages occurring every day, Mr. Glendining was seriously ill and expected to remain on the sick list for three months and the whole hospital was hit with a flu epidemic, incapacitating 'servant staff' and nurses alike, and replacement nurses who reached the required standard proved unobtainable. The following year, Christmas 1917 was once more a time of crisis.

Mary kept a room for herself at the hospital, so that she could slip away quietly to read and write, but also be on hand both to complete her work and to join in with the rest of the nursing staff as an active member of the team, sharing their jokes and fun as well as the work. Somehow she managed to combine being a popular member of the group with retaining her authority and never losing her dignity. It was a difficult road to tread, but she succeeded in striking the balance between aloofness and over familiarity, between colleague and leader. In the middle of the day she would eat a quick sandwich with a slice of cake and cup of tea, then unwind for a few minutes chatting to the Matron or applying herself to the *Times* crossword (she did not appreciate any assistance supplied by those around), then in mid-afternoon, when her shift ended, return to the Abbey for a walk with the Duke. If she was needed at the Abbey, she would sleep there, but, in war-time at least, more frequently returned to her hospital room.

Despite her shyness with the patients, she saw them all as individuals and always put their needs first. One day in the Thirties, she belatedly recalled that an important flying engagement clashed with a scheduled X-ray. She raced back to the hospital in full flying kit, ready to complete the X-ray before going back to her plane. She had accorded the appointment higher importance than had the patient himself: it turned out that he had forgotten his own X-ray.

A patient who became a special favourite was the nine year old boy whom she referred to as 'a delightful little burglar.' Almost an Oliver Twist, he had hit the headlines a year before, according to Mary's diary in 1930, when 'he was concerned in a rather famous London burglary, having been engaged by his friends to throw brickbats at the police from the roof. A philanthropic lady in this neighbourhood having read the account of his case, offered to adopt and reform him (or save him from his friends) so he came on probation for a year. He did very well for nearly a year and then stole a sackful of apples from an orchard of which he is supposed to have eaten an inordinate quantity. The next thing was a violent attack of acute appendicitis and he was admitted for an emergency operation on an almost gangrenous appendix. He has done very well and is a perfect darling with a most innocent face and beautiful manners. All the staff love him. I wonder what his upbringing was? When asked at what hour he went to bed at home he said his mother "kicked him upstairs when she came home at about 1 a.m." Certainly providence never intended him for a criminal with that face. I gave him a little wrist watch and he was seen to rub his cheek against it and murmur "Oh, I have wanted you for a long time!" He is to be sent to a training ship where I hope he may take the right road.' Those who suggest that she disliked children forget her little Oliver Twist, the young members of her bird watching club and her grandson Hugh.

Mary was deeply loved locally. Small gestures, such as personally making a cot blanket for the first baby to be born in the hospital, were still remembered and appreciated a lifetime later. Her hospitals became flagship examples of the standards to which all others should aspire. Visiting high ranking medical and military officials admired and applauded her work in a long succession of reports. Surgeons who had worked at Woburn would return to London and make comparisons which were never flattering to the city hospitals.

Three main factors contributed to her success. First and most important was the depth and consistency of her personal commitment. Her attention to detail was second to none. She was always there, seeing for herself precisely what was happening, maintaining unfailingly high standards herself and ensuring that others did likewise.

Secondly, the lack of financial constraint was clearly vitally important. She appears to have used the money sensibly and effectively to achieve the best possible results for patients and staff alike, and, since she and Herbrand controlled the purse strings and all the important decisions were taken by Mary herself, she ensured that all the money was used for the intended purpose and bureaucratic waste was cut out entirely.

The third important element was Mary's judgement in selecting the right people to fill the important roles. Bryden Glendining and all the matrons were conspicuous success stories, although Mary did describe her pre-War Matron as 'amiable but inefficient.' Some of the later appointments were more questionable, although in some cases, such as Glendining's successor Mr. Ogilvie, the problems merely reflected the realities of a changing world.

Top-class consultants prepared to work in a relative backwater, accepting only a salary and willingly contributing their expertise and time for the good of humanity were fast becoming extinct. Almost as fast as were dukes and duchesses with unlimited incomes.

For, as the twentieth century rolled on, even the Duke found that he had occasionally to think about what he could and could not afford. In 1913, pressure exerted on the owners of the great landed estates following Lloyd George's budget caused him to start negotiating the sale of the whole of the Covent Garden area of London. He eventually received two million pounds for this, although the sum was not paid in full until 1922. Some of the proceeds, though by no means as many as was subsequently believed, were invested in Russian Bonds, leaving Herbrand with the largest collection of Russian Bonds in the world. Unfortunately after the Russian Revolution, they could be used, as his grandson commented, 'only for papering walls, should anyone so wish.'

All the other economic and fiscal changes of the time combined with this meant that Herbrand, for the first time in his life, was under some pressure to effect economies somewhere. There was no question in his mind of making any change in the way in which the house and estate were run. The extent to which Mary was aware of the problem is not clear. Just a year before her death, she was writing to tell Hastings 'my outside charities have to be very limited now.' For this reason and because she knew too much of the committee-managed hospitals in the country, she would not care to spend her money on the hospital if she was not running it personally.

Hastings was not questioning the financial viability of the hospital. He was questioning whether, in February 1936, a year before her death, when his mother was seventy, she should still be working for so many hours in the hospital. He suggested that she should at least reduce the amount of work she was undertaking, and suggested that no-one was missed as much as they expected to be. She responded forcefully, stating that if she did give up working, the hospital itself would have to go. She was not prepared to have it run by the doctors, as had been the case in the past. She was convinced that 'the work could not be so efficient and secondly I hate the idea of giving up the "dirty work" of my jobs to other people and only doing the interesting pleasant part.' She concluded: 'my own humble opinion is that if you take up a thing like Hospital work at all, it must be all or nothing and you cannot do it irregularly.'

Conceited though her views may appear when set down baldly,

they were basically valid. Although, as Hastings pointed out, no-one is indispensable, Mary's position at the hospital was unique. The fact that she was in essence both Paymaster and Chief Executive gave her such power and such responsibility that no-one else could have filled her position. She exercised her power in the interests, so far as she could define them, of the patients and of the medical team. Had she not been working so closely with both, she would have lost her grasp of the situation. As it was, she knew, from hands–on experience, all the issues needing to be considered. The disadvantage was that, having made herself indispensable, when she died the hospital died with her.

It was ironic that, while she was accorded unstinting professional endorsement for her achievements, and immense local admiration, she received no public or popular acclaim. At the end of the War, she was awarded the Order of the British Red Cross Society, Second Class. Not being a professional nurse, she was not eligible for the same Order, First Class. Ten years after the end of the War, she was created a Dame of the Order of the British Empire. By then she was becoming a figure of national renown, not on account of her hospital work, which so richly deserved acknowledgment, but because her flying exploits had caught the public imagination so vividly. She herself emphasised constantly that her achievements in this field would have been impossible without the services of her paid pilots, and were in any case a hobby at which, like so many others, she excelled. But, even then, she believed, perhaps unfairly, that the values of those administering the Honours system were sometimes more closely aligned to the values of the popular press than to those of the leading professionals in the fields of medicine and the relief of suffering.

For Mary, her hospitals, and her work in them from 1914 on, encapsulated the achievements of her lifetime. The gifted amateur, who had been reluctant to devote the time and effort necessary for the serious study of medicine in her youth, developed into the role model for every professional in her chosen sphere. She pursued simultaneously two different career paths in the world of medicine. She trained herself to become a skilled hospital administrator at the same time as Bryden Glendining was training her to progress from junior nurse to theatre sister, to radiographer and radiologist.

Inevitably she sacrificed everything else in her life to this. She struggled to fulfil her duties as a duchess where necessary, but avoided extending them in any way, Her previous interests, and in particular her ornithology, had to be totally abandoned, at least for the duration of the War. Her only child's part in her life had faded long before. Only her relationship with Herbrand developed in consequence. Her gratitude to him for making her career possible and making so many of her dreams for her patients a reality was an all-important influence on the later years of their marriage.

Her work brought out the best in Mary. Her determination, her gentleness, her kindness, her sense of humour, all came to the fore and were fully appreciated by the nurses and doctors, and sometimes by the patients too. John Gore, in his unbiased appreciation of her, written years after the death of Herbrand, concluded that 'If she had never married, she would have risen to the top in the profession of nursing.'[8] She found in her work a true vocation, in a field where her unique position enabled her to achieve something truly unique.

Some, including her grandson Ian, have sought to belittle her achievement, suggesting that, with the resources at her disposal, many might have achieved similar results. It is rare at any time to find those with exceptional resources who are prepared to devote them unstintingly to the welfare of others. Her hospital was a flagship organisation throughout the First World War. Her personal achievements in the fields of both nursing and hospital administration were unusual. At the time they were particularly unusual for a woman. As a duchess, the role expected of Mary did not include any of these achievements. She had exceptional gifts, both of character and fortune, and she used them in a quite exceptional way.

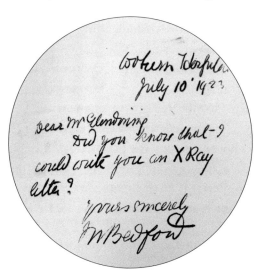

X-ray letter

CHAPTER 9

DUCAL DUTIES

'Right Trusty and Right Entirely Beloved Cousin, We greet you well ... and Command you and the Duchess your wife (all excuses set apart) to make your personal attendance on Us at the time abovementioned, furnished and appointed as to your Rank and Quality appertaineth, there to do and perform all such Services as shall be required and belong unto you respectively. Whereof you and she are not to fail.'

Such were the invitations, or Royal Commands, which Herbrand and Mary received for great state occasions, coronations, royal weddings and funerals. Such historic occasions were a pleasure and privilege to attend, though they were also a commitment which could easily interfere with other plans. On an invitation for a State Banquet for the King and Queen of Spain in 1905, Herbrand wrote:

'We must attend. Most inconvenient.'

Perhaps on that occasion, despite his initial lack of enthusiasm, Herbrand enjoyed sitting next to the Countess of Dudley, who was not only 'beautiful as a marble statue... a carved lily' but also, like Mary, had a keen interest in nursing. The Marchioness of Londonderry, on his other side, was not the great society hostess of the inter-war years, but her mother-in-law. Mary was given a greater challenge for the evening. She sat between the Duke of Sotomayor, who had been the Special Spanish Ambassador for Queen Victoria's Jubilee some years before, and the Turkish Ambassador, with the Russian Ambassador opposite to her. No doubt whoever was responsible for the seating plan felt that this was the sort of challenge to which she might respond well.

Two evenings later, Herbrand and Mary attended a Royal Opera Gala Performance at Covent Garden, also in honour of the King and Queen of Spain. Both Caruso and Nellie Melba were singing, and the programmes were works of art in silk, which included pictures of King Edward VII and the King and Queen of Spain.

Mary was first presented at Court in May 1894, a few months after she became the Duchess, when she attended her first Drawing-Room. A month later, they were both commanded by Queen Victoria to dine and sleep at Windsor Castle. Mary was painted looking extremely elegant in her robes for the Coronation of King Edward VII, which was the last occasion on which the Bedford family coach was used. This painting is the most important one of Mary now on show at the Abbey. The picture of the twelve year old Hastings on the same occasion shows him, somewhat tense but immaculately turned out, in Court dress. He received an identical invitation. A note included with the invitations asking for any spare tickets to be returned indicates that even Royal Commands were occasionally rejected. Other administrative issues were also covered, with detailed instructions concerning the route to be taken by carriages.

Mary at the Drawing Room held by Queen Victoria

Herbrand and Mary with King George V and Queen Mary

Herbrand and Mary also attended the Coronation of King George V. A year later they were invited to luncheon at Windsor Castle following a Service of the Order of the Garter (Herbrand was a Knight of the Garter) when two new Knights were present, the future Duke of Windsor and the future Lord Grey of Fallodon. They were at the marriage of Princess Mary to Viscount Lascelles in 1922, an afternoon party at Buckingham Palace in 1931 ('A quiet and pleasant entertainment. No crowd...'), the Silver Jubilee Thanksgiving Service and a Court Ball in 1935 and the funeral of King George V in 1936. After the Court Ball she commented:

'Met for the first time for many years some of my sister Duchesses who, like myself, had grown distinctly older since I last saw them.'

They also hosted at least two Royal Visits to Woburn. In 1907 the Princess of Wales (the future Queen Mary) came to see the collection of pictures and in 1930 the future Duke of Windsor came to lunch before going to the Bedfordshire Agricultural Show. No doubt Mary enjoyed his visit, for he arrived by plane, landing in the Park.

Mary's attitude to the Royal Family was appreciative and understanding. After witnessing a certain amount of unintentional rudeness by those not used to attending such occasions, she commented:

'Royalties of the future will be reared in a social world which has changed, but one feels for a King and Queen who have been brought up to expect some deference to their high position when they have to tolerate what is not even ordinary civility and thoughtfulness between one fellow creature and another. However, in the little I see of them, they play their part nobly.'[2]

The world had changed dramatically during Mary's lifetime. She commented after the funeral of George V:

'Five Kings were present, and most of those would have been considered Minor Royalties in King Edward's time; the Emperor of Germany, the Czar, the King of Spain, the King of Portugal, the Emperor of Austria, are all gone, and with the King of Italy, owing to Mussolini and the Abyssinian War, we are on strained terms.'[3]

A week after the funeral, Herbrand had a private audience with the King (Edward VIII, later Duke of Windsor) when he was presented with the Zoological Society's gold medal. Herbrand much enjoyed the occasion. He was rather more impressed with the medal itself (Mary described it as a 'medal worth having', large, with animals and birds depicted with great accuracy) than with the King's office. He found that a very dark and indifferent little room and quite as untidy as his own study.

Herbrand was President of the Zoological Society for thirty-seven years. Mary became a Fellow in 1892. She worked with him to introduce many new species to the Park, including the Père David deer from China which later became the sole survivors in the world. Mary and Herbrand would both have been very proud of their great-grandson Robin, the 14th Duke, who arranged in 1985 for some to be taken back to China, where they are now once more thriving.

Mary, predictably, participated fully in county affairs, and in particular those concerned with medical matters. She was County President of the St. John Ambulance Association and played an active part in the Bedfordshire Rural District Nursing Association. Support for the local Scouts in 1935 gave her the opportunity to turn the tables on the Press, who so often caused her intense irritation. The Scouts were planning to hold a mock 'bullfight' as a Christmas entertainment and fund raiser. Mary had a friend who had once taken part in bullfighting in Spain. She persuaded him to come and play the Matador, then persuaded Flight

Lieutenant Preston (her pilot) to be the front end of the bull. Another man was enlisted for the hind quarters.

At this point a reporter telephoned to ask whether it was true that she was arranging a bullfight. Mary replied that the organisation had nothing to do with her, and she was only contributing half the bull (meaning Preston.) The journalist begged for further details but she refused to give any, explaining that it was not her show.

The reporter's next move was to ring the police. He demanded to know whether they were aware that the Duchess intended to hold a bullfight in the Park at Woburn. The Chief Constable wrote to Mary: clearly the whole episode had made his Christmas. Even when the policeman who took the call assured the reporter that the Duchess was pulling his leg, the arrogant young man remained convinced that a real bullfight would be taking place.

Mary was rarely content to make a donation and remain a figurehead. Soon after she came to Woburn, she became a Governor of the Harpur Trust, the Bedford Charity which promotes education, provides relief for the sick and those in need and provides recreational facilities with what they describe as a social welfare purpose. Through this Trust she became actively involved with Bedford High School, where two successive headmistresses had been members of staff at Cheltenham Ladies College. She took an equally keen interest in the Modern School, backing the senior staff at both establishments whenever they developed new schemes for the improvement of girls' education, attended all of the Governors' meetings and went to as many of the school events as she possibly could.

Young people with problems particularly interested Mary, and she invited a group of girls from Aylesbury Borstal to tea at Woburn. She drove them round the Park and after tea took them to see her aeroplanes, finally waving goodbye to them as she flew away.

She played her part too in London, in the Bedford estate in Bloomsbury. Amongst many other contributions, the 'Flower Girls' of Bloomsbury much enjoyed a tea party followed by an evening at Drury Lane Theatre.

All sorts of other good causes and local events, both in London and Bedfordshire, won her support. Some financial support was probably taken for granted from the Duke and Duchess, but with Mary there was always so much more. Not only would she give generously, she would also attend the relevant meetings, take an active role, express her opinions and help with the project in a practical way..

Arriving at Cheltenham Ladies' College by motor car, 1905

After she became a national celebrity, following her record breaking flights in the late 'Twenties, she was in particularly high demand. She rose to the occasion to the best of her ability, and became involved in a number of different flying associations.

Although her fame enabled her to do more to help various charities, Mary not only found it extraordinary and faintly ridiculous, she also constantly found the intervention of the press and petty officialdom intensely irritating, and even over-curious members of the public were sometimes infuriating. On some occasions Mary had the last laugh. When the lodge keeper opened the gates for her to drive through, passers-by would sometimes watch to see who was coming through. One day, in a car, on her way to work in the hospital, she saw a man turn away and mutter something disgusted to his companion. Mary's deafness had made her a competent lip-reader. The man was clearly disappointed.

'It's only a nurse!' he remarked.

Mary, predictably, was years ahead of her time in her use of the internal combustion engine. She was pictured as early as 1904 outside Cheltenham Ladies College in a motor car. She had gone there to present a portrait of her old headmistress Miss Beale in commemoration of the jubilee of the College. The College magazine in 1905 described her visit:

'The Duchess of Bedford, speaking in a strong, clear voice, which was well heard in every part of the hall, said: "During the time that I was a pupil at the Cheltenham Ladies' College, I learned the lesson which was enjoined upon me, that 'Little girls should be seen and not heard.' I do not dispute the value of that maxim, but it is not the best preparation for public speaking. Today we celebrate the jubilee of our College which owes most of its success to Miss Beale's individuality and strenuous endeavour. I am here today to unveil her portrait and to present it to the College." Her Grace then removed the covering from the portrait – an act which was a signal for renewed applause.'

In reply Miss Beale stated that 'our own Duchess has given up her one free day to motor to Cheltenham (may she arrive in safety at home)'.

These were typical of the sorts of duties duchesses at the time were expected to undertake. That Mary performed most of them willingly, regularly and with particular charm was predictable. That she found time, particularly in later life, after her hospital work became so demanding and she struggled to maintain her regular flying as well as her almost daily walk with Herbrand, always to put in more effort than was requested, is remarkable.

Life was in general kind to Mary. She was offered opportunities which are given to few, and made the most of all of them. By nature she was a giver rather than a taker, and throughout her life she strove to put back as much as she took out. Her hospital work was the main vehicle for her exceptional dedication and her generosity, but, in addition, she never omitted to fulfil all the other obligations imposed by her rank as thoughtfully, conscientiously and fully as any of her sister duchesses.

One of Mary's book plates

CHAPTER 10

MOTHER AND GRANDMOTHER

'Henry Davies if you are not wanted at home and have nothing else to do will you come up to dine at 1.30 tomorrow (Saturday) and go out with me again in the afternoon, M Bedford' 20.1.1911.[1] Henry Davies was then 13 years old, the son of a nagsman at Woburn. At the time he was one of Mary's four 'bird boys'. These boys were provided with suitable clothes and accompanied the Duchess on many of her ornithological trips. They went canoeing on the Tamar, stayed on remote Scottish islands, practised the Morse code with Mary and found it all wonderful fun. In return they were expected to work hard, to watch, listen and learn, so that they developed into first class naturalists. The immediate objective was to win the RSPB shield, which Henry achieved in two successive years. Henry's last letter from Mary was dated 1915. In it she acknowledged that his bird list was now better than hers. When the boys did well they were praised, when they made mistakes, they were left in no doubt that higher standards were expected of them. The Duchess drove them hard: some rose to the challenge, others fell by the wayside.

At least one of those who fell by the wayside went on to become a world renowned expert on deer and on parakeets. He was both interested and gifted, but he was intimidated by the Duchess and, unlike Henry Davies, Henry Newbury and her other successful boys, did not respond to her robust, challenging approach. He in turn, convinced that she mistook his timidity for coldness, retreated ever further from her. It was tragic that this wretched boy was her own son Hastings.

Although Mary's greatest failure was undoubtedly as a mother, her relationship with her only son did improve in later years, whereas the relationship between Hastings and his father deteriorated. As a child, Hastings found his mother much less easy than his father. At this time his father made a considerable effort to set aside time regularly for his son every day. Even then, however, resentments started to build up. When Hastings climbed a tree and refused to come down as a protest against going back to school, his father had no compunction about falsely assuring him that he need not return, then breaking his word as soon as the boy was back at ground level. Hastings hated every school he attended: a natural target for bullying, he found little or nothing to interest him. At home, he was bored with his family and acutely unhappy with strangers, but he had a passionate love of his different homes. Time spent away from those three places to which he was most deeply attached, Woburn, Endsleigh and Cairnsmore, seemed to him to be time wasted. Despite occasional brief memories of happy moments with his parents, such as shrimping with them both, making toast with his father, or salmon fishing on the Tay, he found difficulty in building close relationships with anyone. The salmon fishing was more clearly linked in his mind to the keepers who accompanied him than to his parents. His apparent lack of response to anyone left him lonely and unhappy. Neither of his parents succeeded in helping him to overcome his natural difficulties. Herbrand tried within his own limitations, but eventually lost patience with the son who had so much in common with him in his interests, but whose opinions and principles diverged diametrically from his own. Mary made little attempt to bridge the gap until it was too late.

She felt excluded from his life from the start, excluded by her husband and father-in-law from having any say in her son's education, and excluded by her son from sharing any interest with him. Yet he was secretly longing to learn from her. They were quite unable to communicate and their relationship was doomed from the start. The nervous, quiet, unresponsive boy seemed to his mother almost obstinately determined to dislike anything which she liked. Like both his parents, he was fascinated by animals, but his enthusiasm did not extend to horses or dogs: he was much more interested in spiders. His lack of response left his mother feeling baffled and rejected. In turn, Hastings found her impatient and totally oblivious to his yearning for love and support. Mary, who could show such patience and understanding in her work and with animals, was incapable of suppressing her irritation with her son.

The one person to whom Hastings could relate as a child was Jemima. When he grew up, and his views on social and military issues drove an ever deeper wedge between him and his father, he retained his fondness for his former governess. He was not a strong character and his unsatisfied longing for affection made him an easy prey for strong personalities wishing to influence him for the rest of his life. Later Hastings, never a good judge of character, was dominated by a number of people keen to use him for their own ends, political, financial or both. He was fortunate in his early twenties that the head of the family which influenced him deeply was highly principled. Robert Jowitt Whitwell, whose daughter Hastings was to marry, was a Professor of Greek at Oxford and wrote a Greek lexicon. A deeply religious man, he was very involved with the YMCA movement and soon recruited the young man to the cause. Mrs. Whitwell was perhaps less altruistic in her motives. Her oldest grandson, Ian, 13th Duke of Bedford, who had little respect for his parents or grandparents, saw her as a particularly snobbish version of Jane Austen's Mrs. Bennett. With two daughters of marriageable age, she saw the rudderless young heir to a dukedom as a gift from heaven. Ian claimed[2] that the elder daughter Crommelin, Ian's mother, later told him that she prayed that Hastings would propose to her sister rather than to herself. Mrs. Whitwell must have been a formidable woman indeed. For, despite Crommelin's misgivings and her strength of character, she did marry Hastings, thus becoming the Marchioness of Tavistock.

Although eventually the marriage did nothing to bring Hastings closer to his own parents, at first Mary was optimistic that her son's life was taking a turn for the better. Many years later, she wrote to her grandson Ian:

'Your father came under influences at Oxford which showed him a way of devoting his life to work for others instead of thinking only of himself, his likes and dislikes. He also fell deeply in love with a girl who at the time seemed to have kindred tastes. It has been a grievous disappointment to find that she has ceased to care for him and the work in which he was so deeply interested, and has moreover (he firmly believes) been otherwise unfaithful to him...'[3]

Crommelin may never even have visited Woburn at this time. She met her parents-in-law at Endsleigh. The marriage was solemnized at a most inauspicious moment, in November 1914. Tragically, circumstances prevented Crommelin and Mary from getting to know each other better. An impenetrable barrier soon separated them, yet they had so much in common. Both were powerful characters, not necessarily an indication of compatibility, but they shared many interests as well as a down-to-earth approach to life. Both loved animals and country life, neither set any store by social airs and graces. Though both were blessed with good looks, neither, in later life at least, took any trouble to enhance them. The photographs of Mary climbing in or out of her plane show a tough pilot. When Crommelin, to the astonishment of all who knew her, had her portrait painted by Annigoni, she would arrive at his studio extremely dishevelled, dressed in a jersey she had knitted herself. When it was finished, she said,

"You have painted a portrait of an old woman, haven't you? Not really what I was thinking of. I wanted my dog and my garden in it."

"Yes," he answered. "I know exactly what you wanted. A portrait of your dog with you in the background."

A short time later she met Annigoni for lunch in London. She had just had her hair done and looked immaculately turned out and very smart. Annigoni looked at her.

"You know, if you had just looked like that when you came to me in Florence it would have been quite a different portrait."

"Yes, I know," she answered. "But it wouldn't have been me, would it?"[4]

Annigoni himself told the story slightly differently in his autobiography, *An Artist's Life*.

'..... from Cedra Osborne in London I learned that the Dowager Duchess of Bedford was coming to Florence to sit for me. At that time I knew virtually nothing about the ducal Russell family (and even less about their eccentricities); so when the day came to meet the Duchess's train, I and my friend and aide, Riccardo Noferi, went to the station without any idea of whom we were to meet, except that she was a duchess.

'The train came in, the passengers poured out. We scrutinised all the women but none looked at us and none looked like a duchess, young or old. We waited until the platform was empty and had just decided to leave when a woman climbed down from the far end of the train, dumped her baggage on the platform and stood beside it. We walked slowly towards her until we were close enough to see that she was a peasant-woman bringing her wares to town. She was smiling at us in the hope, I supposed guiltily, that we would offer to help her with her bags. I smiled back and then she said, 'Are you Mr. Annigoni?'

'Introductions over we took her to her hotel, a modest one, and then to dinner in a restaurant where she and I discussed a schedule of sittings, the first of which took place the next day. She turned up for it, and for every subsequent sitting, in the same sort of very plain clothes as those in which she had arrived at the station. From the first she was perfectly at ease and made me feel so too. She talked a great deal, pleasantly and wittily, and by the time the portrait was finished I knew everything worth knowing about

The Pietro Annigoni portrait of Crommelin

the Russells, dead and alive. She talked freely about the present Duke, who was then developing Woburn Abbey, the family home, into the number one show-place among the stately homes of England. 'My crazy one', she called him with affection, but I gained the impression she was more fond of another son.

'The portrait went very easily and was as good as finished when, after the eighteenth sitting, the Duchess returned to London. As I was going to London shortly afterwards, I arranged to deliver the portrait myself and, at her invitation, dine with her and some of her friends. She had a flat in the West End to which I went, with the portrait under my arm, immediately after my return to my London studio. When I rang the bell she opened the door herself – and I gasped. She looked magnificent, beautifully dressed and looking ten years younger than she had appeared before. Seeing my astonishment, she laughed loudly, forgetting for a few moments to ask me in.

'Later, over a drink, she explained to me that the peasant pose was part of a naughty joke she was playing on her son. He wanted a portrait of her to hang alongside all his ancestors at Woburn, so she decided to have one that would stand out like a sore thumb among the others. Next time we met – at the dinner, for which she wore a beautiful gown and superb jewellery – she told me that the Duke was duly shocked. However, he must have come to accept it after a time because he commissioned one of my pupils to make a replica of it!'

In different circumstances, Mary could have appreciated a daughter-in-law with a sense of humour who was true to herself, just as Mary herself always was. But in November 1914 she had other preoccupations, and soon Hastings caused his father at least to regard the influence of the Whitwell family as shameful and dishonourable.

Hastings had already, at his father's behest, endured a brief spell in the Territorial Army, when he was attached to a battalion of the Grenadier Guards. The experience encapsulated everything that his father most admired and Hastings most detested. To the irritation of his father, he left at the earliest opportunity.

Now, with his country at War, Herbrand never doubted that the only possible way forward for his son was to rejoin his regiment. Hastings, wretched and appalled at the prospect, perceived army life as a form of slavery. He was also so lacking in self confidence and slow in his reactions that he saw himself as an accident waiting to happen, likely to bring disaster not only on his own head but on the heads of any men placed under his command. Confused and miserable, he felt that he must find some menial duties which he could perform to play his humble part in the tragedy now engulfing his country. Unable to face his father, he left him a note to tell him his intentions.

This was too much for Herbrand. Still himself Colonel of the Bedfordshire Regiment, his quick temper flared and he wrote to his only child to tell him that he never wished to see him again. Only a legal obstacle prevented Herbrand from disinheriting his son. Mary was less surprised. She saw this as the inevitable culmination of the way in which her son had been brought up.

'Of course, I know that it is his upbringing and those at home know I predicted it,' she wrote to Zoë. 'His letters to his Father are abominable. Of course I know he was never taught to treat him with respect, so it is hardly to be wondered at. Still, his Father showed him great devotion as a child and boy, and he has a right to expect a little return.'[5]

He got none. Father and son did not meet again for nearly twenty years. But Mary had one final meeting with her son before the final split.

Jemima, probably the only person at Woburn for whom Hastings still felt any affection, persuaded him to return once, when his father was away, to see his mother. The meeting was not a success. Hastings, who remained a profoundly religious man for the rest of his life (he had his own religion, just as he later had his own political party, because 'there was never anyone else whose views precisely coincided with his own'[6]) learnt what was to his eyes the most shocking fact about his mother possible. She was an agnostic. Apparently he had never discussed the matters closest to his own heart with her before, for the news came as a total surprise. Despite being the daughter of an Archdeacon (albeit a somewhat worldly one), she doubted the existence of God, and was prepared to say so when asked. Neither her agnosticism nor her son's pacifism was a widely shared or popular view at the time. Hastings half heartedly proposed a deal. If his mother would attempt to pray, he would join the army as a private. To his relief, she was too honest to accept the proposal.

Hastings and Crommelin spent most of the War, according to their eldest son, washing dishes in a YMCA canteen in Portsmouth. Ian was born in May 1917, Daphne in September 1920 and Hugh in March 1923. After the war they lived at Warblington House near Havant, on what is now the Havant by-pass, and had a small farm three miles away at

Emsworth, looked after by Charlie Broad, whose brother Norman was valet to Hastings. The two brothers remained in his service for most of their lives. Hastings devoted his time to endless charitable and religious enterprises, and to his famous collection of parakeets. Relations between him and his wife became increasingly strained and bitter. By 1930 their separation was complete and extremely acrimonious. Hastings expected his wife to bear the brunt of rearing the children, but begrudged every halfpenny she spent on the household.

Hastings with parakeets

During the next six years, much of the allowance which Hastings continued to receive from his father was squandered on legal fees. He succeeded in establishing a legal precedent, something at which, his son Hugh remarked, 'my family was always rather good.' He was given permission to live apart from his wife with no obligation to provide her with a home, so from then on they lived separate lives. The children became Wards of Court in Chancery.

Ian was miserable throughout his childhood. Later, when writing about his father's own childhood, he commented 'There were occasional agreeable interludes – certainly more than I ever experienced in my turn.'[7] He felt totally unloved and took no pleasure in any of the activities available to him. Fishing, shooting, riding and playing golf, as well as various forms of exercise organized for him by tutors, were almost equally repellent to him. He had no interest at all in natural history. One of his tutors was dismissed after Hastings convinced himself that he was having an affair with Crommelin. A later tutor took Ian on a series of visits to Europe, but again failed to inspire him with any enthusiasm. The first time that he went skiing, the party 'was formed of the sort of bright, enthusiastic young people who get up at seven-thirty and are always first on the ski-lift in the morning and last down at night, terribly hearty, brash, slap-on-the-back people with whom I had no contact at all. I used to turn up on the slopes at ten, and after two or three days they gave me up as a bad job.'[8]

Ian, largely on account of his expensive tastes, was permanently short of money. Most of the correspondence between him and his father and grandparents concerns this topic. The tendency started early. One of the few relations for whom he showed any partiality was his great aunt Lady Ela Russell, sister to Herbrand and 'Aunt Vermin.'

'At one period (Ela) had twenty-eight coloured photographs of me in her drawing-room and it was always assumed that I would receive her money when she died. However, I went to lunch there one day and she dashed my hopes by suddenly saying, a propos of nothing: "If ever I make a will I won't leave you a penny, I won't leave you a penny."'[9] Ian's affection for her cooled rapidly from this point on.

What Ian was longing to sample were 'the charms of London life', and as soon as an opportunity presented itself he moved to the bright lights, 'painting London red' as his brother later described it, and played no further part in the lives of his mother or siblings for many years.

The two younger children, Daphne and Hugh, got on well with each other and with their mother. Both enjoyed riding and golf. At this time Daphne excelled as a rider and Hugh at golf, although later their roles reversed and Daphne became President of the Rye Ladies Golf Club while Hugh chaired the selectors for the British Olympic Horse Trials team.

The Russell side of the family took very little interest in Daphne. She rarely visited her father, nor, later, her grandparents. Indeed in 1936, when Hastings and Mary were once more corresponding with each other, Mary wrote to Hastings after the completion of one of the interminable court cases, commenting chillingly 'It will make things easier if you have not got to look after Daphne'. Daphne remained close to her mother, though Crommelin was later saddened by Daphne's dabbling in drugs and found it hard to accept her Lesbian lifestyle.

The youngest of the three children, Hugh, later commented that, despite every issue concerning him having to be decided by the courts, he 'had really a very nice upbringing personally.' Crommelin was keen to send him away to school. Hastings, remembering his own misery at Eton and regarding all British public schools as sloughs of despond, was determined to resist and, characteristically, employed not one but both of the two leading Counsel of the time, Sir Patrick Hastings and Norman Birkett, to ensure that Crommelin could not have either of them. As a young man, Hastings had attended a number of trials, including that of Crippen. He became disillusioned with the concept of justice and convinced that everything depended upon having the best advocate.

The judge, most unusually, said that he wished to see the boy himself, so Hugh was taken to his chambers.

"I have been listening to Counsel arguing over what you ought to do," he told Hugh. "What do you want to do?"

Hugh replied that the present arrangement suited him very well. He spent term times with his father, and had a tutor, then spent the holidays with his mother. His father provided him with all the fishing and shooting and his mother with all the riding and hunting he could want. The judge agreed that this sounded an admirable arrangement, returned to court and told them that this was what he and Hugh wanted, so he had made his decision accordingly.[10]

Although Mary did not yet know her grandchildren, she had quietly been building up a relationship with Hastings, quite possibly without even mentioning the fact to Herbrand. In 1929, for example, she flew down to Hampshire for a few days, and visited him at his home at Warblington House. Five years later, she decided to take the reconciliation a stage further.

Hastings, like Herbrand and Mary, enjoyed spending long weeks in the summer in Scotland, and, like them, he rented an estate there for many years. His was called Glentrool, situated some thirty miles away from Cairnsmore, where Herbrand and Mary continued to spend their summer holidays. One day, when Hugh was eleven and was at Glentrool with his father, his grandmother drove over to Glentrool from Cairnsmore and took Hugh back with her to meet his grandfather.

No doubt Mary had been planning this for some time. Some sixteen years had elapsed since Herbrand's bitter parting from Hastings at the outbreak of War. The bewildered small boy soon found himself completely captivated by his grandmother. More than seventy years later, his eyes still lit up as he talked of her.

If, at first, Mary's motive had been to re-establish relations between her husband and son, and to strengthen her own bond with Hastings, she soon became as fond of the small boy as he was of her. Both grandparents were impressed with how well he shot, and Mary was delighted to find how many of her interests he shared. She gladly passed on to him much of her knowledge of ornithology and of mammals. Like her, he was fascinated too with all things mechanical; the training he received from Mary and her chauffeur provided the basis for his professional skill later as a motor mechanic in China and elsewhere during the Second World War. It is often suggested that Mary's bad relationship with Hastings was caused in part by her deafness making his childish treble difficult for her to hear. This defence is hard to substantiate when no such problem arose to mar her relationship with her grandson a generation later. She herself, incidentally, was described as having an 'odd, high–pitched voice.'

Invitations soon followed for both Ian and Hugh to visit their grandparents at Woburn. Ian's later famous declaration that he had no knowledge of his grandparents' existence, before a careless remark by a housemaid when he was sixteen, accorded well with his desire for publicity, if less convincingly with the facts.

Both brothers were warned that their grandfather was 'an absolute stickler for time.' Since their mother Crommelin was quite the reverse, this was a new concept to them. Crommelin, when she was President of the Hastings Music Festival, once met the Lord Mayor of London, who had come down for the festival, and was attending it with the Mayor of

Hastings. When Crommelin learnt that the Lord Mayor would be staying the following day also and had no commitments for lunch, she invited them both to lunch at her home. The Mayor, who knew her well, thought this an excellent idea. Her guests were invited for one o'clock. She brought them in through the back door and a moment later the Mayor was shelling peas and the Lord Mayor found himself peeling potatoes. They eventually sat down for lunch at 3 p.m. The Mayor declared it the most successful lunch they had ever given for the Lord Mayor.

Herbrand was as extreme in his punctuality as Crommelin was in her neglect of it. When the car came to pick Ian up to take him to Woburn, he was half an hour late, and consequently half an hour late in reaching Woburn, for they worked to the clock absolutely. Still he did not bother to get ready for the meal and so was late for lunch also. At this point his grandfather informed him that the car would be ready to take him back to London at four o'clock. He received few subsequent invitations.

Hugh was young enough to feel minimal embarrassment over the style of his journeys to Woburn. The ritual of the two Wolseleys, the two Rolls Royces, the eight chauffeurs and the crowd of bystanders which gathered to watch the performance paled into insignificance beside the excitement of travelling at 80 miles an hour, and of going to see his grandmother. While Ian found life at Woburn 'formal and deadening... grim and monosyllabic,' and rarely stayed a night, Hugh loved every moment, from breakfast at seven a.m. with his grandparents, enjoying bacon, fried eggs, scrambled eggs, kidneys and mushrooms, till he went to bed exhausted many hours later. Ian believed that his 'grandfather and grandmother lived isolated lives of their own': Hugh recorded that 'They walked out at Woburn together every day of their lives, at five p.m. in the summer and three p.m. in the winter, and in all the time I spent with them at Woburn I never had any reason to think that they were anything but perfectly happy.'

The gentle, affectionate little boy was deeply loved by all who knew him. His mother and father's separation (they never divorced, for this was contrary to Hastings' principles) was as bitter and traumatic as was possible. His grandfather had not spoken to his father for some sixteen years when he first came to know them, and the relationship between his father and grandmother was tenuous. His mother was bitterly resentful of her father-in-law, as well as of her husband, no doubt blaming Herbrand for many of the deprivations she was forced to endure. Hugh remained very close to all of them. A reconciliation between his mother and the Russell family was beyond even him, the hatred built up over many years on lies and misunderstandings. Ian later claimed that he had made an attempt to reconcile his father with his grandparents, but had been given no credit for the attempt. Probably this was because the actual bringer of peace was the quiet, sensitive younger brother, not the brash, publicity-seeking older boy. Soon Hastings and Mary were engaged in an extended correspondence which continued until her death. Relations between Hastings and Herbrand never became warm, but the barriers were broken down sufficiently for them to meet and exchange somewhat stilted conversation.

Three Generations: (l to r)
Hugh, Herbrand and Hastings

Hastings later wrote of how he and his mother 'achieved, if not complete understanding, at least that substantial measure of mutual respect and real affection which I am glad to say characterized our relations during the years prior to her sudden death.'[11] This is an accurate description of the letters which Mary wrote to him in the last years of her life. Interestingly, he attributes the improvement in their relations to a specific occasion when, as a young man, in defence of someone to whom he was attached, he fought 'a terrific battle with her, at the end of which, much to my surprise, she broke down and cried (and) the old fear ended.'[12] The description of himself as a young man seems to imply that this was before the major rift with his parents. Perhaps it was only because of this episode that he was able to come to Woburn to see her once more after breaking off relations with his father.

The delight she undoubtedly took in her grandson made her more conscious than she had ever been before of how much she had missed by her alienation from her only son. The surviving letters which Mary wrote to Hastings in the last year of her life reflect a wish to show her son how and why she had lived, and was continuing to live, her life in the way that she did. She tells him of her pleasure in her hospital work and of the commitment which it entailed. She tells him of her relations with his father, openly and without any attempt to minimize the difficulties, which indicates some tact on the part of Hastings: she obviously had no fear that he would gloat over any shortcomings of Herbrand's, or use her criticisms to justify his own position. Indeed, Hastings showed none of the vengeful spirit towards his parents which was so evident in his treatment of his wife. Hugh never remembered hearing Hastings complain of his parents. Ian on the other hand, a generation later, seldom had a good word to say for his.

Hastings was willing to acknowledge his mother's strengths. A naturalist of world renown himself, he later told how he was initially taken in by a claim made by Nepalese naturalists to have discovered a hitherto unknown breed of unicorn sheep. His mother was much quicker than Hastings to perceive that the appearance of a unicorn head had been artificially achieved by damaging the horns.

Mary took a keen interest in her son's troubles, in his ongoing legal battles with Crommelin and in his anxieties over Ian. Her view of the battles with Crommelin was inevitably one sided. She had not witnessed Crommelin's struggles to bring up a family when every penny was begrudged, a situation which inspired Ian as well as Hugh to speak out on behalf of their mother and do what little they could to help her. Mary saw Crommelin as grasping, pugnacious and immoral.

'I am dreadfully sorry about the allowance,' she wrote, 'and think it is a great shame that a woman who has behaved as she has should get such an award, but I suppose it is all due to Sir Patrick Hastings.'

On this occasion Hastings must have failed to brief him as well as his own Counsel.

Hastings must by then have overcome his scruples about divorce, unless in this respect Mary was expressing her own opinion of the situation, but she declared that she 'wish(ed) with all my heart that you could divorce her as the worry for you seems quite endless.., I think the only hope about Crommelin now as her morals do not seem to be her strong point is that she may give you further cause to divorce her.'[13]

Battles with Crommelin continued to concern the children as well as financial issues.

'I have been trying hard to find time to tell you how delighted I was to hear the result of the appeal and that you are at least to keep Hugh,' Mary wrote to Hastings. 'What lies must Crommelin have told to make the judge think that he was backward and of all things in the world 'difficult'? I wish you could have won out and out, and it is indeed strange that Counsel cannot allow you to plead the truth without being considered vindictive. At this rate how do divorces ever come off?'

Mary was hearing only one side and court battles in family cases can be particularly unpleasant, when the washing of dirty linen in public is combined with a conviction by each side that the only hope of success is to show the other party in the worst possible light. Adjudicating between a mother who felt that her son should be sent to a public school and a father of known eccentric tendencies bent on educating the boy himself with the aid of a tutor, the judge showed a greater understanding of the needs of children than the boy's grandmother.

'It must be rather a nuisance to be compelled to get Hugh a boy companion unless you happen to know one of the right sort,' wrote Mary. Fortunately the tutor was able to help, and a boy of just 'the right sort' was found. Hugh and Niall Campbell remained close friends for the rest of their lives.

It is possible that Mary secretly had more sympathy with Crommelin than she openly declared, but that she avoided saying so to Hastings, for fear of alienating him and damaging their fragile relationship. She almost certainly appreciated at least that there was another side to the story. Zoë's daughter-in-law, Marjorie Beaver, strongly took the side of the injured Crommelin, even going so far as to make Crommelin Godmother to her small son Martin. After Mary's death, it became apparent that Mary had been quite fair minded enough not to hold this against Marjorie.

Mary was concerned, too, with the predictably disastrous relationship between Hastings and his oldest son Ian. Two more different men would be hard to imagine. There was no possibility that either could ever start to understand the other's point of view. Many of the issues between them were those which have caused antagonism between countless fathers and sons. Ian wished to amuse himself and wanted money to be able to do so. His father, usually supported in this respect by Herbrand and Mary, expected him to work. Ian did his best to maximize his chances of success by approaching each of the three separately. His needs, as he perceived them, were considerably greater than those of most young men.

'Even she,' he complained of his grandmother, whom he thought the most promising of the three for his purposes, 'did not seem to realize that the standards expected around London of a young man with a title could not possibly be maintained on the sort of allowance I was receiving.'

When Ian wrote to ask for money for new shirts, 'She wrote back a long lecture saying that people should be plainly and simply dressed, and that she simply could not understand shirts costing three pounds. So I never got them. And yet she had an annual income of thirty thousand pounds a year...'[14] He conveniently forgot that out of that income she was financing a hospital.

Mary made a point of passing on to Hastings any favourable comments about Ian which she chanced to hear, from sources as diverse as Lord Londonderry and Flt. Lt Preston, her pilot. She could also be endearingly frank to her grandson about his father. Although the exchange of letters between Mary and Hastings in the later years was generally amicable, each expressed strongly held opinions. She told Ian:

'I have just been telling your father that when I see a thick letter from him, I get the same sinking feeling below my pinafore that I used to get when my mother wrote to me, because I know that I am going to get a lecture and a scolding. However I added that with him I had the satisfaction of answering back. As I have been so much deafer since I had the 'flu, correspondence is now almost my only way of keeping contact with my fellow creatures.'[15]

Despite the criticisms which Hastings levelled at his mother, he was quite prepared to ask for her support, and even, indirectly, that of his father, in dealing with his own recalcitrant son. Mary responded to one such request:

'I will ask your Father to use his influence with Ian and hope he may do it successfully, but firstly I think Ian is almost bound to suspect the source of his Grandfather's information and secondly your Father is not a good hand at writing tactful letters when he wishes to convey a gentle reproof.'

She illustrated this by telling Hastings of her own experience in receiving occasional ferocious letters from her husband, even though both were in the house together and the matter could easily have been resolved by a quick conversation. Hastings in fact inherited more of his father's bad habits than either appreciated. Another criticism of Herbrand which Mary confided to Hastings concerned Herbrand's selfishness in sporting matters:

'Nobody at Endsleigh can row, so your Father would never have anyone but me. He himself has only one cast (or had, for he no longer fishes) and used to waste a lot of the best water, but if I asked him to row me...! It is so strange that, though he has been very keen on shooting and fishing all his life, he never seemed to have an idea how birds would fly in arranging a shoot or when fish would lie and take.'

Ian, unlike his grandmother, had no interest in country sports, or indeed country life. But he attributed this in part to the treatment meted out to him by his father, which closely mirrored Mary's complaint of Herbrand.

The children, Ian said, would carry all the fishing equipment to the pools, and then (Hastings) 'would fish each pool first and leave us to try our luck after he had thrashed it out. I fished for salmon for thirteen or fourteen years and never felt a fish on the line. My father made quite certain that there was nothing in the pool before he let us try it. It used to bore me to death.'[16]

Like father, like son.

It was not surprising that Ian considered, of the three, that his grandmother was the most likely to yield to his demands. His grandfather showed no signs of softening with age and did his best to persuade Ian to be less extravagant and to work harder. He compared Ian to those of his contemporaries who 'go to a university and acquire the education and training you will lack and which will mark you in later life as an ill-educated man. You are doing nothing and not attempting to qualify for any profession.

My opinion is that your father is treating you too generously.'[17]

However when Ian succeeded in passing one exam, his grandfather immediately rewarded him with a cheque for £25.

Although Herbrand showed no signs of mellowing with increasing age, he did become increasingly dependent on Mary. His love for her was as strong as ever, though sometimes Mary found it suffocating. Yet she never for a moment forgot how much she owed to him, and did everything in her power to repay him. She explained the position to Hastings in a letter written just a year before her death. Hastings had evidently been trying to persuade her to take holidays, assuming that it was her hospital work which prevented her from doing so.

'To begin with it is not quite so much Hospital work which prevents my taking more little holidays as your Father. He attaches so much importance to my walking out with him that I feel quite guilty when I miss it & if anything happened to him feel that I should reproach myself for not giving him all that I could in return for all that he has done for me.

Herbrand and Mary with Tu Fu and Ranger

'After I am on my feet from 8.30 am till 2 pm with X-raying or operating then have a sandwich lunch, tidy up & come home & am greeted by "How soon will you be ready to go out?" It is this that makes things rather a drive(?) Sometimes when length of daylight permits, I take a little flight first but the same thing greets me on return. Over & over again I have asked him to go out whenever he feels inclined & leave me a pencil note where I can meet him if he wants me to. But he rarely does it or if he does it is to say he is in the Garden & will come if I whistle. He does not have tea if I am not in.

'I must add that I love my Hospital work and should hate having nothing to do.'

If Hugh were staying, he would accompany his grandparents on their afternoon walks, which he found relaxing and harmonious. His particular delight was to go shooting or fishing with his grandmother, who had a remarkable knack of making any activity fun. She was always introducing some new, additional challenge to whatever pursuit they were undertaking so that the interest never palled, and whatever skills were being developed were tested and strengthened.

Mary recognized that the upbringing of Hastings had been a disaster. She seems to have distanced herself from any responsibility for this, placing all the blame on Herbrand, Herbrand's parents and Jemima. Yet she was living in the house with him and was his mother, even if his formal education was taken out of her hands. She was not an ineffectual creature incapable of exercising any influence. Responsibility for his childhood, as opposed to his schooling, was one of many duties which did not attract her and which she was happy to allow Herbrand to delegate to Jemima.

Perhaps because she did not see this as a personal failure, but rather as something which hardly concerned her, eventually she found it easier than Herbrand did to build up a relationship with Hastings as an adult. She probably recognized that she had missed out on something important and potentially rewarding, and resolved not to make the same mistake a second time. At first, she was thinking only of building bridges with her son: a burgeoning acquaintance with her grandchildren soon showed her that with one at least of them she could in some measure recoup what she had lost.

Hugh's peaceable, affectionate nature made him the ideal catalyst for re-establishing relationships. Mary had no wish for any contact with Crommelin, but Hugh's life was already divided between his two parents, so there was no need to impair the child's close bond with his mother. Hugh himself enjoyed an almost perfect relationship with his grandmother which shone a bright light into the early years of his life and the last years of hers. The incomprehensible rejection of Daphne by her paternal family may have been a greater loss to the family than to Daphne herself: subjecting her to the emotional pressures of the complex tangle of relationships could well have caused greater damage to her fragile personality than the relatively stable affinity with her mother and younger brother. Ian shared none of the interests or enthusiasms of his kindred: he was only happy when he escaped as totally as possible from all family ties. However, the problems he posed acted in some measure as a unifying factor between the hitherto unhappy triumvirate of his father, grandmother and grandfather.

Mary's short drive from Cairnsmore to Glentrool was one of the most important journeys of her life. Despite her earlier failings, she at least had the courage to make the first move in ending the tragic isolation and separations which had beset the family for so long, bringing some measure of harmony back into her troubled family, and creating one of the few truly happy relationships within it, that between herself and her youngest grandson.

Goblin – Mary loved cats, especially Siamese,
but Herbrand once declared that he 'loved the Mary Tribe but not the feline (tribe).'

CHAPTER 11

EMULATING THE BIRDS

Mary delighted in bird watching throughout her life for many reasons. The intellectual challenge of identifying and studying rare species, the thrill of the chase in finding them and the competitive satisfaction of excelling at these skills was but a small part of her pleasure. Mary loved the same wild places favoured by the birds, the remoteness, the isolation from her fellow men. Sometimes as she watched them, sharing, as far as she was able, the lonely isolated spaces they inhabited, she longed to become one of them, free to explore the element denied to her, to revel in the space above both earth and water. But that was denied to all mankind: only a bird could fly.

The achievements of the Wright brothers must have seemed remarkable to her, but so clumsy in comparison with the real thing, as exemplified so effortlessly by the birds. When Blériot first crossed the Channel in 1909, she probably envied him with no thought of ever being able to share his pleasure. The War left her little time to think of anything beyond her work, but the sight of aeroplanes flying over Woburn stirred her imagination.

Before 1925 private flight was not a practical proposition in the United Kingdom. In that year, Geoffrey de Havilland produced his first Cirrus Moth, a light aeroplane suitable for private ownership. Other Moths followed: de Havilland was a lepidopterist as well as an aircraft designer. The Gipsy Moth, Giant Moth, Hawk, Puss, Swallow, Tiger, Fox, Leopard and Hornet Moths all made names for themselves during the Twenties and Thirties. The earliest Cirrus Moths could be bought for £830. Soon the price had dropped to £650 and they were on sale in shops.

The early Twenties were not a happy time for Mary. The adrenaline fuelled days of the War were behind her. The only family members with whom she was in contact, other than Herbrand, were her sister Zoë and her family. Her deafness and the accompanying tinnitus were becoming increasingly oppressive. It was as if she had continually to listen to trains rushing through a railway station. She continued to devote all her energies to the hospital, but old age seemed to be approaching as fast as the trains whirring through her head. There was seemingly little to look forward to, save a steady decline in the quality of her life.

One unusual aspect of her deafness was the way in which her hearing improved rather than deteriorated with extraneous noise. Modern sufferers from tinnitus are advised that if the noise seems to become worse when all around is silent, the playing of soothing music and other sounds may help. Anxiety and stress can also lead to increased problems.

We do not know whose inspired idea it was to suggest that Mary might be happier in an aeroplane, overpoweringly noisy as they were at this time. She did not like the noise, a universal complaint at the time, but the change in atmospheric pressure did bring her relief.

Another practical spur was her hatred alike of trains and of wasting precious time on extended journeys. She was 60 before she experienced her first flight, as a passenger, from Croydon to Woburn. Almost all those involved in the world of flying at the time were young: the Wright brothers, Blériot and Geoffrey de Havilland were all considerably younger than Mary, Amelia Earhart, who died in the same year as Mary, was 32 years younger than her, and Charles Lindbergh nearly forty years her junior.

If in this sense she was born too soon for the activity which was to make her famous, in another sense she was lucky: her flying years were a golden age for the private pilot. Despite, or perhaps because of, the risks, the discomforts and the tragedies of flying at this time, the excitement, romance and glamour were never equalled. There were no rules or regulations: the pilot was free as air, welcome almost, though not quite, everywhere, navigating by identifying landmarks below. On Mary's first flight, she commented that they had flown straight down Watling Street. A passenger could enjoy every detail of the country over which they were flying.

Mary's first flight took place on 17th June 1926. She had written to the Private Hire Department of Imperial Airways, whose initial proposal was that she should travel in a DH.50, a cumbersome machine designed to carry four passengers. She rejected this indignantly: such a means of travel was hardly 'emulating the birds.' Instead she was piloted by Sydney St. Barbe, one of the foremost pilots of the day, in a de Havilland '2-seater 'Moth' (open) machine travelling at 70 air m.p.h.'[1] St. Barbe was at first convinced that he had an exceptionally nervous passenger on board: as they approached Woburn and he started to look for a suitable landing site, she became extremely agitated and seemed to be desperately trying to communicate with him despite the noise of the plane which made conversation impossible. Only later did he realise that her knowledge of the landing site he had selected was greater than his, and, although large and level enough, it was in the middle of the Bison field. Her concern had been that he would frighten the animals.

She in fact enjoyed the experience so much that, for the rest of the summer, whenever she had a long journey to make, she would hire a private plane, complete with pilot. In this way she first got to know Captain Charles Barnard, who was to become the first of her three private pilots in the following spring. Flights that first summer included travelling home from Manchester, where she had been with her hospital surgeon Mr. Ogilvie to watch an operation (Mr. Ogilvie travelled both ways by train), to lunch with Zoë at Lyndhurst, where a small diversion enabled them to look at the *Mauretania* in Southampton Water, and to Cairnsmore. In some respects such flights bore a closer resemblance to a modern car journey than to air travel today. On the way to Cairnsmore, for example, they stopped at both Birmingham and Manchester for petrol (they had to wait at Birmingham whilst sufficient fuel was delivered there from Manchester to enable them to fly to Manchester itself to fill the tank completely.) Stops would be accompanied by delicious farmhouse teas close to the aerodrome. On the journey back home, the weather was bad enough for Barnard to assure her that many pilots would have been ill, but, to her satisfaction, she still arrived home three and a half hours ahead of Herbrand and Jemima, who had travelled by train.

Charles Barnard, in many ways, made an excellent first pilot for the Duchess. Very experienced and capable, he was also an outgoing enthusiast with a great sense of humour who communicated his own pleasure in flying to Mary. He had been a Flight Commander in the Royal Flying Corps, a test pilot with Sopwith Aviation and chief instructor for de Havilland. Unfortunately, he was also a great self-publicist, who no doubt appreciated from the start the interest likely to be aroused by a 'flying Duchess'. Unlike his employer, he delighted in the attentions of photographers and journalists, and frequently submitted his own reports to the press. Eventually this led to a parting of the ways between them, but for the intervening three years it was in his interest as well as his duty to ensure that the Duchess enjoyed her flying. They shared many adventures as well as many jokes together.

His other failing was a daredevil streak to his character which might have deterred many a novice pilot. This was an added attraction to Mary. He also possessed 'that divine thing called luck.'[2]

By March she was allowed to take over the controls for a short time. A month later came her first expedition outside Britain. On this first expedition, Herbrand insisted on sending a ground party consisting of a maid, footman, groom of the chamber and Herr Vetter, a renowned courier who had accompanied Mary on many of her travels over a period of forty years, including mountaineering in the Alps, but was now aged 76. This group was supposed to keep in touch and join up with Mary and her pilot whenever possible. Neither the maid nor Vetter enjoyed the experience, though Vetter admired Mary immensely: he always declared that there was never anybody quite like Mary Bedford.

For more than three weeks Mary and Barnard toured Europe, staying at the Ritz at Le Bourget, visiting Biarritz and admiring Versailles, Chartres Cathedral and other famous sites, many of them new to Mary, from the air. They chanced to be flying over Bordeaux aerodrome when Mary asked why the engine had suddenly stopped. Her pilot said he did not know but thought it was an airlock. They then landed rather quickly as he realised that they had in fact run out of petrol.

'All experiences being new to me and having implicit faith in my pilot, even when short of petrol, I had done nothing but enjoy myself,' Mary wrote in her diary. Her implicit faith was hardly justified. They had flown further than the Moth's fuel tank was expected to last without filling up.

Barnard seems almost to have been trying to frighten his passenger. If so, he was singularly unsuccessful. As they lunched together in Biarritz, he remarked:

' "Tomorrow we go over the Pyrenees, and if the engine fails we crash or else come down where we cannot get away from." (*sic*) I said "Yes; it is strange how calmly one can look forward to it" and asked whether he tried to forget or to remember it. "I am *always* thinking of it," he said. "A pilot who is not always thinking of it is no use"; and I expect he is right.'[3]

Next day, he could not resist showing off, with 'a little spin and a nose dive' over the aerodrome, which terrified the spectators beneath and made even the imperturbable Duchess extremely giddy.

"Rather jolly," he remarked. Mary hoped that she too might get to think so.

Mary dressed for flying

Some days in fact elapsed before the weather allowed them to cross the Pyrenees and when they did so Mary revelled in the beauty of the country beneath them.

'I am indeed thankful that I have had the courage to fly before my course is run,' she reflected. 'Not that any great courage is needed actually to fly, for I had always longed to do it, but one has to run the gauntlet of one's friends and relations, who think it silly and foolhardy and done from a desire to show off... I can certainly say that from the time I took my first flight... no qualm for my personal safety has ever possessed me except for Herbrand's sake.'

In Spain they were greeted by two long suffering members of the Duchess's staff, one of whom had been with her for 40 years and, at the age of 76 'does not appreciate the uncertainties of my new method of travel.' Then it was on to the Ritz in Madrid, with dinner, a theatre and a cabaret.

Next came Cordoba and Seville, where Barnard fortunately found a pilot friend who arranged a hangar for the Moth, as local goats were jumping on top of the wings, and there was a likelihood of bees blocking up the engine. His wife took Mary sightseeing and, to Barnard's delight, the Prince of Wales was there as a guest of the king of Spain. An air display had been laid on as a Royal performance, but Barnard managed to outdo the local talent with a dazzling display of his own. Mary was quietly amused by the advertising stunt which he thus pulled off for de Havilland. Next came Jerez, the inevitable sherry factory and a visit to a bullfight. Mary grieved for the horses more than the bull, but still took pleasure in the spectacular production. When eleven different friends of her hosts came in turn to tell her of the piebald Spanish donkeys which they had sent to Herbrand, Mary became totally confused, knowing that only one had ever reached Woburn. All became clear when she learnt that the old Spanish Marquis who had sent it had eleven sons. She had met them all in turn, and each had laid claim to the donkey.

Next day Mary was invited to lunch at a castle at Arcos de la Frontera, a fairytale building magnificently restored by her hostess. The castle itself, the country in which it stood and the birds she saw there remained a highlight: next day they flew over the castle, where her friends stood waving from the battlements, on their way to Tangiers, catching glimpses of Gibraltar and the Atlas Mountains in the distance. That evening Mary gambled at the 'Casina', losing heaps of francs, which in fact totalled only eight shillings and sixpence. Shopping was not a temptation for there was no room on board for any purchases.

On the way back again, delighting as ever in the scenery beneath, and once spotting a whale, Mary was persuaded by the reckless Barnard to photograph the Rock. He encouraged her to open the side door. With her attaché case, where she kept her camera, open on her knee and the camera in her hand, she had managed a few shots when, as they turned behind Gibraltar, the plane was sucked into a tornado. As they were tossed about 'like a cork in the sea', Mary somehow succeeded in shutting the door before stowing away her camera and attaché case. Meanwhile Captain Barnard had managed to turn the Moth away and bring it back under control. They later learned that the down draught on that corner was notorious and had led to the destruction of other planes.

After an abortive visit to Granada when the Alhambra was closed, they returned there two days later for their visit, having spent the intervening time in Seville, where Barnard had completed some work on the Moth. Wherever they landed, Mary made new friends, expatriate British or old Spanish Grandees. Her real delight was in the beauty of the country and the ancient buildings. 'Once again did I bless the day that I had made up my mind to fly, and blessings also descended upon the head of my young pilot, who was responsible for persuading me to come on this particular flight to Spain.'[4]

Their homeward route took them through Alicante and Barcelona. Because they reached Alicante at lunch time, no-one was available to refuel the plane. Barnard therefore decided to fly on and land on the sands near Valencia to fill up from the spare petrol can they carried. Lettice Curtis, herself an experienced pilot, comments:

'At any time, let alone in doubtful weather conditions, this must have been a somewhat dubious undertaking.'[5]

Mary was required to do some precise calculations from a large map with inadequate space to unfold it. Barnard's temper was frayed, but he declared that if they reached Tarragona in half an hour, they could just reach Barcelona before dark and before running out of petrol. Tarragona took 37 minutes. Mary thought to herself that an emergency landing in the sea was inevitable. They reached Barcelona moments before darkness closed in, with less than ten minutes' supply of petrol in the tank. Mary later asked what he had planned.

"Oh, you can generally crash without hurting yourself much, if you know how," he replied, but later conceded that they would probably have had to make the landing in the sea, as she had anticipated. When she asked what chance the Moth would have had of floating for a time on the sea, he replied "None".

Mary was relieved to find that a virtually perpendicular funicular at Monserrat, dependent on two thin wires, was not yet completed and could not be used. She knew that if it had been operational, Barnard would have insisted on trying it, and she supposed that she would have had to go too.

Next stop was Montpellier, where Mary was presented with an enormous bouquet. Lack of space inside the plane forced them to shred it and drop the pieces from the plane as soon as they were out of sight. The Alps were shrouded in cloud and they found Lyons unattractive, but Paris proved another highlight. They enjoyed all the traditional sights, though Barnard's decision to take Mary to the Grands Guignols – the Paris theatre renowned for its horror productions - in the evening 'by way of a little cheering evening's diversion!', was an interesting one. Next day they lunched at Versailles. Mary had not previously visited it, but found it somewhat run down; neither fountains nor flowers had been restored since the War. They then climbed the Eiffel Tower, took the Moth up to view the rest of the famous buildings from the air, and landed again to go to the Folies Bergeres that evening.

Barnard inevitably could not resist a 'mild, spectacular spin' in front of the 'hornet's nest of Press photographers' awaiting their arrival home from 'the most glorious three weeks' holiday I have ever had and quite the most wonderful experience of my life.'

Mary's confidence in her pilot is remarkable. Despite her comment after the Barcelona episode – 'Thus happily ended our one very narrow "squeak," unless the Rock was another'[6] – the Rock most certainly did qualify, as did the occurrences at both Bordeaux and Valencia. It is hard to regard Barnard as anything but reckless: coming as close to running out of petrol as he did on two occasions (even allowing for the fact that this was a perennial problem for pilots at this time), encouraging his passenger to open the door as they approached an area notorious for its dangerous cross winds, and choosing to land on a narrow beach can at best be described as showing a lack of forethought. Barnard was not a stupid man; he seems rather to have been addicted to taking risks.

Although even her bare outline of facts makes the dangers of such situations quite apparent, Mary's diary certainly minimises the risks. Perhaps this was for Herbrand's sake, who worried enough about her new found sport in any case. Certainly Mary's instinct would always have been to play down, rather than exaggerate, any danger. She was undoubtedly determined to prove to this young man that he would not find her lacking in courage, or holding him back because of any lack of nerve on her part. As a novice, she may have been somewhat naive about the boundary between those risks which were an inherent part of flying at the time and those which could easily have been avoided. Despite this, it is hard to avoid the conclusion that this was an important constituent of her enjoyment of flying.

For Mary, this was a matter which in essence affected only herself and Herbrand. Perhaps Herbrand's dislike of flying, the only one of his wife's activities which he did dislike, and, in fairness, the only one which would be defined as a 'risk sport', was partially attributable to a realisation that she allowed, or even encouraged, the risks to be increased artificially.

Barnard's behaviour is less excusable. As an employee, and with his professional knowledge and expertise, it was clearly his duty to minimise the risks. But perhaps he understood that for Mary, as for himself, that would also have reduced the fun. Judging from their conversations at such moments, as quoted by the Duchess, she is unlikely to have encouraged him openly to gamble with their lives, but this aspect of both their natures formed part of the bond which united them, making them such good team mates in their undertakings. The desire to court danger for its own sake was totally alien to Herbrand's nature. Satisfaction of that need may account in part for the upsurge in Mary's happiness after she took up flying.

Smooth though Barnard's landing of the plane was at the end of their momentous journey, Mary did indeed come down to earth with a bump.

'And so back to X-rays, the operating theatre and a quite appalling accumulation of correspondence,' she wrote in her diary.

Tragedy too, anticipated but no less affecting for that, awaited her. In the preparation for her departure, the person who had taken most interest in every detail was Mr. Glendining. Her first action on her return was to fly over his house, letting off rockets, to tell him of her safe return.

'Alas! He was too ill to be out, and only lived a week after my return. I had been his assistant in the operating theatre since 1915, and had never missed an operation with him since I began...'

Their journey, covering 4,500 miles, attracted considerable interest in the world of aviation. It was seen as providing proof of the reliability and capability of the Moth, which was encouraging for Mary, who had just bought her own Cirrus Moth. This was not delivered to her, complete with its certificate of airworthiness, until July. However it was registered in her name, immediately after her return to England, on the 18th May. On the 20th May Charles Lindbergh took off on his epic flight across the Atlantic in the *Spirit of St. Louis,* landing in Paris on the 21st.

Mary continued to fly throughout the summer whenever she had a long journey to make. She also enjoyed, even when she was not actually visiting friends, flying low over their houses: her grandson Hugh remembered always the fun of seeing her circling low over his head, flapping the plane's wings to him in greeting when he was at his mother's house. She circled low over Mr. Ogilvie, her surgeon, when he was out in his boat. On another occasion, she left Endsleigh to return home for a single night to take part in an operation at the hospital. On the way, she tried to wave to her sister Zoë but could get no reaction. Then, looking for another a friend, she could spot only the friend's Sealyham terrier and not the friend herself.

The fun of travelling to events by plane inspired Mary to attend many functions which she would otherwise have avoided. Journeys were no longer a chore. She had never been to the Derby before 1927, and would have begrudged a full day out for such a purpose. Now she was able to continue working all morning, carrying out X-rays, and Captain Barnard did not collect her until after 2.30 p.m.

'Though it was very foggy, so much so that he had had to abandon a Press job, we flew to Epsom, and arrived a few minutes before the walk past, then saw the gallop past, were alongside at the start, and followed round to the winning-post and returned via Stag Lane' (de Havilland aerodrome) 'to my X-rays! A very comfortable way of seeing the Derby. Even Herbrand was impressed.'[7] It is to be hoped that the runners and riders were equally impressed.

The Derby that year was emblematic of changing times. For the first time, the race was broadcast by the BBC. Mary's plane was not the only one: aerial views of the day were filmed. People arrived on foot, by car, in horse-drawn charabancs and in open-topped double decker motorbuses as well as by plane. Gypsies gathered round a camp fire, feeding their babies, tending their horses and telling the fortune of anyone prepared to cross their palms with silver. A new grandstand was in use for the first time. After a false start, the race was won by a horse named Call Boy, who led from start to finish. The King, Queen and Prince of Wales were all there to see his triumph. So

Mary at Endsleigh –
Gore describes the vehicle as the chericut.

too, appropriately, was Charles Lindbergh, as a guest of Lord Lonsdale, the Yellow Earl. Clearly Mary considered her day a success. The following year she attended both the Boat Race and the Grand National by aeroplane.

Four weeks after the Derby, Mary was one of a tiny handful of people in Britain to witness the total eclipse of the sun, which was the last to be visible from England until the eclipse in 1999. Although the 'path of totality' crossed North Wales and northern England, heavy cloud meant that most of those who had gathered in this area were disappointed, unable to see anything beyond a sudden darkening.

Mary and her pilot spent the night at Harrogate and were up at 4 a.m. They feared at first that the weather would prevent them from flying at all, but the Moth climbed higher and higher, bursting through the clouds, which 'formed a snowy landscape beneath us, whilst above was the clear blue sky and the slowly dimming sun'. It was bitterly cold as they reached an altitude of 10,000 feet.

'As far as the eye could reach was the wondrous panorama of piled masses of cloud... The shadow had seemed to advance very slowly all the early part of the flight, but at the last it appeared to rush across, and totality seemed to last but four or five seconds. One had just time to see the complete corona and a flare of light on the right side and it was gone, and we returned to almost normal daylight as it were in a moment. I had time, however, to note a beautiful rose and pale yellow tinting of the Southern sky, where a few small scirrhus *(sic)* clouds were lit up by it.'

Once again, Barnard's legendary luck had been with him. No other aeroplane which published reports was in an absolutely clear sky: the others merely enjoyed clear views in breaks of the clouds.

At last Mary's own Moth, the 'Emerald', arrived and flights became more frequent. Herbrand wanted to buy her a house of her own as a dower house and one of her earliest expeditions was to look at Old Buckenham Hall in Norfolk. This was not suitable: eventually the house they chose was 'Wispers' near Midhurst. However such excursions gave her a greatly increased opportunity for learning to fly herself. Norfolk was a regular destination: she was paying for the restoration of the sails at Cley Mill, which was lived in by Sister Rachel, a Wantage nun who was a character after Mary's own heart, climbing ladders, slithering over muddy boards and driving a car in her nun's habit.

In August, Mary and her pilot enjoyed a week in Italy. Views of both Rome and Vesuvius from the air proved somewhat disappointing, and airport officials seemed particularly unhelpful, a constant battle. Mary was better at retaining her composure on such occasions than her pilot: she invariably either settled down with a book or found someone to talk to, to keep herself relaxed and interested. But, as always, the pleasure and beauty of flying made it all worthwhile. The drama of the week was provided by flying through the mistral, which Captain Barnard later described as the worst time he had had in eleven years' flying experience. Forest fires were raging beneath them, then Barnard later described how they were suddenly 'drawn into the sort of whirlwind... hurled about like a piece of paper... a cone of water... quite 50 feet high... The Duchess, although badly bruised on the arms by the terrific buffeting, was not unnerved by the ordeal.'[8] At the time his only comment down the speaking tubes was 'It's a good thing I am so well, or I should be ill!'

Mary herself seems, not for the last time, to have contemplated the prospect of seemingly imminent death with interest rather than terror. Her regrets were for Herbrand and for the possibility that the Moth would not accomplish its mission.

The bathos of returning to England was exacerbated by a particularly obtuse reporter who succeeded in meeting them as they landed. He asked whether she was fond of flying, and whether she thought she would fly again. Mary's patience with obstructive officials did not extend to journalists, but she restricted herself to:

"As this is my own machine, I hope so!"

1928 started on a high note when Mary was created a Dame of the British Empire in the New Year's Honours lists. The Order was given for Public Services. Mary would later growl that she had worked really hard for five years without recognition, then been created a Dame for flying as a passenger to India. This was untrue: she had not in fact flown to India at that time. However, she was not alone in suspecting that the celebrity status conferred by her flying exploits had some influence on the distribution of honours.

That spring, Mary and Barnard, with an additional crew member named Alliott, made their first, unsuccessful, attempt on a world record. The aim was to go to India and back in eight days. In fact they were away for three months.

The journey seemed fated from the start. Mary had hired a Fokker, 'Princess Xenia', for the attempt, a plane which had already been used for two major expeditions, both of which had ended in failure. Even Mary's journey to Lympne to join Captain Barnard in the Fokker had been bumpy enough for the newspaper headlines to proclaim that she had nearly been killed. This was gross exaggeration. However, the take-off in the Fokker next morning did constitute one of the most dangerous moments in Mary's flying career.

A crosswind and the heavy load of fuel caused the machine to struggle to become airborne. The undercarriage caught and scythed through some telegraph wires. Fortunately, at the end of the runway, there was a cliff edge with a drop of 500 feet to the marshes beneath. Without this, Barnard later admitted, a disastrous crash would have been inevitable. Mary, in her diary, dismissed the whole episode in half a sentence.

This flight, unlike the European tour the previous year, was no holiday. The Fokker was so noisy that it was not even possible to communicate except through written notes. Mary did not stay at the Ritz, nor in the comfortable houses of friends. On the first night, in Sofia, she was offered the use of a sofa in one of the married officers' houses, in a room which combined the functions of sitting-room, kitchen and, on this occasion, bedroom. In the air she was expected to work hard on complex time and distance calculations, unable to take her usual pleasure in the view beneath. The second night was spent at Aleppo, with a long, hungry wait for food, and no drinking water. Mary promised to call her pilot next morning for a dawn start, but Barnard, never good in the early morning, complained vociferously when she did so that she had not set her watch to local time and was an hour too early. Mary replied reasonably that the sun was rising and it was indeed dawn.

That day they followed the course of the Euphrates between Mesopotamia and Syria, then through Iraq. Below them stretched mile after mile of desert, enlivened only by an occasional train on the Baghdad Railway, cluster of mud huts or extinct volcano. Occasionally Mary was given the controls, but she did not find this easy, with the seat set low for Alliott, a very tall man, and the steering system quite different from the Moth she was used to.

One of the objectives of their journey had been to help Imperial Airways to establish a regular route. This had been planned in 1927, but had to be temporarily abandoned when the Persians withdrew permission to pass through their air space. Before this 'hitch' arose, Imperial Airways had built an aerodrome and hangar at Bushire, on the Persian Gulf, which Mary's crew planned to use: they had been granted all the necessary permits. However, it soon emerged that the Persian officials on the ground had not been informed of this. While Mary passed a relatively comfortable night at the Residency, her pilot spent most of the night trying to convince them 'of the error of their ways.' A sentry threatened him with a rifle when he even attempted to approach the Fokker.

By next morning, the situation had somehow been resolved. They prepared for take-off, with Mary, as was her custom, sitting on the step between the two pilots to lighten the load in the rear. The air became very warm and the cabin started to fill with smoke. Black oil was flying back, covering the windscreen and plane.

Barnard pushed the map into Mary's hand and turned the plane back to the aerodrome. He landed it superbly, despite the weight of 350 gallons of petrol. But the damage caused to the engine by the choking of the oil supply was clearly serious. Barnard, despite declaring as they landed, 'Well that's the end of our flight!' soon regained his customary blithe optimism and was convinced that, with the aid of engineers from Basra or Cairo they would soon be in business again. Mary, ever the realist, wished to send for a new engine from home. Several days elapsed before Barnard acknowledged that she was right. An engine had to be shipped out from England. It took nine weeks to arrive.

Most people in Mary's position would have been deeply despondent, and many angry. Her record-breaking plan was shattered, her hired plane seriously damaged, her Chief Pilot had wasted several days through insisting that he knew better than she did. She had planned to devote just over a week to this enterprise. Whilst she did not then have any conception of quite how long she would in fact have to wait, she realised that there would be no quick resolution of the problem.

The country where they were stranded had already demonstrated its hostility to British aeronautical enterprises. Local officials were recalcitrant and possibly trigger-happy. The heat was excessive: June, July and August were not months which a tourist would select for a visit to that area. The humid climate was rated one of the worst in the world. For several weeks, she suffered from a 'terrible, unquenchable thirst.' Sir Lionel Howarth, the British Resident, departed with his wife for the hills a few days after Mary's arrival. Although he assured her that she could remain at the Residency, the skeleton staff left after his departure soon made it abundantly clear that visitors were not welcome.

Limited space in the aeroplane meant that Mary had a totally inadequate supply of clothing. Everything was permanently damp. The sea was too hot to be refreshing, and the muddy coral painful to walk on. Water for washing had to be brought in from a mile away on donkeys. Towels and sponges were regularly infested with black ants, spiders, lizards, centipedes, sandflies and 'other nameless creatures of the devil.' Snakes, too, were about, though Mary only actually saw one. Worst of all, for someone of Mary's active temperament, she had absolutely nothing to do.

Such situations brought out all Mary's best qualities. Barnard later wrote:

'Her unfailing courage never flagged; in spite of the heat and discomfort she was always cheerful and anxious to continue her flight.'

Mary referred only to the interest of the flight and the kindness of those who were to entertain her.

Soon she was observing with enthusiasm the wealth of local bird life (though she regretted having no books with which to identify them) and mammals. She studied the way local small boys caught crabs, and, in return, allowed them to study the moon through her binoculars.

She also started to look for a suitable place where the three of them could stay. They were lucky enough to find Robert Parkyn, who offered originally to share his small bachelor bungalow with them on a cost-sharing basis. He in fact eventually absolutely refused to accept any payment at all, although they were based there for nine weeks. He was also, to his eternal credit in Mary's eyes at least, the only person who did not let her feel that he considered the whole expedition a risky and foolish one for her. So grateful was Mary to him both for his generosity and his kindness throughout, that she bequeathed £2,000 to him and Mr. Gass, who was also exceptionally hospitable, in her will. Mr. Gass sent an invitation for her to visit him in Abadan, 200 miles away. The temperature was such that water from the cold water tap was too hot to put a hand in, but her host gave her a fascinating visit, showing her the oil wells, pumping stations and all the associated works. The opening of a new oil well was an impressive event, with a flame blazing up 70 feet into the air.

She also visited a hospital, on a day when the temperature reached 125 in the shade. A second hospital impressed her greatly, in particular with the ways in which they contrived to keep patients cool, including a ward lined with cork. The Chief Surgeon had once performed an appendicectomy on King Feisal, and, no doubt wisely, kept an aeroplane waiting so that he could fly off at a moment's notice if the operation was not successful. Mary later had the most up-to-date X-ray equipment sent out from London to the hospital at Abadan.

Mary sent other presents out from England after her return. An Arab member of Mr. Parkyn's staff had taken particular trouble in looking after her. She wrote to ask Mr. Parkyn what he would like and he suggested a pram. There were various delays and, by the time that it eventually arrived, Mary was worried that the baby would have outgrown it. Mr. Parkyn reassured her, saying "Never fear, there will always be others to fill it."

Mary's only regret was that her pilot had not allowed her to bring a camera (although she later discovered that he had brought his own) as they passed caravans with camels, goats and big, long-eared woolly sheep. In the evenings, watching polo reminded her of India, but eventually she felt that she had 'sponged' on her new friends for long enough, and must return to Bushire. Soon after, Mr. Parkyn arranged another visit for her, away from Bushire, where the climate was much worse than in any of the neighbouring areas, to the beautiful city of Ispahan. She derived equal pleasure here from the architecture and the wildlife. A drive through a mountain pass ended with the car leaving the road: enlisting help from the local population proved an interesting exercise.

As usual, doors everywhere were opened to Mary, partly through local traditions of hospitality, partly no doubt through curiosity, and probably too because of her enthusiasm and interest in everything and everyone she saw. If she had reservations about the standard of treatment available in the Ispahan Mission Hospital, she delighted in meeting the Armenian Archbishop, whose diocese was Asia.

At last the engine arrived. Three days later they were able to take off. After a 13 hour flight, they reached Karachi, where Mary stayed at Government House, in great luxury, but embarrassed by what remained of her clothes.

Worse was to come. The new propeller was irreparably damaged. Further delay was inevitable. Mary, by now deeply concerned over her long absence from her own hospital, most reluctantly agreed to travel home by boat. She had a wretched journey, when 'crawling home alone in an old P & O steamer, I should not particularly have cared had we gone to the bottom', though she did enjoy receiving 'a Marconigram from home, giving the latest news from Herbrand.' The last lap was brightened by a sudden inspiration: she arranged for her Moth to meet her at Marseilles, and thus at least flew into England, albeit two days later than Barnard and Alliott: they had succeeded in repairing the propeller. As Alliott was suffering from scarlet fever, perhaps it was a blessing in disguise.

Flying up to Cairnsmore later in the autumn in a very strong wind, Barnard asked if she would like to fly *under* the Forth Bridge: as she never refused 'an experience' if she had the chance, she agreed.

In the circumstances, Barnard showed little gallantry when he published an article comparing men and women pilots, which included photographs of two women pilots and the Duchess, who was not then a pilot as she had yet to fly solo. The article said that:

'When a woman says she is not frightened... she is deficient from a mental standpoint and... unlikely to give that extra touch of brilliance... which means the difference between success and failure... (women) tend more to panic.' [10]

Mary retaliated, pointing out that his distinction between the sexes regarding fear was hard to understand.

'I read that it is mind that matters, and, as I'm not a pilot, my photograph was probably used to illustrate a mental deficient.'

Barnard retracted immediately.

'She herself,' he wrote, 'has shown great ability in the air and in my opinion, is one of the few examples of a woman who is quite capable of flying well.'

He kept his job. He probably also meant it. Mr. Parkyn described her as 'the greatest woman he ever met'.[11]

Mary had written in her diary on the night of her return to England from Persia, 'Shall try again if I get a chance.'

Now she changed the name of the Fokker from *Princess Xenia* to *The Spider*. The plane had failed to fly the Atlantic and failed to fly non-stop to India with previous teams. She had failed to fly to India and back in eight days with Mary and her crew. Like Robert the Bruce, Mary expected the plane to try, try and try again.

'Spider'

CHAPTER 12

BREAKING RECORDS

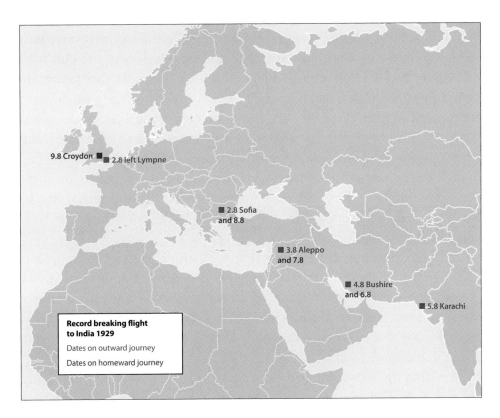

9.8 Croydon
2.8 left Lympne

2.8 Sofia
and 8.8

3.8 Aleppo
and 7.8

4.8 Bushire
and 6.8

5.8 Karachi

**Record breaking flight
to India 1929**

Dates on outward journey

Dates on homeward journey

The route to India

Mary used her Moth for almost every journey she made outside Bedfordshire in 1929, seeing everything from Stonehenge to the R101 airship, and visiting everyone from her Dutch naturalist friend Mr. Blaauw in Holland to Hastings in Hampshire. Finally, at the end of July, the Fokker, now the property of the Duchess, rechristened Spider and equipped with a new engine, was ready. Jemima, accompanied by three senior members of the hospital's nursing staff, came for an inspection and was somewhat shocked by the Spartan interior. Considerable space was now filled with additional petrol tanks. It was Mary's duty to spend much of the journey pumping petrol from one tank to another.

They aimed to do what they had failed to do in the preceding year, which was to fly to India and back in eight days to prove that this would be a viable journey for a passenger and commercially feasible for an airline using a relay of pilots. Since their last attempt, a non-stop flight to India had been successfully completed, and Mary did not doubt that the same crew could have returned non-stop had they elected to do so. Accordingly she was not thinking in terms of breaking records. They had planned to leave on 30th July, but bad weather made this impossible. Conditions were not much improved three days later, but Barnard could bear it no longer and they took off. Almost twelve hours later they landed at Sofia. Next day they flew more than a thousand miles, over Constantinople to Aleppo. Mary would have appreciated a quiet evening's rest, but politeness compelled her to spend the evening sight-seeing, as well as devoting much time to despatching telegrams home. She did resist attempts to take her to a dance that evening, though the noise from it allowed her little sleep. Mary never ate on these occasions until her pilots were ready to join her. On that evening, it was 10 p.m. before they appeared. Mr. Alliott's place in the team had now been taken by Bob Little.

On the third day, they again left at 4.15 a.m. This time, though, their destination was almost a homecoming, as they landed at Bushire, to be greeted by Mr. Parkyn, their host of the previous year, and his bride. Not only was he as hospitable as ever, but, when they found that they had punctured a tyre, he was able to produce the spare wheel, left behind the previous year, and in immaculate condition. Thanks to his care, they succeeded in reaching India within the allotted four days, landing at Karachi that evening. Mary enjoyed a comfortable night at Government House, with what the crew considered the luxury of three and a half hours' sleep, the most any of them had during the flight, but the two pilots had to work for most of the night on the plane, the second pilot fitting in only an hour's sleep.

On the return flight from Karachi to Bushire next day, the cloud was low, forcing the pilot to fly at a low altitude. Mary, while working hard on the petrol pump, secretly revelled in being able to watch the people, animals and birds beneath them. When they landed, even the Persian officials proved more accommodating than usual. The next day, despite a delay in taking off when their hosts overslept, was wonderfully clear and beautiful, and their reception at Aleppo much more friendly than on the way out, for now they had a reputation and the hotel staff were all attention. But breakfast next morning was eaten in semi darkness, until Little, the last to eat his roll, turned on an additional light. Only then did they realise that all the rolls were swarming with black ants inside. Mary and Barnard had already eaten theirs.

That day, in response to more bad visibility, Barnard took the relatively unusual decision for the time of remaining above the clouds and leaving the navigation to Little's skilful use of the compass. To Mary's surprise, despite their altitude, they flew through a big flock of Egyptian vultures and were lucky that none became entangled in the propeller.

On the final day, the weather had deteriorated even further, and with it Captain Barnard's temper. Food, strictly rationed throughout to reduce weight, was in very short supply. Barnard was given the one small tin of Brand's Essence of Chicken. Little was left with a dry biscuit, which Barnard, when asking the navigator to attend to something else, took out of his hand. What, if anything, was left for Mary she does not say.

The flight to India had been undertaken to show that passenger flights on this route were feasible. They were not aiming to break any records, for a non-stop flight to India had already been successfully completed. They were quite unaware of the excitement generated by the press during their eight days' flying, feeling at the time that, if they had been more fortunate in the weather, they could have completed the journey much more quickly. As they approached Croydon, Mary was feeling a little sad that the adventure was over. She felt that she had adapted to the routine of early starts, long hours of flying and sparse meals and could have continued for weeks, though she knew how exhausted both her pilots were.

They expected when they landed to be greeted by the usual handful of journalists, a group of their personal friends and a few bystanders. Their astonishment was total when they found that there was hardly an empty corner inside or outside the aerodrome building, or even on the surrounding roofs. A bewildering array of press photographers and reporters, thrusting cameras in their faces and screaming inane questions, surrounded them: they were dazzled by flash bulbs, invented a mere two years earlier, and overwhelmed with messages of congratulation from officials of every kind.

A telegram arrived from the King: 'The Queen and I warmly congratulate you on accomplishing a record flight to and from India in a week. We trust you are not unduly fatigued by this remarkable feat of courage and endurance. GEORGE R.I.' The Royal Aero Club of the United Kingdom was equally impressed.

A fortnight later, Mary was persuaded to make a broadcast about the flight. She found this a terrifying ordeal, but made a great success of it: a representative of the BBC said that he only wished they could find more speakers with her vigour and enthusiasm. She quoted two verses from a poem by Jeffery Day[1] which summed up all that Mary most enjoyed about flying:

Have you seen the narrow riband, unimportant, half forgotten, that tells you that the Thames is far below?
Have you glanced with smiling pity at the world's most famous city,
A large grey smudge that barely strikes the eye?
Would you like to see things truly and appreciate them duly?
Well, then, do it, damn you, do it, learn to fly!

Have you chased a golden sunbeam down a gold and silver alley with pink and orange jewels on the floor?
Have you raced a baby rainbow round a blue and silver valley, where purple caves throw back the engine's roar?
Have you seen the lights that smoulder on a cloud's resplendent shoulder standing out before a saffron-coloured sky?
Would you be in splendid places and illimitable spaces?
Well, then, do it, damn you, do it, learn to fly!

The *Daily Herald* complained about her use of the word 'Damn' on the airwaves.

After this talk, some elements of the press presumed too much. A Sunday newspaper announced, without any authority, that the Duchess would give an account of an air race she was due to attend as a spectator the following week. When Mary made it plain that she had no intention of doing any such thing, the Manager attempted to resort to blackmail by announcing that he would give Captain Barnard a thousand guineas if she would give even a short message. This was not the way to handle Mary. Infuriated by their pestering, she wrote in her diary, 'Capt. B. had to go without his 1,000 guineas.'

Mary had one further excitement in 1929. Although she regularly piloted both the Fokker and the Gipsy Moth which had replaced her original Cirrus Moth, she received no formal teaching. But in September

Barnard allowed her to do something she had been longing to do for two years: 'Loop her First Loop'.

The following spring, Barnard was increasingly committed to a flying company he had set up. Mary had a number of flying lessons from Sydney St. Barbe, who had piloted her first ever flight nearly four years earlier. One day in April, he jumped out of the plane and said, "Now, your Grace." Mary had not expected this. She asked for one more practice landing with the dual control, then made her first solo flight. Her nerves calmed as she took off, while her instructor belatedly panicked, suddenly realising the responsibility he had taken and saying that if he had had a gun handy he would have shot himself on the spot. The take-off was perfect, and the landing well up to standard.

Barnard was disappointed. He felt that he had worked extremely hard to teach her to handle the plane more smoothly. He acknowledged her patience, keenness and willingness, but emphasised too the problems created by her deafness. Because of her age, and no doubt too her position, he decided that she must complete ten consecutive perfect take-offs and landings. This was a virtually impossible target for a novice pilot, and Mary was beginning to feel that she would never be allowed to take the next step in her career as a pilot by flying solo.

She may not have expected St. Barbe to send her solo on the actual day that he selected, but she was only too glad to take advantage of Barnard's frequent absences, whether about his own new business or in preparing the *Spider* for their next great expedition, to work with a different teacher:

'Without my knowledge, she obtained the services of a well-known instructor Mr. Sidney St. Barbe, who promptly sent her solo after less than two hours dual. He told me afterwards that he would never be able to understand why I had not had the courage to send her off myself. If the truth be known I had intended to do so on the first suitable day.'[2]

The Aeroplane magazine rubbed salt into the wound by congratulating both Mary and her teacher, Mr. St. Barbe.

The timing was in fact perfect for Mary. The boost of personal satisfaction and achievement came the day before she set off with Barnard and Little on their next attempt at a record breaking flight. This time they were heading for Cape Town.

They took off at 5.10 a.m. on the morning of April 10th. Despite appalling weather, Barnard found a way through the Pyrenees and by

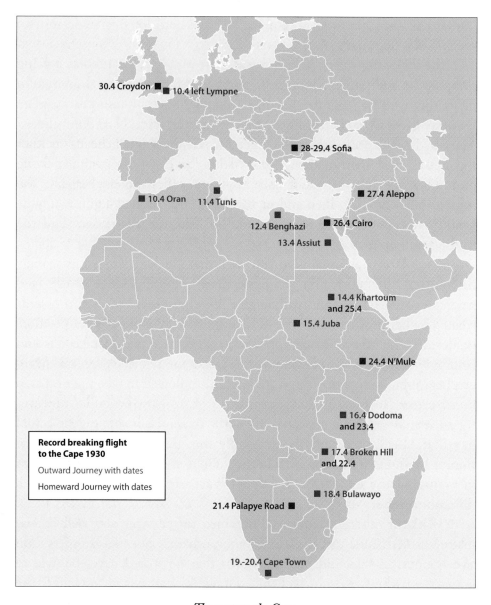

The route to the Cape

evening they were in Oran. Mary piloted unattended for quite long periods: her success solo must have boosted her confidence, and possibly that of the two professionals as well. Day followed day, staying at Tunis, Benghazi, over the Pyramids, flying too high to see them clearly and Assiut on the 13th (landing by special permission), where they dined in elaborate style with the Egyptian Pasha, who depended on his son and daughter to translate into French or English.

The next day, Mary revelled in the beauty of the desert, but her Captain was sunk in gloom, having been warned that he must fly by compass rather than following the Nile, as a previous pilot had been lost when making a forced landing and it cost £6,000 to find him. They reached Khartoum safely, then on to Juba next day, where Mary was pictured looking elegantly dressed beside the *Spider*. This was Mary's first impression of the reality of Africa, with lion and elephant close to the station, though she saw neither and secretly half hoped for an enforced delay. This did not happen, but flying on to Dodoma next day she did see her first giraffes and elephants. Cloud compelled them to fly low: as ever, the chance to watch wildlife and birds on the ground more than compensated to Mary for the danger inherent in their situation. A shrewd observer of everything within her visibility, she finished the day with strong views, not always according with the accepted account at the time, on issues ranging from which types of trees were most widespread to the reaction of native villagers to aeroplanes. They were popularly supposed to be terrified, but the Duchess observed them staring up with the same interest she felt herself whenever she watched an aeroplane fly over Woburn. At Dodoma, the hotel was incomparably filthy, but 'it was the bird-watching of dreamland.'

Next day they reached the mining town of Broken Hill. Wherever they went, Mary was intrigued to find that the English people they talked to unanimously preferred living in Africa to England. Apart from the malaria, and the views of those whom she described as her 'belongings' (meaning, presumably, those closest to her, such as Herbrand and Zoë), she agreed with them. Next day, Mary as usual was delighting in all she could see below them, but both pilots were clearly feeling considerably less relaxed, uncertain of their position and running low on petrol. A succession of messages passed between them, in which the possibility of seeing the Victoria Falls was mooted, but it was evident to the passenger that neither pilot even knew which river was below them. Barnard later admitted that he had been considering the best place to crash. Then they spotted the railway to Bulawayo and followed it to the town.

Mary was unhappy to find that a reporter had managed to join her unidentified in the car while looking for a hotel and her whole conversation was headline news next day. Both professional pilots were in a state of exhaustion, too tired even to eat any dinner, and, as the cook had gone to bed, Mary too was left hungry. Bulawayo was not a place she afterwards recalled with any pleasure, and it was two hundred miles further from Cape Town than their intended resting place at Palapye Road. All the same, Barnard was determined to reach their goal the next day. The cloud cleared, and they were able to fly at eight to nine thousand feet: no more bird watching for Mary, though she did pick out some of the famous landmarks of the Boer War. The 1,250 mile flight was believed to be the longest non-stop flight ever made in South Africa at that time.

On arrival in Cape Town, at a different airport from the one where they were expected, they had completed nine thousand miles in one hundred and one flying hours, taking nine and a half days. Two years later, Imperial Airways brought in a weekly service to Cape Town for which they allowed eleven days. In the photograph of the three of them standing by the *Spider*, even Mary, usually serious to the point of moroseness in such photographs, no doubt in part because of her hatred of the press, is wreathed in smiles.

They were allowed little time for sightseeing. The pilots spent every moment possible of the two nights and a day they remained in the city working on the plane, while Mary had to work her way through a massive pile of telegrams and letters and deal with reporters and photographers. She did enjoy being driven round the city, however, contrasting this with the

At Palapye Road

long, boring hours she usually spent in some filthy, isolated hotel, not even eating until her companions were able to join her. At 5.30 a.m. on Easter Monday, 21st April, they set off on the homeward journey.

The first day passed without incident. On the second day, they flew over the Victoria Falls, too high for a close view: Mary found them from that angle disappointingly unimpressive. Barnard, who rarely took an interest in the country below them, disagreed: he described them as 'easily the most impressive sight from the air I have ever seen.'[3]

After some five hours' flying, high above the clouds, Mary's book fell from her knee. She struggled in vain to keep awake. A few minutes later, Barnard felt overwhelmingly tired. He tapped Little on the shoulder and asked him to take over the controls to enable him to douse his head in cold water. Little replied that he, too, felt so sleepy that he would only be able to fly the machine for a very short time. Barnard stumbled out and was amazed to find the Duchess sound asleep: she was always in touch with all that was happening, ready and willing to take a turn at the controls. He tried to shake her, but, when there was no response, he was too dazed to persist. He decided that the lack of sleep from which they had all suffered during the journey had caught up with them, but there was no possibility of landing: they were flying over dense, uninhabited jungle. The two men took turns at the controls, changing places at constant intervals and putting their heads out of the window in between. They flew for seven hours five minutes that day. The last three hours, after the drowsiness set in, seemed an eternity to the two pilots.

When they eventually landed at Broken Hill, Mary was unconscious. They carried her from the plane and laid her down in the open air. After half an hour, her eyes opened and she slowly sat up. By then all three were feeling extremely sick and ill. They started to go through everything which they had eaten or drunk, but could think of nothing which could have poisoned them.

At last Barnard thought of the heating pipe which ran from the exhaust pipe to heat both carburettor and cabin. Examination showed that there was a large hole in the exhaust pipe: carbon monoxide was pouring into the plane. The doctor told them that another hour would probably have been fatal to them all, and particularly to the Duchess, asleep in the fume filled cabin. Both men were deeply shocked by the episode, which left them all with appalling headaches. Mary brushed the whole incident aside, treating it as a joke.

Askari Guard at Dodoma

Next day both men were tense and irritable as they flew to Dodoma. The engine was also giving some cause for concern and Mary felt that they were in a state of nervous exhaustion, and made themselves worse by refusing all offers of food. She herself thoroughly enjoyed her day, watching rhino, hippo, waterbuck and later elephant, as well as observing with interest the finer points of the anthills. They reached Dodoma in a downpour heavy enough to flood the town.

By morning thick fog had come down. It cleared sufficiently to enable Mary to watch the largest herds of game she had ever seen. But there was no time to sit and stare: she was soon needed for pumping petrol. The big spare tank contained 270 gallons. Mary had to spend fifteen minutes in every hour, pumping petrol at a rate of a thousand pumps every fifteen minutes, from there into the wing tanks. They could communicate with each other only by using the 'printator' – an early form of a child's magic notepad – to write each other messages. As they flew over the shores of Lake Victoria, Barnard informed Mary that they would have to make an emergency landing. After some discussion as to whether they had recently flown over a suitable place, he decided to fly on. Kisumu in front of them was their only chance, but he warned that they had only a matter of minutes, with less than a pint of oil remaining: there was a leak in the system.

They landed safely, only to find that it was the oil gauge rather than the supply which was faulty and there had in fact been no danger. Mary reflected that overcoming feelings of panic in such circumstances was relatively easy for her, for she had no responsibilities, and was thus able to accept that 'Che Sara Sara', what will be will be, which is the motto of the Russell family.

They set off once more for Juba, but they were not destined to reach it that day. They came into mountainous country where the vestiges of fog had given way to torrential rain, the roar of thunder and the country was lit up by constant flashes of lightning. With mountains ahead and storms whirling all around them, Barnard had little choice but to find somewhere to land, and managed to find an airstrip at a place called N'Mule. Crowds quickly gathered, some frightened, some curious. To the intense embarrassment of the pilot and amusement of Mary, they were clad only in beads. The English group handed out chocolates and cigarettes, and were escorted in triumph to the Chief's mud hut, some two miles away. At either end of the procession, flares were carried through the elephant grass, some twelve feet high, to ward off the lions. The travellers collapsed on the little bedsteads erected for them. Mary rolled up her skirt as pillow, and managed a little sleep. At 11 p.m. supper arrived, brought from four and a half miles away. The two chickens had clearly been killed in their honour, but were so tough that they had to resort to fingers and teeth. Mary was soon asleep, regretting only that she could not hear a lion roar. The men lay awake, listening to the eerie beat of the tom-toms. Next morning, a large party turned out to see them off, some wearing the lids of the cigarette tins threaded around their necks.

Juba was only an hour's flight further on. Here they refuelled and overhauled the plane. Mary would have liked longer to explore, but there was no time to spare. They flew on, through yet more storms, to Khartoum, then, after a few hours' sleep at the hotel, on over the desert, with Mary at the controls, to Cairo.

Mary had last visited the city 42 years earlier, on her honeymoon. She was pleased to stay at a different hotel, having 'very lively recollections of the highly undesirable bedfellows I discovered on that occasion'[4], and even more pleased to be greeted by a cousin of Herbrand's, and whisked off to dinner at his lovely house. Just over a decade later, Mary's grandson Hugh found himself in Cairo, suffering from a raging fever and in urgent need of recuperation. He was taken in by the same cousin, Tom Russell, known as

Russell Pasha. He was Chief of the Cairo Police and had been appointed in part to stop the heroin trade. Many of the fellaheen, the agricultural workers, were becoming addicted, first to hashish, which was grown all over Palestine, and then to heroin. Russell Pasha (he was knighted in 1938, becoming Sir Thomas Wentworth Russell) succeeded in driving the drug out of first Egypt and then Palestine.

The main source of supply then shifted to Switzerland. The Swiss indignantly denied being suppliers of heroin to the whole Middle East, claiming that theirs was for medical purposes only. Working through the League of Nations, Russell was eventually able to prove that the Swiss production of heroin was about ten times what they should have sold for medical purposes. The Swiss eventually admitted that there was a problem and took the necessary steps. The trade then moved to Turkey. Russell approached Kemal Attaturk but said that he fully appreciated that with some 10,000 miles of coastline it was going to be almost impossible for Attaturk to resolve the problem. The dictator simply replied "It will be stopped". About a year later, after some 700 people had been shot, the trade totally disappeared. Next it moved to Mexico, where the Mexican government succeeded in cutting off the main sources, driving it into the United States. There Sir Thomas could do nothing, but it became so expensive to import heroin from the U.S. to Egypt that the fellaheen could no longer afford it and he was at last victorious.[5]

After her evening with this remarkable man, Mary was for once able to enjoy a long lie-in as her crew were working to ensure that the problems with the engine were resolved. They finally took off at 9.15 a.m. and flew over Ismailia and the Suez Canal, crossed the frontier of Palestine, along the coast and over Mount Carmel to spend the night at Aleppo, their fourth visit to the city. The flight next day was bitterly cold, with no way of keeping either cabin or cockpit warm: even rugs were not a practical possibility. Mary's host at dinner in Sofia was a senior diplomat who had been a prisoner of war in the city for two years; a curious contrast, Mary felt.

The next morning, April 29th, dawned wet and windy once more, but the crew were cheerful and determined. England was just a day's flying time away. With luck, they would be home that night. But luck was not with them on this occasion. They had been flying for less than twenty minutes when the engine gave some 'ominous thumps.' Barnard had no time to choose his landing ground: although he made a perfect landing, the field was full of potholes and almost a bog from the recent wet weather. They were in the Dragoman Pass, regarded as a death trap for aeroplanes and landing there had been considered a near impossibility. The high winds and appalling visibility made the feat particularly impressive. Once again, Barnard had demonstrated both his legendary skill and his legendary luck.

Both men were deeply dejected: prospects of taking off in even an undamaged plane from such a base were slim, with the weight of full petrol tanks as a handicap. And the Fokker was far from undamaged. The oil supply was choked, and if the oil pipe was damaged in an inaccessible place, all hope of beating the record was gone. They had worked so hard in Sofia to ensure that everything was right. This set-back was devastating.

Barnard set off on foot to the nearest railway station in search of help. Little was in the depths of despair. Yet afterwards his abiding memory was of the way in which the Duchess could think and speak of nothing but the disappointment he and Barnard were feeling 'after so much hard work.' A passing plane saw them and sent a message back to Sofia. The official sent out to help finally understood that they needed a car and the mechanics who had worked with them the previous evening. He was about to drive back to Sofia when he found that his own car would not start. As he too set off for the railway station, matters were assuming the appearance of a French farce. Inevitably, Mary and Little were soon surrounded by a chorus of local Bulgarian rustics. At first they were worried, assuming they were a bunch of brigands, but 'I rubbed off a thick layer of insular prejudice, and was very much attracted by all those with whom we came in contact.'

Help eventually arrived from two different directions simultaneously. Another aeroplane landed to help them and Barnard came back in a car with a member of the British Legation, who promptly scooped Mary into the car and took her back to the hotel in Sofia some thirty miles away. There was nothing she could usefully have done by remaining: she had not even got suitable clothes for the wet, muddy conditions. But, away from her comrades, without means of communication, she felt flat, lonely and despondent. Even a journalist from *The Times* seemed almost welcome: at least she could talk to him. Exhausted, having been up since 3.30 a.m., but unable to sleep, she was utterly miserable.

Evening was drawing on when she was handed a scrap of paper. On it, Barnard had scribbled a brief message. Nothing was broken. The sudden change of temperature from a very hot climate to a very cold one had caused the oil to become like rubber and unable to circulate. They had cleaned it all out, moved anything they could out of the machine to lighten it and hoped to fly back to Sofia that evening ready to set out for home in the morning. The French mechanics had had previous experience of this happening, so quickly diagnosed the problem.

Jubilant and as light-hearted as she had previously been wretched, Mary repacked her bags. The pilots returned to Sofia at ten that evening. Next morning, the rain continued to pour, Mary was paddling through deep mud between the car and the plane and only the mechanics who had been working all night on the plane for them were there to see them off.

Once they were in the air, blue sky appeared over the Danube, though there was more bad weather to come, with rain, hail, snow and thick cloud for the pilots to contend with throughout Austria and Germany and arctic conditions inside the plane. Poor Captain Barnard suffered from bad circulation in his hands, which had been terribly burnt in the past, and was in considerable pain. Both pilots rejoiced to see the White Cliffs of Dover. Mary alone was always a little sad at these moments. She described her long flights, without irony, as 'the one perfect rest I get in the year.' Whenever people praised her for her part in the flights, she would always reply that they were strenuous for the men, but a pleasure cruise for her.

In England the sun was shining. They flew over the aerodrome at Lympne and could see everyone waving from the ground. At Croydon, where they landed at 5.30 p.m., there were so many people that it was hard to find their own friends. Her old friend St. Barbe wrote 'Bravo' in the air in sky writing. Mary described how she was smothered in bouquets and very nearly carried into tea. Tu Fu, the Pekinese, brought along by Jemima, became a celebrity over night and received almost as many invitations to dinners, lunches, teas and cocktails as his mistress. More fortunate than her in one respect, he was not asked to make speeches, broadcast or lecture, though he may have been expected to help with opening fetes and bazaars. Telegrams awaited her from the Air Ministry, Air League and, once again, the King.

They had been to the Cape and back in 20 days (including the day on the ground in Cape Town) with 175 hours in the air. Mary claimed that she was not tired at all and would happily have flown back to the Cape. She felt that the real work came in the days following her return, fulfilling all her commitments. Some she enjoyed. She was invited to Chelsea Flower Show for the day before the opening. A problem with the car bringing her from the aerodrome meant that, to her delight, by the time she arrived the place was virtually deserted. She was quite unrepentant even when she realized that the actual object had been for her to meet the King and Queen.

Soon life returned to its usual routine. She joined Herbrand and Jemima at Endsleigh, fishing and watching birds, but flew home for operating day at the hospital. She continued to dine out more often than she had done for thirty years, but rarely enjoyed such occasions, for, even if the speeches were good, she was unable to hear them, but she willingly accepted the need to support the various causes for which they were given.

On July 10th she recorded in her diary:

'Told Captain Barnard that I should have to find another pilot, as he has too many other engagements. July 10th has ended my flying experiences with Captain Barnard, and it means, I fear, "Goodbye" to my long flights which I have enjoyed so much. I could not possibly have had a better pilot, and it will not be easy to find a satisfactory substitute.'[6]

Mary realised that Barnard's first loyalty was no longer to her. He had his own company to run, with which he established an air circus, and he was too closely allied to the press for her taste. A few weeks after his departure, she referred to a bunch of reporters and press photographers, who discovered that she was briefly in Blackpool, as 'virulent mosquitoes.'

Barnard had never been in any way sycophantic or subservient, and it was the last thing she would have wanted. Early approaches by the press amazed him:

"What an extraordinary idea," he commented. "One would think you were the first woman to fly."

Mary entirely agreed with him. She remained genuinely surprised for the rest of her life by the public acclaim she received, when she considered herself merely a passenger, and was only too glad to give the full credit to the professionals. But she probably felt that his close bonds with the journalists, whom she saw as the enemy, created a risk of treachery. She also felt, with reason, that, if she was paying a pilot, it was not unreasonable for her to expect that his services would be available whenever she required them. This would frequently be for lessons or to accompany her on all the shorter flights she wished to take, and not just for the grand occasions and record breaking expeditions.

On 6th September, less than two months after she told Barnard that, brilliant though he was and much as she had enjoyed his company, he was no longer fulfilling her requirements, his successor Mr. J.B. Allen moved into the Paris House at Woburn. It was a momentous day for her. On the same day, she recorded that Jack came on a visit. Jack was probably her tea planter brother, whom she very rarely saw.

The Duchess had had trial flights with a number of other applicants for the vacant position. Bernard Allen was the ideal candidate. Now aged 33, he had transferred to the Royal Flying Corps in 1916 and remained in the RAF after the War. He had one problem which had already lost him a number of mooted promotions. This very problem may well have been influential in winning him his new job: he was slightly deaf. Mary identified with him from the start. Of her three pilots, Allen was the most attractive character. Now that he was living at Woburn, she was also able for the first time to keep her Moth at home, and a hangar was built for it. She also needed a qualified ground engineer. One of the Woburn chauffeurs, J.W. Todd, had been apprenticed at Woburn before the War, served with the Royal Naval Air Service during the War and returned to Woburn afterwards as a chauffeur. She now arranged for him to have the necessary training to qualify for the position. By the start of 1931, the new team was ready.

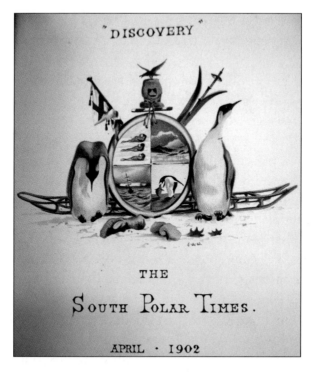

The South Polar Times –
a memento of Captain Scott probably given to Mary by Peter Scott

CHAPTER 13

DIFFERENT PILOTS

Percival Gull outside the hangar at Woburn

The three years during which Flight Lieutenant Bernard Allen was her pilot were the happiest of Mary's flying career. J.B., as the Woburn staff called him, was a charming man, less flamboyant than his predecessor, but a kind, conscientious person who loved his flying. Unlike Barnard, who was always thinking of new schemes which attracted him, then fitting his work for the Duchess around them to the best of his ability, Allen was devoted to his work for Mary. His primary objective was to ensure that she enjoyed her flying. They broke no world records, but they had some delightful flying holidays travelling together, won competitions with the planes and visited all sorts of interesting places. With his support, Mary eventually obtained her pilot's licence in May 1933, at the remarkable age of 67. Allen was unhappy in his private life, and was separated from his wife, though the quiet, unassuming young man made friends wherever he went. He and the Duchess had much in common, with their shared love of flying, of birds, animals and travel and their shared handicap of deafness. He became, as she later wrote, much more than a skilled pilot: he was also a loyal and trusted friend.

She did give a few backward glances. Barnard bought the *Spider* from her to use in his air circus, and, when he took her for a joy ride, she admitted to wishing that she were off on a long tour. Some months later, he invited her to join him and a colleague on a proposed record-breaking flight to Australia, assuring her that he would not be asking her for much money. Whether she was tempted we do not know: the flight never took place.

In April she set off with Flight Lieutenant Allen for a fortnight's holiday in France and Italy, which she enjoyed, and followed up with a similar break to Berlin, Vienna, Budapest, Belgrade and Venice in the autumn. She always had an enquiring mind and flying enabled her to see many events which interested her and which in their turn gave additional purpose to her flying practice. That year they included witnessing the Severn Bore; hovering close as the great German airship the Graf Zeppelin landed; and inspecting a field where a thunderbolt had fallen. That storm was long over before they appeared, but Allen, like the Duchess, revelled in the natural drama of a violent thunderstorm. Even when in the air, they loved watching the flashes of forked lightning. Perhaps the great rolls of thunder were particularly prized as a sound both could hear.

She also acquired a new plane, a Puss Moth. Unlike the other planes, the inside was not open to the elements. It was even possible to take a little more luggage. But Mary had been brought up in a hard school. The plane was supposed to be dual control, but she found the system very frustrating, and preferred fresh air to 'abominable draughts.'

Allen, like Mary, delighted in the beauty of the world above the clouds. One day he took her, in her words, to Fairyland. Mary wrote a lyrical description of sunset witnessed from above the clouds on what was, on earth, a gloomy, cloudy day. Her bird watching expeditions increased too, for this again was something which Allen enjoyed as much as she did. In the spring of 1932, their holiday lasted three weeks, a return for Mary to Spain and Northern Africa.

But, probably for the first time ever, the economic crisis in Britain was having a direct impact on Herbrand. The taxation introduced by the new National government, which had taken power following the election in October 1931, was so hard hitting that Herbrand was forced to consider reductions in his lifestyle. Mary's contribution at this stage was to restrict her activities in the autumn to British soil.

Herbrand's own reaction to the need to economise was remarkably unselfish. He proposed to give up his lease of Cairnsmore, where he had enjoyed so many happy weeks ever since his marriage 44 years before. His main reservation was that this could cause hardship to the owner of Cairnsmore, who would find it difficult, if not impossible, to find a replacement tenant at such a time. In the event, they did not give up Cairnsmore, and for a time economic pressures relaxed once more, though for the rest of their lives they were both aware that never again would even a Duke and Duchess enjoy virtually limitless resources, as they had done till then.

The financial pressures were not sufficient to curtail activities for long. In March 1933 Mary set off with Allen on a venture lasting just over three weeks, which contained the best elements of all her flights. They visited some of the greatest places in the world, including Constantinople, Jerusalem, Petra, the Pyramids and the Valley of the Kings, and delighted in all they saw. At Jerusalem, the agnostic Duchess was deeply moved by Gethsemane. Next day as she piloted the plane over the desert to Petra, her thoughts were of T. E. Lawrence: she reflected that, had his troop been Europeans not Arabs, during the summer months they 'would certainly have deserted to go to Heaven.' She herself risked doing likewise for different reasons. At one moment she was certain that she could not have been 200 feet from the ground, but her diplomatic pilot declared that he had not been looking just then.

The vicissitudes of weather, hotel staff, obstructive officials and of the Puss Moth herself presented sufficient challenges to satisfy them both. They also, as so often, made some remarkable new friends. At Constantinople, the nephew of the Chief of Police collected them from the Aerodrome. When Allen asked if the banks would be open, the young man asked why. Allen replied that they needed Turkish money to pay their hotel bills and other expenses.

"But you will have no expenses; you are the guests of the Turkish government, and all your expenses will be paid."[1]

Mary, who had been told beforehand that Turkish officials were likely to prove exceptionally recalcitrant, was amazed as well as grateful, even when

Mary with Herr Blaauw and Flt. Lt. Allen at Gooilust

she later learnt that her kinsman Tom Russell (Russell Pasha) in Cairo had many good friends in Turkey. Tom Russell himself was waiting for them later when they landed in Cairo.

At Petra, there were only two other visitors, 'an obvious German or Austrian professor... with black hair standing straight on end for some four inches, and a black beard... and a bright little lady who had obviously travelled a great deal who made herself very pleasant.'[2]

The bright little lady was in fact Freya Stark. She later remembered the Duchess, never a believer in wasting time, sitting in the Mess tent knitting a black sock.

On their way home, they stopped at Barcelona for petrol and met a young man named Captain Lancaster, who was trying to set a new record time to the Cape. (Mary's own had already been superseded.) They did what they could to help him but were concerned that he had only so far completed eight hours' flying and was already a physical wreck and bundle of nerves. He indeed got lost and ran out of petrol three days later. His skeleton in the plane was not found until 29 years later, with a diary beside him showing that he had survived for more than a week.[3]

Mary and Allen knew nothing of this. When they stopped at Cannes and were driven to Monte Carlo, they narrowly escaped being involved in a car crash, their second altercation in a car since they left home. Mary jubilantly declared that it was extraordinary that anyone should think flying a greater risk than motoring. But only a fortnight after their return home :

'We passed over Hendon Aerodrome, where we saw the wreck of Lord Knebworth's machine; he was killed there yesterday.'

Throughout their travels, Allen had proved himself the most delightful of companions. He was also an excellent teacher, prepared to take endless trouble with his pupil. Thanks to his training, Mary had passed all the tests necessary to be granted her Pilot's A Licence two years before. But the Air Ministry Medical Board had refused to allow her to pass her medical, ostensibly because of her deafness. Mary suspected that it was in fact on account of her age, but now, when she was two years older, (she was 67) she was finally granted it. She was triumphant. Without it, there were severe restrictions on where she was allowed to fly solo. She celebrated four days later by winning a special *Concours d'Élegance* Cup at Brooklands for the smartest aeroplane owned and flown in by a lady. When the Prince of Wales wished to see her, she was eventually found helping her pilot to polish the two aeroplanes. Characteristically, she gave all the credit to Allen and Todd.

1933 was a glorious spring for both of them. They continued to fly all over Britain during the summer – once, they inadvertently landed on the Isle of Man, which Mary declared she had always wanted to visit, but not at that precise moment. Flying encouraged Mary to attend all sorts of different events, from spaniel and sheepdog trials to Highland Games, all of which gave her pilot as much pleasure as Mary herself.

Mary, despite her deafness, was a good listener. She soon learnt of the problems of her pilot's private life. Within a week of his marriage, he had learnt that his wife had deceived him in every direction and had contrived to make his life a misery ever since. He had believed, for example, that she was eight years his senior but it soon emerged that she was very considerably older than he had appreciated. Mary was totally sympathetic, though she worried that he did not have good judgment about women. There was a new woman in his life who seemed likely to cause almost as much trouble in the future as his wife was already causing him. She realised that there were no easy solutions for him, but her support undoubtedly helped him to get matters into perspective.

Their next plan was to enter for an international flying competition called 'The Tour of the Oases Trophy' in December. The General Aircraft Company, makers of the Monospar twin-engined monoplanes fitted with Pobjoy engines, built them a special Monospar for the event. It was on loan to the Duchess, painted in her green colours and registered in her name. No doubt the company saw this as an excellent investment for obtaining publicity for their machines. A fortnight before the event, Allen flew it to the Pobjoy factory at Hooton Park on the Mersey for a final engine check. Mary had an appointment that day so was unable to accompany him. The engine was passed by the engineers and Allen was looking forward with pleasure to flying out to Cairo with the Duchess that Saturday.

Unfortunately, there were a few hold-ups at Hooton Park and he left later than he had planned. He did not contact Woburn to tell them of his movements, but had previously arranged for Todd to light a petrol flare if he was arriving late. Visibility that evening was bad. Todd heard him approaching and lit the flare, but Allen turned the plane due east to Lidlington, where he was confronted with a row of high pylons and cables. Moments later, the monoplane crashed. Allen was terribly injured and died in Bedford Hospital a few hours later.

Mary was devastated, knowing that she had lost 'not only a skilled pilot, but a loyal and trusted friend.' Everyone in the world of aviation and at Woburn was deeply saddened. As his obituary in *The Aeroplane* said, 'He was liked wherever he went, and he made numbers of friends wherever he worked.'

Todd's young daughter later recalled that a gipsy woman had called at the house where he lodged, for he was separated from his wife, three times on the morning of the crash, saying:

'It's absolutely imperative that I see the Master to stop him going on a journey.'[4]

Mary described him as having a 'wonderful personality.' She noted in her diary that she had now flown 1819 hours, most of which had been with him. An unselfish and generous hearted man, with him Mary had always come first.

After his death, all the problems in his life came to the surface. Mary found herself involved in a maelstrom of bitterness and jealousy, which seems to have emanated from his wife but also caught up his new girl friend, his parents and even Mr. and Mrs. Prestwood, the couple who had cooked and cared for him, as well as Mary herself. Some very unpleasant scenes took place, including one in the mortuary. The labels on the wreaths given by Mary and Jemima were removed. Even the dead man's mother declared:

"I am afraid my daughter-in-law is a *very* peculiar woman!"

When Mary learnt the full details of the tragic events of the evening, she began to question whether it had in truth been an accident. There was no evidence of any mechanical failure, and, although night flying was not a common practice at the time, she was convinced that Bernard Allen's navigational skills, combined with his detailed knowledge of the area around Woburn, would not have allowed him to make such a mistake as was suggested. The journey also seemed to have taken him around half an hour longer than it should have done. Mary came to believe that he had spent the flight, perhaps including a diversion, thinking about his problems and had eventually become convinced that they were insoluble. Knowing that he was on his own and flying a machine which belonged to a commercial company and was fully insured, he decided to end his life. She concluded:

'I do not blame him and am glad he is at rest. There was no other hope of happiness for him.'

She was the more concerned now to do all that she could to protect his memory. She longed to erect a suitable memorial for him, but found herself once more in conflict with his widow, so eventually withdrew her offer. But something appeared in the press, apparently once more through the machinations of the widow, which was so detrimental to his reputation that both Jemima and even Mary herself were offered spurious sympathy:

'How sad that the poor Duchess should have had that dreadful man for a pilot,' people started saying.

Mary was relieved at least when the comments were as open, enabling both her and Jemima to set the record straight and clear his name. His widow also conceived a wish to take his dog, which was settled happily with Mr. and Mrs. Prestwood, but there was little that Mary could do. There were a few mementoes which Mary would have liked to keep, most of which she had given to her pilot, including photographs where she had given him the camera and paid for film, developing and printing, and would willingly have bought from Mrs. Allen, but again the woman was obstructive.

Worse was to follow. Before Mary could come to grips with the tragedy, she was shocked to find that she was being held legally responsible for his death. This seems to have been based on an issue of inadequate insurance, although Mary pointed out that insurance companies included so many restrictions in their policies in relation to private flying that it was impossible to obtain proper cover. However her own lawyer advised her that she probably was legally liable. She resented this deeply, particularly when it emerged that there was some question over the validity of Allen's marriage: it was possible that his wife was already married at the time of the ceremony. Mary commented that 'One can scarcely believe in such a depth of wickedness,' although of course, if this had been proved in the end, nothing would have been due to Mrs. Allen at all.

In the months following his death, Mary was involved in a lengthy correspondence with his executor, his closest friend, Colonel Pillers. The correspondence was friendly and sympathetic throughout. Mary was very sorry for Colonel Pillers, who found himself placed in an extremely difficult position. At first she was inclined to refuse to pay up, even though she knew that she would probably lose any court case, until Mrs. Allen had taken her to court. Eventually she changed her mind and gave Mrs. Allen a thousand pounds, with both sides remaining responsible for their own costs. Her comment to Colonel Pillers summed up her attitude:

'It is a strange world where his best friend has to take action against a woman he served so loyally to support the woman who drove him to take his life!'

Bernard Allen's funeral took place on 9th December, three days after his death. Two days later, Mary received a letter from one of the test pilots with General Aircraft who had known Allen and met the Duchess. He expressed his sympathy, offered to bring back the Moth which had been left at Croydon on the morning of the tragedy, and applied for Allen's job. Mary wrote back emphasising the disadvantages of the position. She explained her own commitments:

'I am a radiographer for this district and a pretty wide area, and also Assistant to my two London surgeons at all operations in the hospital. I am frequently at work there most of the day and look upon flying as my almost daily recreation.'

Because her own hours were so unpredictable, she would make plans with her pilot on a day-to-day basis, informing him at the last moment of the time when she would be able to fit in a flight. She also emphasised how dependent she was on her pilot when travelling abroad, on account of her deafness.

Flight Lieutenant Raphael Chevallier Preston was not deterred. A married man with children, at 41 he was considerably older than either Barnard or Allen. Unlike them also, he had a public school education and had travelled extensively. He joined the Royal Flying Corps in 1917. He stayed on after it became part of the RAF, working as a flying instructor for some years after the War. He had then become personal pilot to the former Secretary of State for Air before joining General Aircraft. He was a competent and experienced pilot. Flying was his area of expertise. He now needed a secure position with a suitable house for his family and an interesting job, ideally including both flying and social and managerial responsibilities, where he was in sole charge. He had little doubt that he could organise both the Duchess's flying activities and her private life when travelling abroad for her to the highest standard. Indeed, he was confident that his superior experience would enable him to fulfil the commitments of the position to a higher standard than either Barnard or Allen. He had no conception that the Duchess did not need or want anyone to take charge of any aspect of her life.

Mary suggested that he was likely to find her style of travelling somewhat lonely. Preston was not deterred: he was quite capable of developing his own social life in the places they visited. Mary, who had always been concerned for the welfare of her pilots, raised a number of other issues, small matters where she was worried that he would not enjoy her way of life. Preston brushed them aside. She knew that, for her, time was short: she could not afford to delay in finding a successor to Allen, and none of the other candidates was suitable. Besides, Preston had been a friend of Allen's: that was a major recommendation. On 6th January 1934 she offered him the job.

In February, Preston persuaded the Duchess to attend the British Industries Exhibition, which she accepted, though she turned down an invitation to speak. She was somewhat surprised to find herself the only woman in a gathering of between 300 and 400 leading businessmen.

In April they set off on her now traditional Easter holiday, travelling through Europe to West Africa - Senegal and the Gambia - and the Canary Islands. The difference in their interests soon became apparent. Preston arranged for Shell Company representatives (whom Mary referred to as the local 'Shell' fish) to meet them everywhere. Mary was polite but frequently bored. They walked by the sea, but 'with a companion who is devoid of ornithological leanings, it is impossible to watch birds.' Preston liked to spend long hours sketching. Both enjoyed playing Backgammon, which filled some long evenings. Mary was always thrilled when people at airports she had visited before came to greet her, frequently producing photographs of her with Captain Barnard.

When they landed at Cabo Juby for petrol, Preston discovered two bullet holes in one of the wings. Fortunately the shots had caused no damage, missing the petrol tanks. Without their knowledge, tribesmen had fired at the plane with a rifle. Mary was impressed with the standard of marksmanship: when hit, they were flying at an altitude of between three and four thousand feet at a speed in excess of a hundred miles per hour.

She was less impressed with the Canaries. When she asked an Englishwoman, who had been there for three months, what there was to do and the woman replied "Nothing!" Mary was astounded that anyone should choose to waste their life in such a way. On their flight on to Marrakech, they had the first 'narrow squeak' which she had encountered with Preston. They were some twelve miles off Fuerteventura when a major problem in the engine developed.

'We had the interesting experience of feeling quite certain that our flying career was about to end in a very rough sea,' Mary wrote afterwards. As the engine showed some signs of recovery, Preston indicated that he thought they might reach land. Mary replied that she thought the sea looked preferable to the wild, rocky mountains inland, and Preston, taking her point, turned seaward once more. Mary resigned herself to the conclusion that their end would be quick, though she was mildly disappointed that those at home would not hear about their flight.

'At all events I should have gone down knitting a prosaic sock and the reporters would have pictured me clinging round Flight-Lieut. Preston's neck and imploring him to save me!'[5]

In fact, the engine eventually recovered, and they were flying at a sufficient height to be able to afford a drop of over four thousand feet. A strong wind made them decide to land at Agadir, where they were advised that landing would have been impossible an hour earlier, and conditions required that one of the wings should be held on to from the runway. As none of the men in attendance volunteered, the Duchess climbed out to do this herself.

No full explanation was ever found for the engine problem. At the time they suspected a grain of sand had penetrated the filters, but later a vapour lock in the fuel lines was considered a more likely cause.

Many of Mary's comments in her diary at this time relate to food, which assumed considerable significance for them after long hours in the sky with little to eat. But the quality varied immeasurably. At Granada it was so horrible that 'my lack of appetite aroused comment, and they wanted to know if I were ill. It was difficult to explain that I was not, but should have been if I had eaten the lunch.'

When their return flight home was delayed by a day with fog, Mary made her usual comment, '*L'homme propose et Dieu dispose*,' her personal variation on the Bedford family motto, *Che Sara Sara*. Back in England, she was amused to note that:

'All our friends, with the exception of Mrs. Preston, are greatly thrilled by the bullet-holes in the wing, of which we knew nothing till we landed, and entirely ignore the airlock (?) over the sea when we both thought death inevitable in a few minutes.'[6]

During the summer, Mary pursued her usual eclectic range of activities, which she reached by air. A particular highlight was the Oberammergau Passion Play, which enthralled her from start to finish. But in Zermatt on the way home, the differences between her and her pilot surfaced once more. They took a train to Gornergrat, where the view was wonderful but there were too many people for Mary's taste. She decided to walk down alone, leaving Preston there to continue sketching, with strict instructions that if he did not find her at the top at lunch-time he was not to bother about her.

She had no intention of meeting him but wished to avoid an argument. After a pleasant walk down, visiting the Gorge on the way, she returned to the hotel. Just before dinner time, she received word that Preston was still waiting for her at the top and had missed the last train down. He had a long walk and rubbed his toes.

'As I did not feel responsible I proceeded to eat my dinner and it did not disagree with me.'

Next morning she was up for a walk at Zermatt at 7 a.m. and finally reached Woburn at 12.45 that night. She was not in bed until 2 a.m.

A highlight of the summer was the twenty fifth anniversary of the first cross channel flight by Louis Blériot. Mary recalled with amusement how Herbrand's sister Ela had prophesied at the time that Blériot would be the last as well as the first man to do this. She also enjoyed attending the launch of the Queen Mary, which brought back memories of *Sapphire,* built by the same builders.

Mary in the Puss Moth, 1931

Strained relations between the Duchess and her pilot reached crisis point early in 1935. The catalyst was discussion in the aeronautical world about the safety of Puss Moths, following a number of crashes. Preston, who, for all his superficial charm, lacked any understanding of the way to handle his employer, advised her to exchange the Puss Moth for a different machine. He felt that he had picked a good moment, when it was going to need a considerable amount of money spending on it. However she needed the Puss Moth to be available for her annual holiday in March, which could not be delayed this year because of the royal Silver Jubilee celebrations which she would be required to attend in May. Her financial situation was restricted because of the pay-out to Mrs. Allen. She also expected the machine to be properly cared for and maintained from an aesthetic as well as a mechanical point of view. Preston took none of the care over its presentation which, in Allen's time, had won both her planes so many Concours d'Élegance, but which demanded hours of painstaking work, with which on occasion the Duchess had willingly assisted.

Preston felt that it was his duty to explain the position regarding Puss Moths to Mary, to ensure that she did not incur what he perceived as unnecessary risks. He considered that others might blame him if an accident occurred and he had not taken steps to avert it. Not only did he express his point of view somewhat pompously. There was a fundamental difference in their perception of the role the pilot was employed to fulfil. Mary had never previously had, and did not now require, someone to take the major decisions for her. She was a mature and highly intelligent woman with many years' flying experience who was well aware of all the issues now raised.

An extended and acrimonious correspondence followed. Mary took care to give her pilot full credit for all that he had done to help her, but she concluded that he was not happy with either of her two machines. He did not like the Gipsy, which he found draughty, though to Mary one of the pleasures of her short flights was that it was open to the air. He replied by saying that he accepted that it was not always possible to have the best of everything: just as he could not afford the Lagonda he would like to drive because of his family, so he realised that the Duchess could not afford more up to date planes as well as running her hospital.

Mary now responded that, since he did not consider the Puss Moth safe, she could never ask him to fly in it again. She therefore felt that he would have to leave her service. She undoubtedly found him overbearing and dictatorial towards her. She missed the companionship and delight in shared pleasures of both her previous two pilots. Preston never enjoyed, as she and they had done, such things as flying above the clouds to watch a beautiful sunset. But Preston had no wish to leave his comfortable position. Eventually the disagreement was patched up, mostly because time was so precious to Mary. She feared that, by the time he had served his three months' notice, it would be too late for her to have a proper holiday that year. Finding a suitable replacement for him would inevitably take time, and that was the one thing which, however much Herbrand helped her, she could not afford.

The reconciliation enabled her to have one final aeronautical adventure. Mary read an article about a flight across the Sahara and felt that here was exactly the sort of venture she was searching for. Uncertain as to how her pilot would react, in the light of their current relations, she left the magazine out for him to find. Thus the proposal came from him not her, and on 20th March they set off in the Puss Moth.

Mary lacked the total confidence in her pilot's professional judgment which she had always had with his two predecessors. No doubt this was partly because her increased experience enabled her to form her own opinions, but it owed something also to their impaired relationship. The first issue was an administrative one. Not until Oran, on the edge of the desert in Algeria, did Preston admit that he had not obtained the permits for crossing the Sahara, but that they would find them in Oran.

'This of course we did not, and being Sunday there is no possibility of doing anything and a blessed uncertainty as to whether we shall get them, at least in reasonable time.'[7] Late the following afternoon, the necessary telegram arrived, although there were further delays next day.

They were advised to leave at dawn next day, but Preston preferred to wait for weather reports, so that they did not in fact take off until 8.50 a.m., a habit which Mary considered dangerous. Next came a navigational error, requiring a retracing of tracks. Mary felt that they would have benefitted from flying lower, but again her companion differed. Soon, inevitably, Preston was forced to admit that he was lost. Mary fortunately enjoyed the resultant unscheduled stop at an oasis in the desert. But she saw clearly that the desert was no place for a novice pilot. Dust storms made the country particularly inhospitable and made visibility constantly poor. Later on in their holiday, Mary suspected Preston of coming rather closer to running out of fuel than he was prepared to admit, but also complained that he could sometimes be over cautious.

They decided to visit Timbuctoo, where there were few motors and nowhere to stay except by invitation. The town blended in so well with its surroundings that they at first overshot it. On the flight in, Mary had been reading the biography of *The White Monk of Timbuctoo*, a well-known character who had originally arrived as a missionary but had now 'gone native' and played a full and important part in local affairs. Mary much enjoyed her meeting with him, and he in turn was delighted with the copy of the book about him, which Mary gave to him and which he had never previously seen.

At Kano they were most hospitably entertained by the Resident and his wife. Next day she visited two hospitals, which particularly interested her, the school, printing works and barracks, before being received by the Emir in his mud-walled palace. He was dressed in a high turban and stately flowing black robes, but had elected to furnish his palace incongruously with modern English furniture from Maples. Mary was convinced that she had seen him the previous year, being escorted round Harrods and the Army and Navy Stores. Mary and the Resident's wife were then taken to see the harem. The gloomy, dark, confined apartments appalled Mary.

With a tame cheetah at Fort Lamy

To Mary's delight, they were introduced to the writer of the original article which had inspired their journey. She was shattered a few days later when they reached Cairo to learn that he had been killed in a crash the day after they left Kano. Otherwise, Cairo was as always a favourite city for Mary, largely on account of the hospitality of Russell Pasha and his wife. Their remaining few days were spent in Benghazi, Tripoli and Tunis, then home through Italy and France.

In Rome, Mary's thoughts turned, as they so often did, to Flight Lieutenant Allen. Preston was impatient throughout their visit, irritated by customs officials and keen to see everything as swiftly as possible. Mary recalled that her first visit, on her honeymoon, had been equally rushed, but compared both unfavourably with a relaxed visit with Edith Tribe and, more particularly, the more recent one with Allen.

'I thought of him with regret as we stood looking down at the Forum, where he and I had studied it all so carefully together. He would have loved to have done all our flight this time, if only Fate had not been too hard for him.'[8]

Despite her reservations about her pilot, Mary returned home well satisfied with her trip. Once again, this had been a true pioneering expedition, for only three years had elapsed since the Sahara was first flown. It proved to be her last major flight overseas. That summer and the following year brought the usual interesting mix of places and events to visit by air. She flew over to France on a number of occasions, including twice visiting to Le Touquet, which gave her her first chance of flying across the Channel, her pilot relegated to the role of passenger.

Mary derived immense pleasure from flying for many different reasons, the challenge, the excitement, the pleasure of visiting interesting places, the convenience of crossing Britain without wasting time and the beauty of so much that she saw, to name but a few. Inevitably, though, when restricted to a single companion for so much of the time, the personality of her pilot and the way in which his relationship with her developed was of vital importance. Captain Barnard first enthused her with the joy of flying, his sparkling dynamism enlivening her life, their shared reaction to danger, where excitement left little room for fear, an additional delight. In Flight Lieutenant Allen she found a true soul mate, a gentle man who understood so well all the different facets of her enjoyment. After his tragic death, she was never again to know the pleasure of sharing all she loved about flight with one who did his utmost to enhance her enjoyment. Flight Lieutenant Preston could never understand the aesthetic, sometimes almost spiritual nature of her happiness in the air, nor indeed of what that old friend of her youth, Rudyard Kipling, described as "Satiable Curtiosity'. For Mary, unlike the Elephant's Child, this was a quality which rarely got her into trouble, but rather led her to some of the finest experiences of her remarkable life.

Moth, by Mary

CHAPTER 14

THE BEST OF DEATHS...

'For him, it has been the best of deaths for an airman to die.'
Mary, on the death of her pilot, Flight Lieutenant Bernard Allen, 1933

1936 started on a sad note for the Duke and Duchess. Their old Dutch friend, Mr. Blaauw, who had shared so much with them both relating to animals and birds, died in January, forty years almost to the day after Lord Lilford introduced him to them. Two days later, he was followed by the King. Neither Mary nor Herbrand had ever been on terms of close personal friendship with the King or Queen, but they had attended many of the great State occasions throughout his reign, and his telegrams of congratulation to Mary had been much prized by her. She had admired the way he had done his duty and believed that he had worked hard all his life. She rejoiced that, at the end, he had had 'a peaceful passing to the Great Beyond.'

In February, Mary had a pleasant week bird watching at Cley Mill in Norfolk. She enjoyed her break there, as did the team of staff she took with her, including two chauffeurs, her lady's maid who took charge of the house and an additional kitchen-maid who was temporarily promoted to cook. The chauffeurs also helped in the house, but, as they were former members of her Bird Club, they too delighted in their change of scene. Mary probably felt that this was a good opportunity to give those who accompanied her an unofficial paid holiday. She is unlikely to have considered such a large staff necessary, although Herbrand may well have deemed it appropriate. Mary took pleasure in their company and felt that the whole group enjoyed escaping from the formalities and discipline of the Abbey life. For her it was a true holiday, allowing her, as she wrote in her diary, to bird-watch, idle and read.

Endsleigh, by J. Bourne

Herbrand became ill soon after her return to Woburn, which probably accounted for her failure to travel abroad that spring, restricting herself to occasional short breaks for more bird-watching (other trips included Winchelsea in Sussex, Hayle in Cornwall and Seahouses in Northumberland) and Endsleigh, which was handed over that summer to Hastings. She also went to a selection of events relating to aviation: air displays, air races (including judging in the Isle of Man) and the Aviation Service in Canterbury Cathedral, and even entered a competition to test efficiency in aviation for women. Mary scored 76%. Her planes also won some of the *Concours d'Élegance* for which they were entered, though they were not as successful now as in the time of Flight Lieutenant Allen: Preston still preferred not to spend his leisure time polishing aeroplanes. Mary was also keen to complete 200 hours solo flying, but the weather was against her and in September her total stood at 197 hours 25 minutes.

Early in December, Mary much enjoyed a visit to Woburn by Peter Scott, son of Captain Scott of Antarctic fame, who came to see their geese and wildfowl. The young man was not only very knowledgeable about them, but also painted them most beautifully and he and the Duchess had an immediate rapport.

Ten days later, King Edward VIII abdicated. Mary reacted robustly:

'A good thing too, he would have been for ever discredited even if he had given up the woman... we have shown the world that we do not tolerate immorality in high places.'

The new year found Mary somewhat depressed. Winter that year was murky and wet, the temperature rarely dropping below freezing. The crisp sharpness of a hard frost would have invigorated the spirits; gloomy dampness, fogs, rain and gales did nothing to lighten hearts and left few days when flying was possible. Every day lost seemed especially important, for Mary was now seventy-one years old and there were indications that, when her pilot's licence came up for renewal, the medical board might well turn her down.

The hospital, too, was an increasing source of anxiety. During the previous decade, her prodigious energy enabled her to combine her work in the hospital with her enjoyment in flying to a degree which amazed those close to her. The general public, no doubt, fed on exaggerated press reports, pictured her devoting all her time and energy to flying. For Mary, herself, flying could never be more than a hobby she loved, as well as a means of transport which enabled her to come as close as is humanly possible to being in two places at once. Hospital hours and routines always took priority, but flying enabled her to fit in brief visits or times of relaxation almost within her working schedule, and conversely to slip back to Woburn to take part in an operation in the middle of a week away from home, and enjoy the journey itself as much as anything she did at either end. Her diary at the end of 1934 recorded that, during the preceding sixteen years, she had X-rayed between 200 and 409 cases every year. In addition to her radiology, she continued to act as Theatre Sister for operations. Thus, in the years when she did most of her flying, she was still carrying an immensely heavy workload of cases. It is hardly surprising that, just occasionally, her work and her hobby merged in her brain, as on the occasion when, in writing a report about a patient with a smashed patella, she referred to his smashed propeller.[1]

Whilst the pressures on Herbrand's finances might not seem great by modern standards, the burden of taxation was increasing and his financial advisers were starting to indicate gently that the present level of expenditure could not be sustained indefinitely. In turn, Herbrand warned Mary that in the end the hospital might cease to be a practical proposition.

For Mary, two separate issues were closing in on her hospital in a pincer movement. She had long resolved, as she told Hastings in February 1936, that if she dropped the hospital work in her lifetime, the hospital itself would have to go. She had no confidence in hospitals managed by committees and would prefer to invest such money as she had available for charitable purposes in a different charity. She also accepted the point made by Hastings that it was too large a commitment of time, preventing her from taking as many little holidays as Hastings wished her to do, though she also made the point that Herbrand's wish to have her with him constantly was a greater tie than the hospital. Hastings may have been suggesting some form of holiday with him and her grandchildren, or he may simply have been commiserating with her for some flying expedition which she wished to take. She was 70 at the time, ten years past the retirement age for women.

No-one ever dared to suggest that her workload was too much for her physically. She would breakfast at 7 a.m. before going to the hospital. There she would work from 8.30 till 2.00 on radiology cases, as Theatre Sister for operations and on a myriad administrative issues. Lunch was a quick sandwich. Even while she ate it, she would be resolving some problem with one of the nursing staff or simply completing the crossword puzzle. She never failed to have a comforting word and a smile for any patient in need. One and all, they felt better for a quiet word from Sister Mary.

On her return to the Abbey, if there were sufficient hours of daylight, she would go for a short flight. But always, before or after her flight, Herbrand would be waiting for her.

"How soon will you be ready to go out?" he would ask.

For him, their walk together was the most important event of his day. If for any reason she missed it, conscious as she was of his reluctance to have his walk or tea without her, she felt guilty all day. She was determined to do all that she could for him in return for all that he had done for her. They rarely had guests other than cousins, but if there was a cousin staying, or perhaps Hugh, she would always find time to include them in the walks or drives and listen to their stories of the other things they had done during the day. Despite her deafness, she could always hear what Hugh was telling her. She could also lip read reasonably in such circumstances.

In the evening, there were letters to write or photographs to develop: she always developed all her own. She would never sit idle; if nothing else required her attention she would work on a jigsaw. Kipling could have had Mary in mind when he wrote of filling 'the unforgiving minute with sixty seconds' worth of distance run'. If she sometimes felt weary at the end of the day, she never mentioned it.

Mary's relationships with her own family had never been better than in the last years of her life. She had been quietly rebuilding her relationship with Hastings for several years, visiting him at least from 1929 on, staying with him at Glentrool in 1930 and taking him for his first flight two years later. Afterwards, since Herbrand was still at Woburn, he came back to lunch at Cairnsmore. She was on sufficiently relaxed terms with him to look in unannounced when driving past Glentrool, and stay to tea with his guests when Hastings himself happened to be out. When her little sunbird died, she recollected how Hastings had given it to her 22 years earlier, long before the split.

The real breakthrough came in October 1934, when she took Hugh back to Cairnsmore with her to meet his grandfather for the first time. Soon, they were all meeting regularly for family tea parties (Mary used the word 'family' in her diary, with special pleasure) and days shooting. That year, both Hastings and Hugh spent Christmas at Woburn. Two years after Herbrand first met his grandson, he finally went to Glentrool to see Hastings, Daphne and Hugh. It was his first visit to Glentrool for over forty years, when it was tenanted by old friends of his. Hastings had been going there regularly since soon after the War.

Despite the improvement in relations between Mary and Hastings, mother and son never found each other easy. Hastings felt that the account of her life which Herbrand commissioned after her death, which was written by John Gore, lacked balance. Gore accepted that this was true. The Duke decreed that no criticism whatever of his adored wife was to be made. Hastings longed for a less biased account, which was only written, in a few short pages by John Gore himself[2], in 1965, after Hastings was dead.

Mary remained close to her own family always, her sister Zoë in particular. Zoë was a regular visitor throughout the years at Woburn, Cairnsmore and Endsleigh. Zoë's husband Fred (the 'Beefsteaks' of their youth) died in 1928. By then he was a General. Zoë lived on into her late nineties, and she, both her sons Philip and Noel Beaver, and their wives remained close to Mary throughout her life. Indeed, Noel's wife and son were the main beneficiaries under Mary's will. Mary enjoyed Philip's wedding to a 'very sweet bride' in Exeter Cathedral, when the bridegroom was 48. Zoë had had two daughters as well as two sons, but both girls sadly died in infancy in India. Mary and Zoë also continued to keep in touch with their sister-in-law Alice, widow of Charles Tribe. Their brother Jack lived on the other side of the world, but probably kept in touch and visited on the rare occasions when he was in England.

Many activities which had previously given Mary much pleasure were starting to become a burden, in part because of Herbrand's failing health. Shooting was a case in point:

'The Duke used to be a very good shot but is now quite blind in one eye and sees very little with either,' she had written three years earlier. 'He is also very decidedly getting on in years. Still, when he can see birds well against the sky he still shoots well. He does not like inviting outside guests to help with our big shoots, partly because it almost compels one to go out whatever the weather, and partly because he is naturally rather sensitive about his shooting. It therefore all devolves on me and it is a pretty hard job at times especially as I can so seldom go out.'[4]

After the warm, wet winter, at the end of February (on a date curiously recorded in Mary's diary as 30th February), snow began to fall. Two weeks later it was still lying. When the thaw eventually came, Mary and Preston flew out over the Fens to see the 'almost unprecedented' floods.

'It all looked very chilly and miserable for the poor inhabitants, many of whose houses are standing in the water,' she wrote, concerned as always for the welfare of others. That was the last entry she ever made in her diary.

Mary had just fifty-five minutes of solo flight left to complete her two hundred hours. She had been keen to do this ever since the previous autumn, but a combination of weather conditions and shortage of time meant that she still needed the final fifty-five minutes. Preston helped her to work out a triangular route from Woburn to Buntingford, over Girton College at Cambridge and back to Woburn. He estimated that this would take just about an hour. She took off in the Gipsy Moth at 3.30 in the afternoon in calm weather conditions.

At 4.30 snow began to fall. Soon the world once more turned white, but there was no sign of Mary. Herbrand, worried, came down to the hangar to talk to Preston and Todd. Todd had helped her on take-off but neither had any reassuring suggestions to make. The Duke decided to ring the Chief Constable.

Lieutenant Colonel F.A.D. Stevens had been the Chief Constable of Bedfordshire for many years. During the First World War he had been responsible for the County Emergency Committee and was fully aware of all that Mary had contributed. He also liked and admired her personally, as was evident when he derived so much amusement from the 'bull fighting' episode. Soon police in all the neighbouring counties were aware of the position, and search parties were mobilised from ten different RAF stations. Ships at sea were also alerted. Not a trace of the Duchess or her Gipsy Moth was found.

At first, there was hope. Perhaps she had been caught up in bad weather and found somewhere different to land and take shelter. Perhaps... Herbrand had known from the start that the situation was serious and had allowed no time to be wasted. Her flight, by definition, could not be less than 55 minutes, yet within 90 minutes of take-off the police were mobilised.

The immediate action was followed by a long period of waiting. Eventually, hope faded and a memorial service for Mary was held on 31st March. On 2nd April one of the struts from the plane was washed up on the coast at Yarmouth. In the course of the next few days, the three remaining struts were washed ashore at Gorleston, Lowestoft and Southwold. Todd, who had lavished such care on the Moth, went down to Yarmouth to identify it. He was devastated: he had worked at Woburn ever since he left school, except during the War years when he joined the Royal Naval Air Service. All his opportunities in life had come to him through Mary. She had arranged his training, respected his professional skill and treated him as a friend. When his daughter had an operation as child, Mary not only brought her books and jigsaws but held her hand as she was given the anaesthetic and, as soon as the operation was over, went straight to reassure her father. When the planes won prizes, she gave them to Allen but always had special mementoes made up for Todd as well.[5] He had been the last person on earth to see her alive.

Perhaps his only consolation in his grief was the knowledge that, given the location of the spars, the crash had not been caused by any mechanical failure which might have been his responsibility. Either the Duchess had made a mistake in her navigation, or, as people were already beginning to suggest, she had not.

A number of theories have been put forward to explain what happened on that cold March afternoon. Keith Spence, writing in *Country Life* fifty years after the event, suggested that when she reached Cambridge she decided to make a diversion over Norfolk, perhaps to take a further look at the flooding there. Deteriorating weather conditions caused her to make for refuge at Cley, where she could stay at the Windmill, but somehow she overshot it and headed out to sea. It is possible, though not altogether convincing. She had landed so often at Cley that she would have been unlikely to overshoot, and, had she done so, would quickly have realised her mistake and circled back.

The theory put forward by Lettice Curtis, a very experienced pilot herself, in her book *Winged Odyssey*, published in 1993, is much more plausible. The type of compass used at the time in Moths was operated by

Herbrand at home

lining up a compass needle on a grid where North was indicated by a large, red arrowhead. On the needle itself, the only distinction between the north end of the needle and the south was a small cross bar at the north end of the needle. So frequently did pilots confuse north with south on this compass, that there was a name for the mistake. It was known as setting black on red, and was a mistake which was particularly likely to happen to an elderly pilot with failing eyesight in bad visibility.

Had Mary made this mistake, when she imagined herself to be flying south west from Cambridge towards Woburn, she would in fact have been flying north east over Mildenhall. The weather at Mildenhall that afternoon was particularly bad, with low cloud and poor visibility. She would then have crossed the coastline in the area where the wreckage was eventually found.

If this was what did happen, with the weather deteriorating fast, there were only too many ways in which disaster could have overtaken her. A minor misjudgement whilst flying low in search of landmarks, an engine problem or simply running out of fuel: all these issues had occasioned 'narrow squeaks' in the past: on her own, with increasing age and bad weather conditions, 'luck' was less likely to be on her side than in the past. None of these increased risk factors would have induced her to be more careful. Mary was always true to herself, and her nature was to rise to challenges.

In the long days of waiting, before hope was finally extinguished, Hastings wrote to a close friend:

'Thank you so much for your very sweet and helpful letter – I so agree with what you say – and, like you, my grief would be for Father, not her – I know too that in spite of the affection and help we have tried to give her, her deafness has always been a barrier in her own eyes – And she has always dreaded the time when her disabilities will force her to give up all the amusements and interests she has loved.'

It was not long before people began to wonder whether this was no accident. The threat to the hospital, the likelihood that Mary's pilot's licence would not be renewed, the further recent deterioration in her hearing, all left Mary with little to live for. Nor was there any doubt of her physical courage. She had so often made clear that she had no fear of death, only of the manner of it.

'I am sorry to say my long experience of doctors & surgeons makes me hope but not expect that I shall die without them,' she once wrote.

She had rejoiced that the King had had a happy death.

'A few days of almost painless illness, decreasing strength lapsing into unconsciousness only in the last few hours, and a peaceful passing to the Great Beyond. What better, happier end could one wish for him?'

But for herself, a better death still, she knew, would be in the element she had come to love so deeply, far from the trappings of modern life, alone, quite natural, like the birds. She had envisaged it all on the flight between the Canaries and Marrakesh.

'I thought it quite an agreeable way of finishing up compared with most ends which are the lot of man, and certainly the one I had most desired; for, with not a boat in sight, and a very rough sea, the process could not have lasted long.'

So it was the right death at the right time. But whether or not she planned it no one will ever know. That, in itself, is probably how she would have wanted it to be. She had no moral scruples about suicide in principle. She was an agnostic, and when she believed that that was the decision her pilot had taken, she did not blame him. For such a caring person, she gave relatively little thought to the feelings of his parents.

But what of Herbrand? He whose day was ruined if she did not join him for his walk, who would not start his tea until she was there to keep him company, was he to be left alone in his old age, after all that he had done for her? If she did indeed so plan, she did her best to ensure that he did not know. It has sometimes been suggested that such an organised, efficient person would have left everything in orderly fashion. To have done so would have made plain her intentions. For Herbrand, there would never have been an appropriate moment for Mary to go, so long as breath remained in his body.

Hugh, the young grandson who loved her so deeply and whom she had grown to love as she never had her own son, kept an open mind for the rest of his life. His fourteenth birthday was just a week after she disappeared, when hope was finally abandoned, two days before the celebration of her life at her memorial service.

Perhaps the truth lay somewhere in the middle. It is possible that she had no such plans in advance, but that in the air, alone, her final goal in the world of flying achieved, as she completed her 200 hours solo, she felt that the moment was right. At the time of Allen's death, she had conjectured that he had reached his decision only after he started his final flight. Up alone amongst the clouds, there was time for reflection. If she did indeed unintentionally 'set black on red,' her reflections when she realised her predicament would not have been so different. Either way, her instinct would have been to head further out to sea, away from land, as she had advised Preston to do when both felt there was no hope. She was not afraid, rather curious and ready, as always, for the next challenge. Like Peter Pan, she believed that 'To die will be an awfully big adventure.'

One of Mary's book plates

CHAPTER 15

RETROSPECT

*The Memorial Window to Mary
in the Church of St. Mary, Woburn*

Herbrand had always known that this was how it would all end. He had supported Mary in all her other activities throughout their life together. He never stopped her from flying. He did not interfere with the ways in which she chose to spend money, but he made it clear from the start that he wished that she would give up the aeroplanes. In fact he made a habit of taking cuttings from newspapers whenever he read of a flying accident, and leaving them on Mary's desk. Perhaps this showed a misjudgement of her character: the risk was undoubtedly part of the attraction for Mary, and emphasising it in this fashion was not likely to act as a deterrent. This was the only respect in which she seriously flouted his wishes.

The only way in which Herbrand could assuage his grief was by doing all that he could to protect her memory. He commissioned a stained glass Memorial Window for the church of St. Mary, the Victorian church built by the 8th Duke which stands between the town of Woburn and the Abbey. The window shows St. Francis of Assisi holding out his hands to birds of many varieties. Herbrand insisted that every feather should be correct. Underneath is written:

'Saint Francis of Assisi. In memory of Mary Duchess of Bedford 1865 -1937 Whose work was in the Hospitals Whose delight was in the Birds.'

The Duke also commissioned a biography to be written by John Gore, a professional writer but not someone who had known the Duchess personally. The book was published by John Murray for private circulation, restricted to family and close friends, in three volumes, a year after her death. The third volume was 'A Bird-Watcher's Diary' and was edited by Arthur Duncan. Gore was required to cover the most minute details of her life but there was to be no hint of criticism. The main source was Mary's own diary. The biographer was allowed greater freedom in relation to her hospital work; at the most important moments, such as during the War, exigencies of time meant that the diary lapsed. This enabled Gore to broaden the picture with independent reports. Herbrand founded a scholarship at the Cheltenham Ladies College in her name for a college leaver to read medicine, one of the few opportunities in life which Mary herself had failed to take. He had copies made of all sorts of documents connected with Mary: letters, bird watching notes and even an old school report, which indicated that she was either 'Satisfactory' or 'Very Satisfactory' in almost everything she attempted.

He was personally devastated. In his eightieth year, he had lost the woman whom he had adored for half a century. He suddenly found himself at the centre of a storm of publicity: the "Flying Duchess" had become an icon of the press, and now her sudden disappearance prompted a furore of excitement amongst journalists. Mary had hated all the press attention she had had, but gradually became used to it. Herbrand had kept well away from the media circus: whenever Mary returned from a well-publicised flight, Jemima was there to welcome her but Herbrand waited until she came home. Miserable and confused, he hid from the limelight unless he felt that he could in any way promote her memory. Inevitably, he was labelled reclusive and eccentric.

As soon as Ian read of his grandmother's disappearance in the newspapers, he decided to go and see his grandfather. He was now approaching twenty. Herbrand had had a somewhat desultory correspondence with him in recent years. He had done his best to persuade the young man, without conspicuous success, to work sufficiently hard at the crammers to which he had been sent to pass some exams and try to obtain a place at Cambridge. Ian was incorrigibly idle academically and even the financial carrot and stick system operated by his grandfather was inadequate for inducing him to work for exams or earn the money he craved.[1] His rare visits to Woburn had been singularly lacking in warmth on every side. Grandfather and grandson had no interests in common, their attitudes were diametrically opposed and the guest made no effort at all to conform to the conventions of his host's house, ignoring such customs as punctuality for meals. Nor had he ever given the impression of being deeply attached to his grandmother, whom he had considered latterly to be 'a rather sad old lady... in a very depressed and miserable state.'[2]

In his grief, Herbrand, impatient by nature, was unlikely to respond to a young man who had been a source of considerable irritation and anxiety to him for some years. However, he kept his temper and spoke to him briefly, but showed no wish to spend much time with him. Ian took offence, considering him 'just as stiff and unbending as ever', and marvelled that 'At a time like that it was still impossible for his own flesh and blood to get anywhere near him.'[3]

In the Woburn community, the reaction was quite different. Mary had been deeply loved, and Herbrand himself commanded a respect and deep-rooted affection which would not only have amazed his grandson but remained evident for as long as anyone survived who had known them. The old man's heartbreak was shared by almost all the staff and villagers. At the hospital, sorrow for an adored colleague, combined with anxiety as to what the future would hold for any of them, engendered wretched despair. Their world was crumbling even faster than the outside world. The last time that the sound of German armies on the march had reached Woburn, Mary had brought the hospital to life in response to the impending tragedy. Now, before most of them had even heard the first sounds of those same armies once more on the move, Mary had gone. They knew that their hospital, her hospital, could not long continue without her.

They were reminded of Mary's personal care and affection for them when the contents of her Will became known. Each of her employees at the hospital, who had worked there for at least ten years, was left £200. There was some discussion as to whether she had also intended to include her employees at Wispers, or even all the staff at Woburn. Robert Parkyn and Mr. Gass, who had proved themselves such good friends when she was stranded in Bushire, were not forgotten. There were legacies for the Royal Society, to be used for research, Our Dumb Friends League and the Guild of Air Pilots and Air Navigators: scientific research, animals and flying. Jemima was left £5,000.

Some etchings and engravings went to her old school, and her superb collection of books was left to St. Hugh's College, Oxford. Why she selected this College no-one knows: perhaps she confused it with St. Hilda's College, which was founded by her old headmistress Miss Beale, possibly through some subconscious link with her grandson's name, or perhaps the decision was the result of some recommendation of which no record remains. The books in this collection are superbly bound, include a selection of the different bookplates which Mary used and cover a wide range of subjects. There are many books of natural history, outstanding among which is the five volume set of John Gould's *Birds of the British Isles,* but the collection also includes many magnificent books on art. A particular treasure is the three volume set of the *South Polar Times,* an in-house magazine produced in 1902-3 by the expedition led by Robert Falcon Scott. The magazine was edited by Ernest Shackleton while the ship the *Discovery* was icebound in McMurdo Sound. This treasure may have been a gift to Mary from Peter Scott, son of the explorer, on one of his visits to Woburn.

Many of her personal possessions were left to Herbrand to keep or distribute amongst her friends and servants. The main beneficiaries of the Will were members of Mary's own family: Zoë and her descendants; and Jack. Others left specific sums of money included Russell cousins, key members of staff and old friends. One other person benefited: Flight Lieutenant Ralph Chevallier Preston received £3,000 (for comparison, Jemima's legacy was £5,000, Jack's £10,000 and Zoë's £20,000). In addition, provided that he was still her Air Pilot, he was left her aeroplanes and their accessories.

Preston knew that he had not always given total satisfaction to his employer. Yet she had treated him with exceptional generosity. He responded by pointing out that one of the two aeroplanes was not available: only four struts had ever been recovered. He himself had written in the last page of the log book 'To the Sea!' The exclamation mark made it a particularly insensitive comment. He now put in a claim for the value of the Moth.

The legal issue was complex and, at least in the opinion of Preston's lawyers, depended in part on the question of whether or not Mary had intended to commit suicide. The lawyers explained that Preston's case for claiming from the insurers was only valid if the crash was an accident, but went on to indicate that it would be necessary for them to establish the truth of this issue in a court of law. Should the Duke prefer not to have this matter publicly discussed, there was a way round. This cruel form of blackmail achieved precisely the result Preston wished for. Had the matter in fact gone to court, Preston might easily have lost. Herbrand's advisers, after considerable discussion, decided to give way to this emotional blackmail.

The biggest surprise arising from Mary's Will was her choice of residuary legatee, the person who inherited everything that was left after the individual legacies had all been paid. Although little cash remained, Wispers was a large and very valuable property, and the Duke surrendered his life interest in it so that it could be sold and the proceeds could immediately form part of the estate. Mary no doubt felt that Hastings and his children would be fully provided for by the Duke, so turned to Zoë and her family.

Zoë's two sons, Philip and Noel (Noel's middle name was Herbrand), were both now married. Philip was a professional soldier who was almost fifty before his marriage, one of the last social events which Mary attended. He went on to have three children. He was a somewhat formal, conservative man, quite different from Noel, a naval Commander who later became a Dartmoor farmer. Noel was jovial and robust to the family, although others found him aloof and terrifying until they got to know him better. He had a son, Martin, and a stepson, David. Noel's wife Marjorie was a strong and unusual personality, and it seems that Mary, in her relatively brief acquaintanceship with Marjorie, must have recognised a kindred spirit. Marjorie had nursed in a hospital in France throughout the First World War, with responsibility for Nissen huts containing more than 200 wounded. At all events, the residue of Mary's estate was left, not to either of the two brothers, her nephews, who each received generous legacies, but to Marjorie. Had Marjorie died before Mary, the money would have gone instead to her son Martin, Zoë's only grandchild at the time of Mary's death.

The choice of Marjorie was the more remarkable, for Marjorie had taken the side of Crommelin in the bitter struggle between Hastings and

Crommelin. She had gone so far as to make Crommelin Martin's Godmother. Perhaps Mary admired the independence of spirit shown by this action. Perhaps she had a sneaking sympathy with her daughter-in-law which she dared not express for fear of alienating Hastings. Either way, Mary showed remarkable judgment of character in her decision, for Marjorie made what Mary would have considered excellent use of the fortune she so unexpectedly received. She bought the former vicarage in Whitchurch in Devon, thus providing her family with a marvellous home, and ensured that Martin had the best education possible. On the outbreak of the Second World War, a year after moving there, she opened the doors of the house to all the refugees for whom she could find space: for most of the war there were two families with seven members staying simultaneously at Whitchurch House in addition to the Beavers. They were joined at various times by soldiers who had escaped from Dunkirk, Austrian and Czech refugees and many others. Marjorie probably worked almost as hard as Mary had done in the previous war to ensure that the atmosphere was as happy as any home in England. She continued to provide open house for many temporarily without a home after the War for the rest of her long life.

Mary's choice of Marjorie was certainly not initiated by Zoë, who disapproved of the decision. Zoë excelled at a number of her sister's gentler pastimes, sewing magnificent tapestries until she became too blind to continue and enjoying playing patience and completing the *Times* crossword. Unlike Mary, she was also a keen and knowledgeable gardener, although here again her failing sight let her down when she could no longer distinguish plants from weeds. She lived in the houses of both her sons in turn, walking the narrow village lanes with her silver handled cane stuck out in front of her, in imminent danger of being run over. Two such independent minded elderly ladies inevitably had their disagreements, but Zoë was the only person who remained close to Mary for the whole of Mary's life.

Mary had expressed a wish to be cremated. In the event, her body was never recovered and the issue did not arise. She would have hated the formality of a traditional family burial at Chenies. She had the full support of Herbrand in this matter. There were two strangely juxtaposed traditions in the Russell family concerning funerals. Generations of Russells had been buried in the family mausoleum at Chenies, and Jemima later had the distinction of becoming the only person who was not a member of the family to be buried there. On the other hand, cremation had been the subject of much controversy for many years. It was only declared legal in 1884, but the cause had received support from successive Dukes of Bedford, including Herbrand's father, and Herbrand counted, amongst the many offices he held, the Presidency of the Cremation Society of England. Herbrand himself eventually honoured both traditions: he was cremated, then his ashes were interred at Chenies.

Of all the people who knew and loved, respected or admired Mary, two were pre-eminent. Her sister Zoë left no written account. Herbrand did record his own appreciation of her.

Mary in 1925 at 60

'It is not easy to show wherein lay the magic charm of her personality. Perhaps charm is too elusive a gift to explain or define, but I think in her it sprang partly from a union of contrasting qualities. Her strength of will was softened by her gentleness of heart; her rather austere and severe manner was contradicted by her genial, humorous smile, and infectious laugh. No one would have suspected that one who seemed to be the embodiment of common sense and logic could, on occasion, startle her friends by a sudden act of pure impulsiveness. Yet so it was. Her wrath was highly disconcerting to its object; but it passed, leaving no sting behind. And, though I never heard of a formal apology coming from her lips, her friends were made aware by some special little act of kindliness that the crisis was over! I have heard her say that she did not "suffer fools gladly", and I think, in the main, this was true. Her own intelligence was too quick for her to have much patience with the slow-witted, especially if that slowness hampered or obstructed her plans. But again, as I myself can testify, the resentment and impatience were short-lived. Anyone as highly gifted as the Duchess could not but be aware of her fitness to lead and rule, but she was never self-assertive. Indeed, occasionally she was strangely diffident and distrustful of herself, a rather pathetic trait in one who was usually so self-reliant and independent.

'She was indeed nobly blessed in her gifts and circumstances. But she had one cross to carry which no affection could lift from her shoulders. For nearly fifty years she suffered from a very trying form of deafness, with constant noises in her head. It was a cruel handicap which, had she not faced it with unusual patience and fortitude, might easily have spoilt both her life and her life's work.

'Her religion was essentially a practical religion of duty and service, not of dogma or ritual; but if she did not profess orthodox Christianity in its entirety, she obeyed through life its golden rule of charity.

'One thing is certain, she never wished to be put on a pedestal; her sense of humour was too keen, and, for all her cleverness, she was too innately simple and unaffected for any pose.'[4]

Herbrand's words vividly describe the contradictions in Mary's character. One characteristic which remained constant was her dynamic energy. She was always doing something, not a moment was ever wasted, which was how she achieved so much. There was also a constant desire for change, for new challenges, which in her younger days could make her seem lacking in constancy of purpose. When she reached the age of sixteen and decided to leave school, this seemed to her teachers and contemporaries as if she was turning her back on all that the brave new world of Cheltenham Ladies College had to offer. For them, the chance for a girl to continue with her academic education and go on to achieve professional qualifications was a new and remarkable opportunity. The only alternative was to go home to their parents for a brief interlude and await a proposal from some young man within the restricted circle of their parents' friends, as their mothers and grandmothers had done. For Mary, the position was different. She hardly knew her parents. The chance to get to know them in itself was something new. India was, in every sense, a world away from Aunt Fanny's house at Pulborough. Continuing her education seemed to her simply that: a continuation of her current way of life. Cheltenham had given her a sound academic grounding, but the subject which most attracted her had formed no part of her curriculum. A rightful place listening to the lectures on anatomy, which had so enthralled her, part heard from another room, still lay a long way in the future, even had she decided to stay on at school. This at least was how matters seemed to the young girl.

She probably never regretted the decision. At the end of her life, she looked back on her years in India as 'a gloriously happy time'[5]. She needed variety in her life and the range of challenges India offered provided the stimulation she sought. Riding across miles of wild, open country with her father, playing cricket against the men or rounding up loose jackals in a railway carriage, Mary developed skills and demonstrated qualities which were to stand her in good stead for the rest of her life. Nor did she become simply a hoyden or a tomboy. From the start, she won admiration for her grace, elegance, good looks and charm. The romance with Carpy helped her to mature and see more clearly the direction in which she wished to move. Unlike the Cheltenham girls whom her father had mocked, Mary did indeed shine in society. The Viceroy welcomed her at all the functions he hosted, never suspecting that, quite unwittingly, she would sabotage his dreams for his own daughters by winning the heart of the most eligible bachelor in India.

After her marriage, Mary threw herself with gusto into every activity which presented itself. At that time, she would devote herself with absolute concentration and unquenchable energy to each new sport or interest, at least until she had attained a level of skill and knowledge that came close to satisfying her. When John Gore wrote his critical appraisal of her life on the centenary of her birth, he concluded that, of all her achievements, there was only one which 'she could have achieved in essentials without the help of unlimited means. If she had never married, she would have risen to the top in the profession of nursing.'[6]

Gore argues that, in shooting, constant practise, firing sufficient cartridges a year and a naturally very good eye can turn anyone into a first rate shot. This is true, but the leading men with whom she is compared – she was generally accepted as the pre-eminent female shot of the time – were also shooting constantly. When the ice rink where she skated was under threat, Herbrand bought the lease. Other leading skaters of the time did not own their own rinks, but they almost invariably had regular access to a rink. Her study of birds was made more convenient by the use of her yacht for longer journeys, and as a supply base when she was staying in rough conditions on the islands. Those who devoted their whole lives to bird watching made their own arrangements for spending time in the lonely places best suited to observation.

The Duke's money did not buy her skill or knowledge in any field. It bought her the time and opportunity to work at attaining the highest standards in many different worlds. The top shots with whom she was compared, for example, were not noted for excellence in other activities such as skating, ornithology, nursing or flying. Herbrand's generosity, combined with Mary's extraordinary energy and ability, enabled her to reach the top in several diverse activities and excel in many others. His sponsorship of important projects linked to his wife's interests inevitably brought her into closer contact with the acknowledged experts in a particular subject, to the benefit of everyone. The great ornithologist Dr. Eagle Clarke encouraged and helped Mary in her study of birds. If he was initially inspired in part by the Duke paying for the development of Fair Island as a migratory station, Mary's enthusiasm, dedication and charm soon turned gratitude into lifelong friendship.

In a life so filled with success, it was tragic that Mary's only conspicuous failure should have been in the upbringing of her own son. At this distance of time, it is impossible to form a reliable judgement as to why this happened. Mary herself believed that the whole matter had been taken out of her hands. Up to a point, this was true. Herbrand and his father decided that their views on the education of the future Duke must prevail. This need not, in itself, have been disastrous, had it not been for a serious flaw in Mary's character.

Her tendency to give single-minded, almost obsessive, concentration to the topic of the moment had its reciprocal disadvantage. When she realised from the outset that she would be unable to take over a matter completely and follow it through to its resolution, she was always reluctant to become involved at all. As soon as she realised that Herbrand wished to retain the ultimate authority in all matters relating to the Abbey and the estate, Mary abdicated all responsibility. Jemima made an excellent second in command. Mary needed to take control or play no part at all. This was a tenable position so far as the house was concerned. When applied to her only child, it was deeply shocking. Mary was an immensely strong woman who rarely had difficulty in bringing her husband round to her own point of view, even when this ran contrary to his own considered opinion. Herbrand hated her flying, yet he continued to support her wish to participate. It is inconceivable that she could not have brought him round to her point of view in the handling of their son.

Mary possessed all the necessary qualities of sensitivity, judgment, perception, intelligence and kindness to have made an excellent mother. She enjoyed the company of children through her Bird Club, with young patients in her hospital, with the children of employees and with her grandson Hugh. Yet, while the bond between mother and child is usually strong, in early childhood at least, somehow the one child for whom she developed an antipathy was her own. She found him irritating and he brought out all her worst qualities.

The circumstances of his birth did not give their relationship a good start. She seems to have suffered from post-natal depression, and probably received little support or sympathy, even from Herbrand who, devoted as he was to her, would have found such a condition hard to understand, particularly in one who was otherwise so strong. No doubt it reinforced his belief that Mary was not the right person to bring up their son.

The character of Hastings was not compatible with that of his mother. Her direct, open, positive nature was mystified by the nervous little boy, who seemed to her to be rejecting her, while the child himself was silently crying out for her love. It was a vicious circle, every emotion exacerbating the incomprehension which divided them. Both parents were proud people. Herbrand was the more patient of the two because he was determined to justify the stance he had taken concerning his son's education. Only when the boy became a man could Herbrand reject the man he had become, dissociating him in his own mind from the little boy for whom he had done his inadequate best.

Mary, on the other hand, attributed every failing she perceived in her son to a system of education which she had opposed. Thus, there was an underlying satisfaction in all that was wrong. She was unable to resist pointing the finger at those who had been responsible for his education. Uncharacteristically, sometimes she was almost gloating, revelling in the pleasure of pointing out 'I told you so.' It was only after Hastings was grown up that she began to appreciate all that she was losing. Her quiet work, concealed at first from Herbrand, in the end had some limited success. She succeeded in building sufficiently strong bridges to bring her son back into her life, and to give her the joy of an excellent relationship with her youngest grandson. But for Hastings it would always be 'too little, too late.'

Despite their disagreements over the upbringing of their son, Herbrand and Mary remained close to each other all their lives. Mary was truly grateful to Herbrand for all the opportunities he had given her in life and felt a deep affection for him. He, in his turn, loved her as much at the end of her life as he had done at the time of their marriage. He admired her even more than he had done then. At the time of their marriage, he admired her character and believed her to be as capable as any girl from her background could ever be. Nearly fifty years later, he knew that neither her sex nor the difference in their backgrounds placed any limitations on Mary's ability to achieve almost anything to which she set her mind.

There is no documentary evidence to clarify precisely what role Jemima played in their lives. A very sweet, gentle person, she treated her ladies' maid almost like a daughter. She was undoubtedly an able administrator, working under Herbrand's command in the departments which he chose to keep within his control: the administration of the house, and to some extent of the estate, though Jemima was rarely involved in the latter, and the education of his son. She undoubtedly came to fill the role of close friend and confidante, accompanying Herbrand on all his holidays and travelling with him, usually by train, when latterly Mary would fly. She was also very close to Mary, who trusted her implicitly, and shared the bond of their love for dogs, Pekinese in particular. Jemima, unlike the Duke, was always there at the start of Mary's flights to see her off, and when she landed, to welcome her home, usually with a Pekinese in her arms. Mary's recorded reflections on her were always kindly and appreciative. She liked to find some small item on her travels which would give Jemima pleasure on her return, and often expressed concern over some issue which she thought likely to upset the other woman. She, in her turn, showed

Mary and Jemima both loved dogs, especially Pekinese

in her writings an unequalled understanding and appreciation of Mary's qualities and character.

Despite this, it was widely believed at Woburn at the time that Jemima was Herbrand's mistress. His decision when she died to have her buried at Chenies, the only person who was not a member of the Russell family to be so buried, did nothing to reduce speculation. If the rumour was untrue, the decision about her final resting place was an odd one for Herbrand to take. If it was true, it casts a remarkable light on Mary. Herbrand's love letters to Mary before their marriage made clear that he was much more highly sexed than she. Her reluctance must have been exceptionally strong for a young man at that time to have remarked upon it openly, even before they were married. It is possible that Mary recognised this as a problem from the start. Once she had fulfilled her duty by producing an heir, she might then have seen the advent of Jemima as a solution. Even if this were the case, few women would have been able to accept their husband's mistress as a friend, without bitterness or jealousy. Mary was no fool: either she accepted Jemima unreservedly on those terms or else the rumour mongers maligned both Herbrand and Jemima.

While each had many interests which the other did not share, they also gave each other strong, active support in some of their projects. In particular, Herbrand's collection of animals and breeding of wildfowl was something which gave them both immense pleasure and which they worked on together. Herbrand's knowledge of mammals, and deer in particular, was even greater than Mary's knowledge of birds. Amongst the many offices which he held, he probably took more interest in his Presidency of the Zoological Society of London than in anything else. A particular delight was the creation, on land which he had donated, of Whipsnade, in which he played a leading part, supported by the Duchess.

Mary's close friendship with her sister Zoë and Zoë's family had the full support of Herbrand, who continued to invite Zoë to stay at Woburn and Cairnsmore even after Mary's death. Mary, on the other hand, was never on particularly good terms with either of Herbrand's sisters, but his own relationship with them had never been close.

Their grandson Ian described Herbrand as 'a selfish, forbidding man, with a highly developed sense of public duty and ducal responsibility, he lived a cold, aloof existence, isolated from the outside world by a mass of servants, sycophants and an eleven-mile wall.' That opinion was not shared by the majority of Woburn estate staff and tenants, with whom he was extremely popular. Perhaps this was because of his highly developed sense of public duty and ducal responsibility. He did indeed live in a bygone age, which made him appear eccentric and could create an illusion of selfishness, but he was also generous, kind and loving. His hot temper and an obstinate, stubborn touch which made him unforgiving to those who had transgressed made him a bad enemy and a difficult man to live with, but his unswerving loyalty made him a true friend. The somewhat pretentious traditions and excessive formality which he upheld bored and irritated Mary. Excessive pomp always grated with her. But she tolerated his foibles, just as he tolerated her passion for flying.

Perhaps because of her flying, and the difficulties created by her deafness, there was a popular conception of Mary as a tough, hearty woman, excelling at field sports but altogether lacking in social graces and cultured tastes. The examples which survive of her fine needlework and her delicate watercolours of flowers, foliage and toadstools still cause surprise. As recently as 1994, the purchaser of a bookcase which had once belonged to Mary contributed a somewhat mocking piece to *The Times,* ridiculing the fact that it contained numerous items such as fishing rods, but not a single book. Mary's reputation was defended by an answering letter to *The Times* from the librarian of St. Hugh's College, Oxford, who pointed out that there were no books because her college had inherited them:

'The collection reflects her deep interest in art and natural history (particularly ornithology) and contains numerous limited editions with fine period bindings. It is the library of a well-educated, cultured and highly civilised individual and greatly enriches our collections.'

Mary marvelled at the way her flying won her such fame and admiration. She herself had no illusions about her achievements. Flying was a hobby which gave her immense pleasure and was made possible because the Duke paid for her planes, her pilots and her expeditions. As she once answered when questioned, she 'felt sure her flying could not be accounted unto her for righteousness!'[7] Popular imagination was stirred because the image of flying in its early days was of an activity for wild and dashing bright young things. The very incongruity of a sexagenarian duchess taking part, much less establishing world records, made her exploits newsworthy. The pursuit of records meant little to Mary, who did not even consider, in the case of India, that there was a record to be broken. She appreciated the importance of this aspect to Barnard, however. Besides, any additional element of challenge always made an undertaking more exciting for Mary and brought out the best in her. Bob Little, the navigator on the India flight, considered her 'the greatest woman he ever met.'[8]

Her courage, determination and endurance were remarkable. Neither idle luxury, nor even calm relaxation, had any appeal for her. Her working life was hard and physically, as well as mentally, demanding, yet she chose to spend her precious holidays in conditions of extreme discomfort as well as danger. She loved her visits to all the different places where they landed, and if at first the welcome she was given was attributable to her rank, very soon people wanted to offer her hospitality and show her all that there was to see because of what she had achieved and the force of her personality. She certainly preferred the company of those who shared or at least admired her enthusiasm. With officials who regarded her as a dignitary to be offered protection, there was almost invariably an element of intense disapproval which she found irksome.

The world to Mary was such an exciting, beautiful place. She always wanted to see more, discover more. Flight itself was a new and dramatic challenge. It combined so many of the elements which delighted her, the chance to visit remote and inaccessible places, the scientific interest of the mechanism of flight, the danger. For a woman keen to fit as much into her life as Mary was, it was also, by the standards of the time, amazingly fast. Above all, she felt with Leonardo da Vinci:

'When once you have tasted flight, you will forever walk the earth with your eyes turned skyward, for there you have been, and there you will always long to return.'

Her three pilots, and in particular the first two, were an important part of her enjoyment of flying. Both Charles Barnard and Bernard Allen, their different characters and their own enthusiasm for all that Mary enjoyed about flying, contributed much to the enjoyment she derived from the whole experience.

Flying provided a glamorous and exciting escape from what, to Mary, was the real world. The glamour meant nothing to her. She found it incredible that such exploits won her world renown and admiration, whereas the hard work of a lifetime remained unnoticed, rewarded only with an Order of the British Red Cross Society, Second Class. Her achievements in the medical world were truly amazing. She later belittled her establishment of the original cottage hospital in Woburn, at first in the centre of the town and later at Maryland, which she so carefully designed and lovingly created. Yet most people would consider that the provision of a hospital for a town which previously had none, built to the highest standards and offering the skill of a leading London surgeon, was in itself a worthwhile lifetime's achievement. This was certainly an unusual, if not unique, success for a woman in the late Victorian period.

Mary's true life's work began with the outbreak of war in 1914. It is interesting to consider whether, without the War, she would ever have identified so clearly a single committed path of service. She could easily have spent her whole life floating butterfly-like from one venture to another, all individually worthwhile, all performed to the highest standard, but lacking the steady, solid day-to-day devotion which she offered to her patients from 1914 to 1937.

For nearly a quarter of a century she worked as hard as any modern career woman, doing things for which she had previously had no formal training. She was not only willing but keen to undertake the most menial tasks, but, with the guidance of Mr. Glendining, she also realised her full potential as a nurse, and in particular as a Theatre Sister, and as a radiologist. Somehow, in a way which seems unbelievable to a generation brought up with the full cumbersome machinery of the National Health Service, she also managed to take responsibility for the administration of her group of hospitals. The concept of Chief Executive, Theatre Sister and Radiologist, with commitments in the latter field stretching county wide, combined in a single person, defies belief. Yet there is no doubt at all that the standards she maintained far exceeded those in most other comparable sized hospitals and departments in her time or since.

Mary was modest in her own analysis of her achievements. She once wrote to the editor of her old school newsletter,

'So you see, even a Duchess may be useful!'

But in reality she had always aimed to be the best in everything she undertook. Time and again, she achieved this, especially in the areas which meant most to her. She was a high-flying Duchess.

Fly Agaric, by Mary

NOTES

N.B. All quotations from letters come from those in the collection at Woburn unless stated to the contrary throughout.

The reference 'HHR' in these notes relates to the unpublished account of his life narrated to the author by Lord Hugh Russell.

A FAMILY TRADITION

1. State Trials
2. *The Russells in Bloomsbury* p158
3. Rachel Trethewey: *Mistress of the Arts* page 111
4. Rachel Trethewey: *Mistress of the Arts* page 72
5. Rachel Trethewey: *Mistress of the Arts* page 110

CHAPTER ONE

1. *1871 Census*
2. *Cheltenham Ladies* (Gillian Avery) p.18
3. *Cheltenham Ladies* (Gillian Avery) p. 21
4. *Cheltenham Ladies* (Gillian Avery) ps. 40-41
5. *Cheltenham Ladies* (Gillian Avery) ps. 17 and 44
6. *Cheltenham Ladies* (Gillian Avery) p. 235 though Gore, in *Early Years* p.6 indicates that it was a year later
7. *Cheltenham Ladies* (Gillian Avery) ps. 22, 45
8. *Cheltenham Ladies* (Gillian Avery) p. 83 quoting Amy Lumby and Elizabeth Raikes (formerly Elsie Higgins)
9. *Cheltenham Ladies* (Gillian Avery) p. 76-7

CHAPTER TWO

1. *Plain Tales from the Raj* (ed. Charles Allen) p.46
2. *The Flying Duchess* (John, Duke of Bedford) p.21
3. *Plain Tales from the Raj* (ed Charles Allen) p.43

4. *Mary Duchess of Bedford* (John Gore) p.5
5. *Mary Duchess of Bedford* (John Gore) p.4
6. *Cheltenham Ladies* (Gillian Avery) Ps.235-6

CHAPTER THREE

1. *Plain Tales from the Hills* (Rudyard Kipling)
2. Balliol College Library: Jowett Papers Index 1
3. *Mary Duchess of Bedford* Vol I Gore pages 7-8
4. *Mary Duchess of Bedford* Vol I Gore page 7
5. *Mary Duchess of Bedford* Vol I Gore page 12
6. *A Silver Plated Spoon* pages. 16-17
7. *A Silver Plated Spoon* page 18
8. *Plain Tales from the Raj* (ed Charles Allen) page 159
9. *The Flying Duchess* John Duke of Bedford page 22
10. Letter from Mary to Hastings dated 17th June 1936
11. *The Years of Transition* p 78

CHAPTER FOUR

1. *A Silver-Plated Spoon*, pages 17-18
2. *Flying Duchess* p 23
3. Gore p 11
4. *Flying Duchess* p 201
5. *Flying Duchess* ps 196-7
6. *A Silver-Plated Spoon*, pages 69-70
7. *The Years of Transition* p. 9

8. *The Years of Transition* p 11
9. *The Years of Transition* p 26
10. *A Silver-Plated Spoon*, p. 29, Gore p. 144
11. *The Years of Transition* p 15
12. *Flying Duchess* p. 64
13. *A Silver-Plated Spoon*, p.16
14. *A Silver-Plated Spoon*, p.23

CHAPTER FIVE

1. Gladys Scott Thomson: *Woburn and the Russells* page 46
2. Gladys Scott Thomson: *Woburn and the Russells* page 51
3. *The Flying Duchess* page 68
4. A *Silver-Plated Spoon* page 15
5. HHR
6. HHR
7. HHR
8. Lady Victoria Leatham: *The Life of a Great House*
9. Catherine Bailey: *Black Diamonds*
10. HHR
11. HHR
12. *A Silver-Plated Spoon* page 9
13. HHR
14. Mark Girouard: *Life in the English Country House* Inside back cover
15. The Duchess of Devonshire: *The House* page 58
16. The Duchess of Devonshire: *The House* page 36
17. Mark Girouard: *Life in the English Country House* page 298
18. *A Silver-Plated Spoon* page 11

CHAPTER SIX

1. Gore Vol.1, page 15
2. Diary for 5th June 1912, quoted by Gore, page 25
3. *The Flying Duchess* page 204
4. HHR
5. HHR
6. Gore Vol. I pages 129-136 for all quotations from letters to Dr. Long in this chapter

7. *Bird Watcher's Diary* page 15
8. *Bird Watcher's Diary* p. Viii
9. *Bird Watcher's Diary* pages 7-10
10. *Bird Watcher's Diary* p.17
11. *Bird Watcher's Diary* p.63
12. *The Years of Transition* p.15
13. *Bird Watcher's Diary* p.200
14. Gore Vol. I page 31
15. *The Years of Transition* p.54
16. Gore Vol. 1 page 89
17. Gore Vol. 1 page 57
18. *The Years of Transition* p.54
19. *The Flying Duchess* p.72

CHAPTER SEVEN

1. Letter to Hastings 23.2.1936 (Woburn)
2. Gore Vol. 1 page 104
3. *The Flying Duchess* p.56
4. Gore Vol. I page 103
5. Letter to Hastings 20.2.1936 (Woburn Collection)
6. Gore Vol. 1 page 102
7. Gore Vol. 1 page 85
8. Gore Vol. 1 page 98
9. *The Flying Duchess* p57
10. Gore Vol. 1 pages 105-6
11. Gore Vol. 1 page 124
12. Gore Vol. 1 pages 125-6
13. Gore Vol. 1 page 127
14. Letter to Hastings 20.2.1936 (Woburn Collection)
15. Gore Vol. 1 pages 106-7
16. Letter to Hastings 20.2.1936 (Woburn Collection)
17. Gore Vol. 1 page 111

CHAPTER EIGHT

1. Gore page 121
2. Letter to Hastings 23.2.1936
3. Gore page 141
4. Gore page 110
5. Gore Pages 108-09
6. Letter to Hastings 23.2.1936
7. Gore pages 138-139
8. *The Flying Duchess* page202

CHAPTER NINE

1. Gore page 18
2. Gore page 18
3. Gore page 443

CHAPTER TEN

1. Original note quoted in article in *Country Life 6.5.1982*
2. *A Silver-Plated Spoon* page 30
3. *The Flying Duchess* page 16
4. H.H.R.
5. *The Flying Duchess* pages 63-4
6. H.H.R.
7. *A Silver-Plated Spoon* page 27
8. *A Silver-Plated Spoon* page 46
9. *A Silver-Plated Spoon* pages 36-7
10. H.H.R.
11. *The Years of Transition* page 59
12. *The Years of Transition* page 59
13. Letter dated June 15th 1936
14. *The Flying Duchess* page 15 and *A Silver-Plated Spoon* page 69
15. *The Flying Duchess* page 17 and *A Silver-Plated Spoon* page 71
16. *A Silver-Plated Spoon* page 35
17. *A Silver-Plated Spoon* pages 54-5

CHAPTER ELEVEN

1. Gore page 154
2. *Winged Odyssey* page 24
3. Gore page 161
4. Gore page 176
5. *Winged Odyssey* page 32
6. Gore page 178
7. Gore page 182
8. *Winged Odyssey* page 41
9. *Winged Odyssey* page 52
10. *Winged Odyssey* page 57-8
11. Gore page 151

CHAPTER TWELVE

1. Quoted in Gore page 255
2. *Winged Odyssey* page 75
3. Gore page 278

4. Gore page 286
5. H.H.R.
6. Gore page 296

CHAPTER THIRTEEN

1. Gore page 326
2. Gore page 333
3. *Winged Odyssey* page 150
4. *Winged Odyssey* page 161
5. Gore page 374
6. Gore page 379
7. Gore page 402
8. Gore page 433

CHAPTER FOURTEEN

1. *The Sky's the Limit* page 32
2. *The Flying Duchess* page 198
3. *A Silver-Plated Spoon* page 71
4. *Winged Odyssey* page 165
5. *Winged Odyssey* page 248

CHAPTER FIFTEEN

1. *A Silver-Plated Spoon* Chapter 3
2. *A Silver-Plated Spoon* page 71
3. *A Silver-Plated Spoon* page 73
4. Quoted in *The Flying Duchess* pages 196-7
5. Gore page 424
6. *The Flying Duchess* page 202
7. Letter to Cheltenham Ladies College
8. *The Flying Duchess* page 203

Bibliography

Allen, Charles (Ed.): *Plain Tales from the Raj* Andre Deutsch Ltd. (London) 1975

Avery, Gillian: *Cheltenham Ladies* James & James (London) 2003

Bailey, Catherine: *Black Diamonds* Viking Penguin (London) 2007

Barstow, Phyllida: *The English Country House Party* Equation (Wellingborough) 1989

Bedford, John Duke of: *The Flying Duchess* Macdonald & Co. (London) 1968

Boase, Wendy: *The Sky's the Limit* Osprey Publishing Ltd. (London) 1979

Curtis, Lettice: *Winged Odyssey* Air Research Publications (Walton-on-Thames) 1993

Devonshire, the Duchess of: *The House – a Portrait of Chatsworth* Macmillan (London) 1982

Diver, Maud: *The Englishwoman in India* W. Blackwood & Sons (Edinburgh) 1909

Duncan, Arthur (Editor): *Mary Duchess of Bedford: A Bird-Watcher's Diary* John Murray (London) 1938 (for private circulation)

Girouard, Mark: *Life in the English Country House* Yale University Press (New Haven and London) 1978

Gore, John (Editor): *Mary Duchess of Bedford 1865-1937 Vols I and II* John Murray (London) 1938 (for private circulation)

Jennings, Tim: *The Flying Duchess 1865-1937* Jarrold Publishing (Norwich) 2001

Kipling, Rudyard: *Plain Tales from the Hills* Macmillan & Co. Ltd. (London) 1890

Leatham, Lady Victoria: *The Life of a Great House* The Herbert Press (London) 1992

Mason, Philip: *The Men Who Ruled India* Jonathan Cape (London) 1985

Somerset, Anne: *Unnatural Murder: Poison at the Court of James I* Weidenfeld & Nicholson (London) 1997

Thomson, Gladys Scott:

Family Background Jonathan Cape (London) 1949

Letters of a Grandmother 1732-1735 Jonathan Cape (London) 1943

Life in a Noble Household 1641-1700 Jonathan Cape (London) 1937

The Russells in Bloomsbury 1669-1771 Jonathan Cape (London) 1940

Woburn and the Russells The Pilgrim Press Ltd. (Derby) 1956

Two Centuries of Family History Longmans, Green & Co. (London) 1930

Trethewey, Rachel: *Mistress of the Arts* Review (London) 2002

Woodcock, Gerry: *The Book of Whitchurch* Halsgrove (Bath) 2004

INDEX

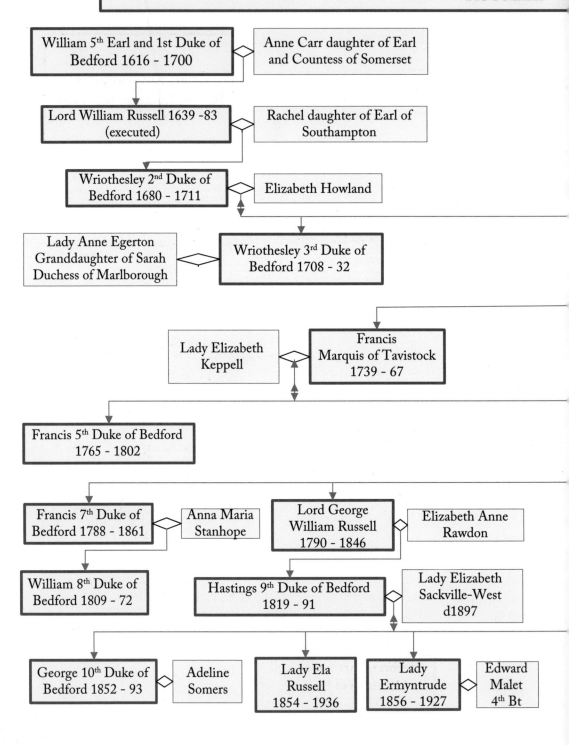

RUSSELL

William 5th Earl and 1st Duke of Bedford 1616 - 1700 ◇ Anne Carr daughter of Earl and Countess of Somerset

Lord William Russell 1639 -83 (executed) ◇ Rachel daughter of Earl of Southampton

Wriothesley 2nd Duke of Bedford 1680 - 1711 ◇ Elizabeth Howland

Lady Anne Egerton Granddaughter of Sarah Duchess of Marlborough ◇ **Wriothesley 3rd Duke of Bedford 1708 - 32**

Lady Elizabeth Keppell ◇ Francis Marquis of Tavistock 1739 - 67

Francis 5th Duke of Bedford 1765 - 1802

Francis 7th Duke of Bedford 1788 - 1861 ◇ Anna Maria Stanhope   Lord George William Russell 1790 - 1846 ◇ Elizabeth Anne Rawdon

William 8th Duke of Bedford 1809 - 72   Hastings 9th Duke of Bedford 1819 - 91 ◇ Lady Elizabeth Sackville-West d1897

George 10th Duke of Bedford 1852 - 93 ◇ Adeline Somers   Lady Ela Russell 1854 - 1936   Lady Ermyntrude 1856 - 1927 ◇ Edward Malet 4th Bt